Barbara Fox is the daughter of Gwenda Gofton. She grew up in Newcastle then moved to London where she worked as a journalist for the *Radio Times* and the *Telegraph* newspapers. She lives with her family in Crawley, West Sussex.

Gwenda Gofton (née Brady) was born in Newcastle upon Tyne. She trained as a nursery nurse in 1949, before beginning general nurses' training in 1952. She later qualified as a midwife, as well as taking a course in tropical diseases nursing. In 1957 she travelled to Cleveland, Ohio, where she spent a year working at the city's Mount Sinai Hospital before embarking on the adventure she recalls in this book. She and her husband, Alder, have four children and nine grandchildren, and live in Ponteland, Northumberland. She has lost count of the number of people who have told her they would like to read a book about her exploits!

SPHERE

First published in Great Britain in 2011 by Sphere
Reprinted 2011 (twice), 2012

A CIP catalogue record for this book
is available from the British Library.

ISBN 978-0-7515-4404-6

Typeset in Bembo by M Rules
Printed and bound in Great Britain by
Clays Ltd, St Ives plc

Papers used by Sphere are from well-managed forests
and other responsible sources.

MIX
Paper from
responsible sources
FSC® C104740

Sphere
An imprint of
Little, Brown Book Group
100 Victoria Embankment
London EC4Y 0DY

An Hachette UK Company
www.hachette.co.uk

www.littlebrown.co.uk

Bedpans & Bobby Socks

Five British Nurses on the American Road Trip of a Lifetime

BARBARA FOX AND GWENDA GOFTON

sphere

To the five who went, the one who stayed behind, and everyone they met on the way

And to everyone who still writes letters

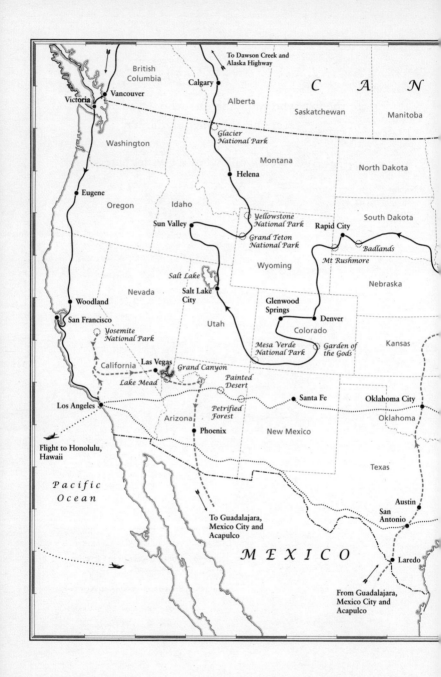

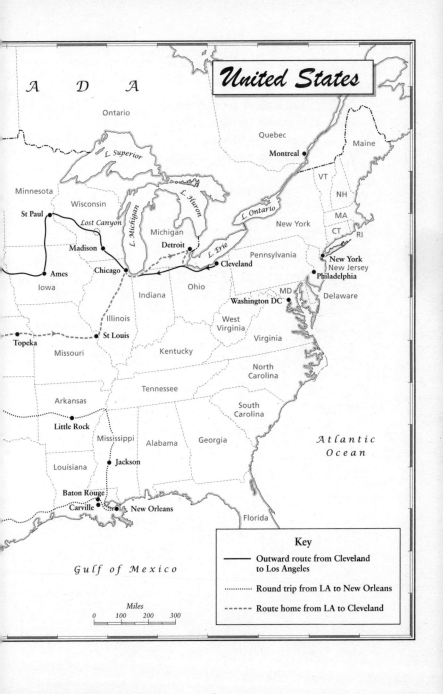

United States

Ontario

Quebec

Maine

Montreal

VT

NH

Minnesota

Wisconsin

L. Superior

St Paul

Lost Canyon

Michigan

L. Michigan

L. Huron

L. Ontario

New York

MA

CT

RI

Madison

Detroit

L. Erie

New York

Pennsylvania

New Jersey

Ames

Chicago

Cleveland

Philadelphia

Iowa

Indiana

Ohio

MD

Washington DC

Delaware

Illinois

West
Virginia

St Louis

Topeka

Missouri

Kentucky

Virginia

North
Carolina

Arkansas

Tennessee

South
Carolina

*Atlantic
Ocean*

Little Rock

Mississippi

Alabama

Georgia

Louisiana

Jackson

Baton Rouge

Carville

New Orleans

Florida

Gulf of Mexico

Key

⎯⎯⎯ Outward route from Cleveland
to Los Angeles

·········· Round trip from LA to New Orleans

- - - - - Route home from LA to Cleveland

Miles

0   100   200   300

You'll never get to heaven
In an old Ford car
Cos an old Ford car
Won't go that far

Traditional camp-fire song

1

Everyone's a Honey

Cleveland, Ohio, Winter 1957

We arrived in Cleveland in the middle of a tea-party. Nobody would ever let us forget that. Trust the English, they said, to fly across the Atlantic Ocean and still turn up in time for tea!

It was Pat who saw the advert first, in *Nursing Mirror*. An American hospital was offering the equivalent of ninety pounds a month for a one-year contract, she read. She looked up at me, widened her eyes in surprise, then looked back at the magazine. 'Ninety pounds a month,' she repeated slowly.

'It must be a misprint,' I said, putting down my cup of coffee and going to peer over her shoulder. 'I've never heard of anyone paying a nurse that much.'

No one went into nursing to get rich, that was a fact. But it had been a good life so far, even if we lived it on a shoestring. As long as we had enough money to eat and to put petrol in the car, we were happy, and we had driven or hitched our way round Britain as well as large parts of Europe in our off-duty. Now, after twelve months of midwifery, we were studying tropical diseases in London, a subject we both loved, though working our way through patients' stools to identify the worms they were infected with wasn't exactly glamorous. We had been talking about going to Africa next, to nurse leprosy patients, but we had written our application letters before we had even found where Cleveland was on the map.

The entrance to the hospital had sliding doors that parted like magic before us as we looked in vain for a handle. We stood there, feeling rather foolish, a rush of warm air and chatter washing over us. Several nurses jumped up and came to help with our cases and bags. Others took our coats and pulled up chairs. Tea was fetched from a long trestle table, presided over by a girl with a broad Yorkshire accent, wearing an overall that appeared to have been plucked from my mother's peg behind the kitchen door. 'Milk and sugar, ducks?' she called.

The nurse who brought me my drink perched on the arm of the chair opposite, and watched me closely as I tasted it.

'Sorry, it's not exactly English tea, but you'll get used to it. At least we've managed to get hold of a pot.' She leant forward and added in an exaggerated whisper, 'Just wait until you see what passes for tea in the canteen!'

It was the last day of February, and bitterly cold outside. I'd been thankful for my winter coat and boots, even for the short walk between car and building, but now I wished I wasn't wearing the suit that my mother had thought would be the correct attire for the journey. I felt my face grow hot. The heat in the lobby was almost tropical, and I longed to change into a short-sleeved dress.

Curious nurses drew up their chairs, others bobbed like white-stemmed flowers around my table, teacups rattling on saucers as they chattered and joked. Occasionally an intercom would call someone's name, but nobody paid it much attention. Pat had been shown to an adjacent table but was now invisible behind a wall of white. Everyone wore a fitted nylon dress, though I could hardly believe the varied styles – U-,V- or heart-shaped necklines, embroidered or plain bodices, pleats at the back, frills round the bottom . . . I thought of the heavy cotton button-through dresses in the colours of our training schools, and the white aprons we wore over them, that made up our uniform at home. Things were going to be very different here.

Everyone was talking at once.

'You're both from Newcastle? Oh, Mary here's from Liverpool. Same neck of the woods. I'm from London.'

'There *are* some Americans here. Honest!'

'You must be exhausted after your journey.'

'You might even meet one if you're lucky!'

'But how fresh you look!'

'What's the weather like back home? Oh, I do miss an English winter when it gets as cold as it did here last week.'

'And you thought today was cold!'

'Don't scare her, Bunty! Honestly, it comes in fits and starts.'

'And the summers – oh you'll just die!'

'Poor girl's only just got here and—'

'They'll just love your accent!'

This produced a murmur of agreement all round, though apart from some one-word answers I had barely been given the opportunity to open my mouth.

One of the girls put down her cup and opened a packet of cigarettes. She removed one and held it between her long fingers as she spoke. 'You won't believe this, darling, but one of my patients said to me, "Haven't you learned the language quickly!" I just agreed and said I was a fast learner.'

We all laughed, and she shrugged, then lit her cigarette, aiming a neat puff of smoke over her shoulder. 'Well, what do you say?'

'Fancy arriving in time for tea!' said a tall girl with an Irish accent who had just appeared. She had an open, friendly face and laughing eyes, and I liked her immediately.

'Is it the same time every day?' I asked. The others found this very funny.

'You're not in Newcastle now!'

'Every Thursday,' said the Irish girl. 'Supposed to help us all feel at home. But daily would be more the ticket.'

'The Americans love it, too,' said someone else. 'Even the doctors pop down sometimes – but they've probably got ulterior motives. One of the girls got herself engaged to one last week, and she's only been here two months!'

'Three, I think, Agnes.'

'Did you hear,' began another voice, 'the director bought the first girls to come over a brand new radiogram for their apartment. He thinks English nurses are the best.'

Agnes, who had a strong Scottish accent, put down her cup, folded her arms and pretended to be offended by this.

'Sorry, Agnes. British, I meant. And Irish, too, Celia.'

A few minutes later, most of the nurses began to drift away. Pat moved across to join me and Celia, who introduced herself properly as Celia Greene from Mullinahone in County Tipperary. She told us that she had arrived two weeks ago, and that everyone was terrifically friendly.

'It's all very informal,' she said in a hushed voice. 'It does take some getting used to.'

We were talking to Celia when a tall, shapely glamour puss sashayed up to us and said she was Mitzi, the manager of the nurses' home, and that she would show us to our rooms. We followed her down corridors lined with vending machines, out of one building and into another, trailed by a gum-chewing porter.

On the ground floor of the nurses' home, Mitzi pointed at a cigarette machine. 'I restock every morning,' she said in a light, fluttery voice. 'I like to look after my girls.'

When Pat told her that we didn't smoke she stopped walking and turned to look at us both with a mixture of pity and amusement. 'You don't?' Then she smiled and carried on sashaying down the corridor. I wondered what the porter would make of her, but he seemed more interested in the television screens that hung on the walls, and walked with his neck permanently craned.

A few yards further on, Mitzi stopped, triumphantly, at some more dispensing machines. 'Coke and gum,' she announced. 'One on each floor. Now everybody likes Coke!'

We smiled at her and nodded feebly. Neither of us told her how that very morning, in Idlewild Airport, New York, we had sampled Coca-Cola for the very first time. Pat had said she rather liked it – though 'It's not Tizer, is it?' – but I found it medicinal-tasting, and couldn't help wondering what all the fuss was about.

I lay on the bed in my underwear, too tired to look for my night-dress. After more introductions and a quick tour, we had been left in peace. My room was small and simply furnished with a bed, a wardrobe and a chest of drawers. I suppose I had expected something a little more modern, but there was nothing wrong with it, in fact it was just like a room in an English nurses' home. A table and chair stood at the window, which looked across a busy road to a large park. Like the lobby, it was unbearably hot. A radiator thrummed in the corner and gave off a smell of burning dust. I could smell cigarette smoke, too, but that seemed to be on my hair and my discarded clothes.

Someone walked along the corridor in squeaky shoes. The noise stopped, and I heard a door open and close. I had no idea what time it was. Apart from the comforting hum of traffic drifting up from the road outside, it was all strangely silent after the liveliness of the tea-party.

A leaflet on the table declared Cleveland to be 'The Best Location in the Nation'. It showed pictures of skyscrapers and handsome shop fronts, and talked about making dreams come true. But in my dreams of America, I was not in a city at all but driving on long straight roads in a landscape so vast it had no edges. Always driving. How my heart had lurched when I saw those very roads from the plane window that morning!

'Only three meals a day,' Pat said, as we went down to breakfast the next morning. We had greeted each other in summer dresses, dug out from the bottom of our suitcases. 'Do you think we'll survive?'

We had grown up with four meals a day: a cooked breakfast and lunch, afternoon tea with bread and jam and a selection of cakes (all home-made), followed by another, lighter cooked meal in the evening. But when we saw the food in the canteen, any fears of going hungry quickly vanished.

'It's like a Lyons Corner House, only miles better.' Pat's eyes lit up.

Spread out before us were dainty boxes of cereal, one-portion big, stacked into pyramids; mounds of apples, oranges and bananas; bread rolls pitted with seeds; bagels filled with cream cheese and speckled red meat; pastries dripping in white icing;

doughnuts; piles of pancakes; trays of sliced ham; eggs in wire baskets, waiting to be cooked any way we wanted them. Having missed supper the previous day, we felt hungry enough to dive straight in.

After demolishing a plate of ham and eggs, I took a nibble – rather guiltily – from the corner of a pastry I had been unable to resist.

'Ah!' I closed my eyes and pretended to swoon.

Pat eyed it suspiciously. 'Are you really going to eat that now? It's seven-thirty in the morning.'

She stole a look around the room, where several people were tucking into pancakes that sat in pools of thick dark liquid. 'It's enough to send me back to bed.'

A nut as sweet as toffee crumbled in my mouth. 'I don't know what it is, but I've never tasted anything so delicious in my life.'

'Pecan rolls,' said an older woman, placing her tray on our table and beaming at us both. 'I do like to see our new arrivals enjoying their food. May I join you?'

She laughed at my embarrassment, and declared herself delighted to meet us again. We both recognized her from the tea-party, but when she introduced herself as Miss Harrison, the director of nursing, we had to hide our disbelief, especially when she offered to accompany us to town later that morning to buy our uniforms. Director of nursing was the equivalent of matron back home, and matrons most certainly did not fraternize with new girls. Matrons didn't really fraternize with anyone.

'What a charming lady,' said Pat as we made our way back to our rooms. 'She was at my table yesterday, but nobody said she was matron. They all looked the same anyway in their white dresses.'

I nodded. 'I don't think rank is so important here. Did you notice how that waitress was calling everyone "honey"? Even the doctors! Imagine that at home!'

I put on my sternest face and said in a voice that Pat knew only too well, 'You must not speak to anyone more than three months your senior unless – Nurse Beadle, that means you, too – unless they speak to you first.'

We giggled. Pat and I had met doing our preliminary nurses' training at Walkergate Hospital in the East End of Newcastle, an outpost of the city's General Hospital. Pat said that she had noticed me on day one, sitting in the lecture room with a broad grin on my face that I was trying unsuccessfully to hide. I think it was Sister Gunn's demonstration of how to squeeze out a dish-cloth that did it – I had never known there was an art to it before. Pat said she knew immediately that we were kindred spirits. We had been more or less inseparable ever since.

The course started in January. It was freezing that winter, and our full-length navy cloaks were the most welcome part of the uniform we were given, much of which was unflattering and designed to fit the largest girl. Nobody showed us how to fold the tailey caps – made up from a rectangle of starched cotton – so those of us who were nursery-trained had a busy time folding everyone else's.

The streets of Newcastle turned a dirty brown in the slushy snow that refused to shift. The sky hung over us all like a grey overcoat with the sun lost somewhere in its folds. Not that we saw much daylight during those first three months. We sat all day in a large, draughty classroom in our short-sleeved dresses and plain navy cardigans, and shivered. We had to remove our cardigans for practical assignments.

A small coal fire flickered reluctantly in the centre of one wall, and our lecturers stood in front of it, greedily swallowing any heat that might have come our way. On the chimney breast was a thermometer. Sister Gunn would burst into the room several times a day, go straight to the thermometer and cry out, 'It's sixty degrees, nurses!' before flinging open the windows. One of my strongest memories of those days is of wondering if my feet would ever warm up again. The girls in the back row were so cold, one of their fathers wrote in to complain, not that it did any good.

We had been there for almost a week when one of the trainees ran away in the middle of the night. Sister summoned us to the classroom before breakfast, so we knew that there was trouble.

'Something has happened that disgraces you all,' she announced, her voice trembling with barely suppressed rage. My face coloured, though I was sure I had done nothing wrong. I could hear my heart thumping in my ears.

'You all know that certain responsibilities are yours, and yours alone. We all do our own dirty work here. If anyone is too grand to get their hands dirty,' here she stuck her chin in the air and waved her hand majestically, 'they should walk out of that door now.'

She paused. Her cheeks quivered. She was a tiny woman who always stood as straight as a plank, yet managed to give the impression of a tiger about to pounce. Her head swivelled round the room, looking at each of us in turn. I focused on a spot of soot on the wall and kept my eyes there. Somebody coughed nervously. Nobody moved. The second hand of the clock was the loudest thing in the room. It shuffled its way from one position to the next, each second slower than the one before.

'You, Nurse Farrier. When you are on lavatory duty, who performs the sanitary duties pertaining to your task?'

Rose, my old friend from nursery training, horrified at being singled out, swallowed hard, considered the question for a few seconds, then replied, hopefully, 'I do, Sister Gunn.'

'Exactly.'

We all breathed a sigh of relief.

'Then we are all in agreement, and you will be as shocked as I was to learn that one of your number decided to depart last night without a by-your-leave – *and without stripping her bed.*'

Our beds had to be stripped every morning, the sheets and blanket folded into three and laid on a chair, ready for Sister's inspection. We took it in turns to clean the toilets at each end of the corridor. One morning, as we stood to attention in our rooms, we heard the cry, 'Nurse McElhennon, go to the lavatory!'

I tried not to laugh, wondering what terrible accident had befallen the poor girl. We were all so tense, the slightest reaction from one of us would have set the others off into hysterical laughter or tears. It turned out that Sister had decided to inspect the toilets before the bedrooms that morning, and poor McElhennon, who was on duty that day, was instead waiting by her bed in the first dormitory.

Every Thursday Sister inspected our dusters, which had to be washed and hung on the towel-stand ready for her arrival. (Knowing that I would never get a yellow duster clean again, I brought a spare one from home and simply rinsed through the new one each time, saving myself a lot of bother.) On the first Thursday, she had only just begun her rounds when a shout echoed along the corridor. 'Nurse! You did not introduce your duster!'

We learned that from now on we were to greet her with, 'Sister, my duster.'

'One day,' I told the girls during our coffee break, 'I'm going to add, "Duster, meet Sister."'

'You wouldn't!' said Rose, wide-eyed with a mixture of horror and excitement.

'Don't even think about it,' said Pat. 'She doesn't have a sense of humour. You never know what might happen.'

'Just wait,' I said, and I did intend to do it, but common sense prevailed on that occasion and I eventually decided that the amusement it would give my fellow students might not outweigh the consequences.

Just once, I thought I saw a glimmer in Sister's eyes that might have been laughter. A large ball of fluff had come dancing down the passageway and deposited itself in front of our dormitory, just before her visit. I was darned if it was going to sully my clean piece of floor, and after quickly checking that she wasn't in sight, I got down on my hands and knees and blew it away. It seemed unwilling to co-operate at first, lifting in the air before returning to its resting place beside me, until it caught in a sudden draught, and scurried across the corridor, where it landed in front of our male tutor's door, just opposite.

Saved, I thought.

But you could never underestimate Sister. I think she spotted that blemish from twenty yards away.

'Nurse Brady, I don't think Mr Woodward wants a piece of fluff outside his bedroom, does he?'

'No, Sister.'

There was a stifled giggle from somewhere in the dormitory. I sucked in my cheeks and looked straight ahead. Sister pretended not to notice. But was she holding back a smile? Had she thought, along with the rest of us, that Mr Woodward might prefer a piece of fluff *in*side his bedroom?

On Saturday afternoon, two days after our arrival in Cleveland, Pat and I went for a walk. It had snowed in the night, but the snow had melted and the pavements were black and glistening. We passed the shop where we had bought tea, coffee and biscuits the day before, and the Italian owner, a bear-like man with wild curly hair and an apron drawn tightly across his large stomach, greeted us from the doorway.

'Ciao, bellas! What you want today? You want meet my sons?'

A doctor we had been introduced to on our tour of the hospital smiled and said, 'Hiya, kids!' as he walked by us, and we tried not to look at each other and laugh when he had passed, but failed miserably. I thought my heart would burst with pleasure just to be here.

A young man stood outside a building, his eyes closed, swaying to sounds coming from within, as if in a trance.

A skinny coloured girl, struggling with a shop door and a pram, beamed at me when I rushed to help her.

'Why, thank you, ma'am,' she said, with a note of genuine surprise, and I felt a surge of affection for her.

The sun poked out through the clouds and a blast of heat took us by surprise. We loosened our coats, then removed them altogether, but noticed that the locals remained bundled up in theirs.

We kept on walking. The city began to change. The crowds thinned out. Shops and restaurants became grim buildings of indeterminate use. An empty children's playground was barred like a cage in a zoo. We were about to turn back when we spotted a used car lot on the other side of a busy road. We waited for ages for a lull in the traffic, grabbed each other's hands and ran for our lives. Someone shouted at us from a passing vehicle, but I couldn't tell if it was in anger or fun.

The car lot was closed but we stood, our cheeks pressed to the railings, inhaling the smell of cold metal and revelling in the sight before us.

I sighed. 'Ah, if I had all the money in the world . . . Oh, look at that beauty!'

'What do you think of that little Hillman? It looks just the job.'

'I can't write home and tell Dad we've got a Hillman. We're in America! It's got to be a Cadillac.'

'Well, Miss Yanky Doodle, if you can find one for under a hundred dollars . . . In fact, why don't we get one each?'

My father had slipped twenty dollars into my pocket on the platform at Newcastle Central Station as we waited for the London train. He and Mum both insisted that the first thing I do was save up enough money so that I could come home if I wasn't happy, and I suppose this was a starter for that fund, or at least emergency money of some sort. Instead, after our first day at work, Pat and I returned to the car lot and handed it over – along with seventy dollars of our savings – for a 1949 Ford V8 in a queasy green with a peeling chrome trim. 'The colour of phlegm,' said Pat later. 'It was meant for us.'

It was dark as we took the car through its paces along the Lake Erie shoreline. I could feel my shoulders relax as I drove, my grip on the wheel lightening with each new mile. I was always happy at the wheel of a car. Just like my father and brother. When Doug and I were children, we would cling to the back of my father's seat as he drove, one in each ear, crying, 'Go on, Dad! Faster! Faster!' My mother, in the passenger seat, remained strangely unperturbed, passing round bags of toffee as we flew down country lanes, sending sparrows chattering into the hedgerows.

I turned the heater to full and it blasted us with air so hot we had to turn it down again after only a couple of minutes.

'A heater that works!' said Pat.

'Oh, this is grand! Where shall I take you, madam?'

'Don't get stopped for speeding on our first drive.' Pat looked across at the speedometer. 'It *is* working, isn't it?'

'Ninety-six miles an hour,' I said, straight-faced. 'Flatus always flies like the wind!'

It was the third car we had bought together, and the name Flatus – the medical term for wind – had been passed on from one to the next, ever since Flatus the first, a draughty old Hillman Minx that had no windows until we stuck in X-ray plates we had scrubbed clean.

'Well, just remember where we are, and policemen carry guns here.'

We turned back for the city, almost euphoric, but when I saw the rooms lit up in apartment buildings, each one a fleeting snap-shot of family life, I had to force myself not to think of home.

Mount Sinai, a large Jewish hospital, was a handsome red- and white-brick four-storey building on East 105th Street, built forty years earlier and added to ever since. Inside, everything was bright and modern. I marvelled at the sliding doors on the wards – even though I found that I moved too quickly for them at first. At the fact that every ward had its own dishwasher. That the wards in the new wing were more like hotels, with private rooms, ensuite bath-rooms and intercoms to the nurses' station. And that the patients in these rooms even behaved as if they were guests, refusing to take their tablets if they didn't want to, and calling up their own doctors from bedside telephones with petulant demands.

Our first day of work was spent in Central Supply, which housed all the sterile equipment. I could hardly believe the gadg-ets: rubber-tube dryers, glove-powdering machines, something to shake down thermometers. It was somebody's full-time job to look after all the thermometers in the hospital.

And the disposable equipment! Tubes and syringes, cups for medicine and water, towels and gloves. I thought of all the hours we'd spent at the General, collecting and stacking glasses, wheeling teetering trolleys to the kitchen, down corridors where cleaners leant on their mops and dared you with the set of their mouths to dirty their floors. All those hours washing and patching rubber gloves – blowing them up to check for holes, mending them with glue and bits of rubber if necessary – then powdering and packing them ready for sterilization in the autoclave.

I'd always loved new technology, and I thought with pleasure how all this labour-saving would mean more time to devote to the patients. However, when I moved on to the wards, I saw that the reality was rather different. The paperwork seemed to be the *raison d'être* of the job, with each patient's chart prepared in triplicate, price lists consulted with alarming regularity and bills constantly flying off to the cashier. Everything had to be paid for, and if it wasn't the insurance company paying, it was the patients themselves.

'Oh no, you don't give them this one unless they're fully comp.'

The nurse wagged her finger at me and flattened her chewing gum behind her front teeth with her tongue. I was so transfixed by this that I barely registered what she had said. A nurse chewing gum on duty! What would the staff nurse say? I braced myself for the reprimand – the staff nurse was coming towards us – but when none came I realized that she, too, seemed to be working something around in her mouth. I tried to imagine a nurse chewing gum in front of any of the staff nurses or sisters I had worked for in England, but the idea was too preposterous.

I returned my thoughts to the matter in hand. As I was only preparing a drip, I thought there might be a misunderstanding, but the nurse came closer, shook her head and said, 'That's the most expensive one. Their insurer won't pay for it, and they sure as hell won't pay for it themselves without a fight.'

When she saw my baffled expression, she lowered her voice. 'This is the charity ward,' she said, not unsympathetically. 'That's life, isn't it – you get what you pay for.'

The charity ward! I had a sudden vision of workhouses, and despair, and stale, shuffling bodies that was totally at odds with the pleasant conditions around me. Did I really want to work in a country where certain patients were deemed more worthy of treatment than others? Where there was not just a second class of patient, but a third and even a fourth class? It went against all my ideals and niggled at me for some time.

I was troubled by the same thought later when I identified a woman showing signs of a bedsore. This would have been considered a disgrace at home, and I pointed it out discreetly, not wanting to get anyone into trouble.

The student nurse I had spoken to shrugged her shoulders in a way I would never have dared do to a senior colleague. 'Whaddya do? That's what they pay a private nurse for.' She snapped her gum. 'Seventeen dollars a shift. I can't wait to graduate.'

Much later, I learned that the queue of people who stood every day at a counter on the ground floor, close to where I collected my fortnightly pay cheque – a queue that never got any shorter, and that included the smartly dressed as well as the more down-at-heel – was comprised of former patients waiting to pay their bills. Or, far more likely, to pay off a small portion of their bills. Some would be paying them off for evermore.

'What happened to putting the patient first?' I asked Pat, as we sat drinking tea in the kitchen at the end of our corridor and eating a slice of my mother's fruit cake. Two irritatingly enthusiastic voices discussed some sporting event on the radio that was playing in the background.

If Sister Gunn had succeeded in anything, it was in drilling that philosophy into us. I could hear her still: 'What comes first, nurses?' And us chorusing, 'The patient. Always the patient.'

'What happened to holding hands and mopping brows, and just sitting listening? A sick patient is specialled day and night at home, regardless of who they are. It's shocking that in this country the level of care depends on how much money you have.' I shook my head, and wiped a crumb from my lip.

'And those blooming charts!' I continued, flushed with annoyance. 'They have more time lavished on them than the patients do!'

Pat sighed. 'I know, it drives me mad, too, but at least we'll be on our own wards in a couple of weeks. Do things our way.' She was about to pop another mouthful of cake into her mouth when she stopped suddenly, and added, 'It's not all bad, is it? Remember how we had to refold every single piece of bedlinen when it came back from the laundry for that grumpy old sister at the General? Sixty sheets a day. Talk about time-wasting! And that time I was pulled back by my belt because I was about to overtake a more senior nurse in the corridor!'

We finished our cake in silence, then Pat pointed a finger at me. 'I hope you're not forgetting what we said before we came here, Nurse Brady. We've come to see America – not to change things.'

'Yes, I suppose so. They've managed well enough without us up until now. Mind you,' I did some quick maths in my head, 'if we *did* do a couple of private shifts, just occasionally, well, think of the money we'd make . . .'

Pat raised her eyes at me over her teacup and was about to say something when a voice from the radio boomed out, 'Here's Chuck's Crazy Price Store, bringing you the news right into your home. Yes, it's only Chuck who brings you twenty-eight newflashes in one day. Chuck's Crazy Price Store. It's totally cra-a-a-zeeee!'

And we both burst out laughing.

One day during that first week, a man who had come to visit his wife thrust a bunch of flowers at me, and with barely a break between each word, commanded, 'Poodeez enwodder.'

I was so taken aback by his manner that even when I had managed to work out what he was saying, I simply stared at him with disbelief.

He repeated it. 'Put these in water.' Then, seeing my reaction, hastily reached into his trouser pocket, obviously thinking I was waiting for a tip.

I grabbed the flowers. 'There's no charge,' I said, and flounced off.

Pat had a more embarrassing exchange, when a trainee nurse asked her if she should pass water before she went off duty.

'I was a bit surprised at being asked such a personal question, so I just said it was really up to her,' she told me, wiping her eyes before she could continue. 'But she wouldn't let it rest. "Do you think I'll have time?" she went on. I was getting more and more embarrassed, and in the end I told her that I really couldn't see why not, and hurried away. A few minutes later I saw her handing out fresh water to the patients, and remembered that they talk about "passing" when we would talk about "giving out". I told her about my misunderstanding, but she didn't see the funny side so that made matters worse!'

Miss Harrison had told us she would do her best to put us on the same rota, and she had been true to her word. When our period of 'orientation' was over, we were given our own wards, next door to each other, and put on night duty. Miss Harrison was slightly apologetic over this, but the truth was we loved working nights. Eleven to seven was a doddle compared to the twelve-hour night shift at home. And with just ourselves and an aide, we could run the wards the way we wanted to, the English way. The paperwork had to be done – that was the American way – but if a patient needed special care or someone to talk to, there was time to do it and no one to tell us otherwise.

My ward was a large, high-ceilinged room with twenty beds, plus a few smaller rooms off the passageway where the nurses' station was situated. It held all the rawness of life. I had seen some strange and exotic cases during my tropical diseases training, but in some ways the patients with malaria and leprosy and once – horrifically – rabies had been a cushion from reality. Now, I was back in the real world, and things did not come much more real than inner-city Cleveland.

One night, a few weeks into my stay, I was in the middle of charting, while my aide, Lillie – a hard-working coloured woman with a sharp sense of humour and a laugh that never failed to set me off too – had gone to the canteen to fetch us both a drink. Three o'clock in the morning can be a desperate time on nights, when you fight against your own tiredness, conscious of the fact you are still only halfway through your shift. But here – with all the paperwork to keep me busy – it was rarely a problem, and it wasn't unusual to see some of the worst admissions in the small hours. Indeed, I was waiting for one now.

I had been aware of a noise for some time before it began to arouse my curiosity. It sounded like a burst from a distant television set or radio – a wailing, interspersed with terse speech. The sound grew louder and I realized it was my new patient, heading my way. Not wanting my sleeping ward woken, I jumped up from my seat and went out into the corridor.

'Who did it? Just tell us who did it! Pfff! Stupid bitch!'

Coming towards me was a porter pushing a trolley flanked by two policemen. One of the policemen was bent so low over the trolley, he might have been about to kiss the patient, who turned out to be a young coloured woman. Her crying reminded me of a siren, stopping and starting with a mechanical regularity.

I marched to the trolley to stop it getting any closer, putting a finger to my lips and what I hoped was my sternest expression on my face. Both the officers regarded me for a second. Then the one who had been shouting carried on, perhaps not quite so roughly. 'Come on, kid. It's for your own good.'

And his colleague added, 'We go pick him up now, and teach him a thing or two.'

'Please, officers, I—' I began to speak, but now the patient sputtered out between her sobs, 'I ain't telling you nothing, you goddam—'

Lillie, who had just returned from the canteen, took the woman's hand and tried to calm her. 'Shhh, honey. Shhh.'

I breathed in and drew myself up to my full five feet four inches, looking from one man to the other in my most regal manner. 'This is my ward and my patient. I am sure there is a time and a place for all this, but for now please leave her to me.'

The shouting policeman took a step towards me. He was the taller of the two, at well over six feet. I was so close to him that I could smell the cloth of his uniform, and the strong scent of male skin inside it.

'Can't you see what a state she's in?' I continued, suddenly aware how small and vulnerable I was. 'You're not helping matters.'

The other officer held out his hands in an appeasing manner. 'We understand that the kid's upset, ma'am, but she's been shot and she's withholding information. All we need to know is who done this to her, then we leave her alone.' He turned to the patient. 'He doesn't love you, kid, don't fool yourself. Next time it happens, you're dead.' He pointed at his head with two fingers, and made a popping sound with his mouth.

The girl began to howl even louder, and mutter words I couldn't make out.

I spoke more angrily. 'Porter, I'll take over now, thank you. Could you please escort these gentlemen off the premises.'

How English I sounded! I reminded myself of a character in an old-fashioned play, where everyone spoke with plums in their mouths. Not that I had ever spoken like that in my life, but it was surprising how prim and proper even my Newcastle accent could sound here at times. And when Americans playfully imitated us, we always came out sounding like some member of the aristocracy. (Though, strangely, patients often took us for Swedish or Dutch, much to Pat's annoyance.)

I saw glances pass between the men, and after a scornful look at me they finally turned round and set off down the corridor, their boots creaking as they went.

But before they had gone far, the taller one said in a loud voice, without looking back, 'She ain't worth it. They're all the same. Let 'em kill each other, that's what I say.'

His companion laughed. 'But we'd be out of a job without the niggers!'

I could feel my blood rising. I was on my way after them when Lillie grabbed my arm. I looked at her, and she shook her head.

I knew she was probably right. That they weren't worth wasting
time on. That my patient was the only one who mattered. But I
did regret not giving them a piece of my mind.

Nina was nineteen years old. Luckily, the bullet had merely grazed
her leg. Whether her boyfriend had wanted to harm her more
seriously, I didn't know, or want to know. She loved him, she told
us. He loved her. It had all been a mistake. The next minute she
was 'gonna kick him outta that door' if he so much as 'shuffled his
dumb ass' anywhere near her. I dressed her wound, and after the
doctor had prescribed a sedative, left her to sleep, her body con-
tinuing to heave with sobs.

'Poor kid,' said Lillie, as we drank tea together at last. 'What sort
of a man does that to his woman? And good on you, Miss Brady,
for telling those officers enough was enough. They need putting
in their place some time, they do.'

I wondered how it must have felt for Lillie, listening to their
abusive talk about coloured people, but it was a question I didn't
know how to ask.

Instead, I said, 'What worries me, Lillie, is what sort of people
have guns in the first place?'

'Guns? Why, lots of people have guns. Need to protect themselves. It's a violent world.'

Having already tended more gunshot wounds in my first
weeks in Cleveland than I had seen in my lifetime, I was doubtful about the logic of this. The latest craze, according to the local
paper, was to jump into someone's car at traffic lights, pull a gun
on the occupants and demand money from them. It was a story
I hoped wouldn't reach the press – and my parents – back
home.

'It sounds like a way to make it even more violent, if you ask me.'

I took a sip from my lukewarm drink, and made a mental note not to ask Lillie for tea in the future. She was now tucking into the foot-long salami roll she ate for her breakfast. I usually tried to keep my distance when this was going on, finding the smell alone enough to turn my stomach at this hour.

She put down the roll and pushed her glasses down her nose so that she could see me over the top of them. She had large expressive eyes, flecked with yellow, that reacted to everything. 'There's two old gals live on the floor above me – sisters, never been apart. And one night I hear a terrible bang, sounds like it come right through my own window. I don't dare move. Convinced someone's taken a pot-shot at me. I lie trembling all night long, saying, "My good Lord, I don't know what I done, but I sure am sorry if I upset you any way." Well, next morning, Sadie – that's the older one – she come down and she say, "Sorry about last night, Lillie, but I was polishing my gun and it went off clean in my hands." And doggone me if it didn't go right through the wall of her kitchen, out through the bedroom closet and into the headboard on her own bed!'

Her eyes were brimming with laughter now. She began to chuckle, shaking her head with disbelief, and soon her whole stout body was shaking, too.

I couldn't help joining in. Then I shuddered. 'I could never even touch a gun, Lillie.'

Lillie dried her eyes and picked up her sandwich. 'Well, I guess you'll never need to.' She took a large bite and began to chew it with satisfaction.

I got up. It would be time to wake the patients soon. Lillie pointed to my cup and waved her hand to her lips apologetically. When she had finished her mouthful, she said, 'Now look here –

you've barely touched your tea. And they say you British drink it straight out of the faucet.'

Through the high windows of the main ward, I saw the sky beginning to lighten in one corner. The sound of a siren cut through the stillness, but I felt strangely at home.

2

Open House

Cleveland, Ohio, Spring–Summer 1957

Hospital grapevines are the same the world over. A doctor stopped me in the corridor one night with, 'Hey! Are you one of the pair who bought a car after four days?' Miss Harrison, who we continued to dine with whenever we saw her in the canteen, had clapped her hands in delight at news of our purchase. Having a car felt like a necessity to us, but we soon realized that while other foreign nurses at Mount Sinai talked about buying a car one day, very few of them actually did so. Needless to say, many of them had been working at the hospital for months yet hadn't been out of Cleveland.

Tom and Bill ran an automobile repair shop on Ninth and St Clair, and I turned up there, soaked to the skin, one evening in March. Pat and I had decided to drive out to Sandusky, a beauty spot on Lake Erie, before going on duty. We were with Joan Peutrill from Leicester, one of the newest arrivals. Joan's flatmate,

Tommy, was engaged to Ralph, an American boy, and Joan spent a lot of time with us.

We had only just set off when it began to rain. Drops clattered on to the roof of the car like someone emptying a bag of baking beans. We thought it might be hail. But no, it was simply the heaviest, noisiest shower we had ever experienced. Then, just as we reached Public Square, where it felt as if all the shops and offices of downtown Cleveland had emptied at exactly the same time and every driver in the city was now behind the wheel of his vehicle, weaving in and out of the traffic lanes with gay abandon, we got a puncture.

We took our life in our hands to push Flatus into a side street, then I left the others with the car and set off to find assistance. I was wearing only a thin jacket over my blouse and skirt. Soon I was so wet I might as well have taken off my shoes and stockings and walked barefoot in the puddles. In fact, I was sorely tempted to do so, but it seemed a little too unladylike. It had always been the bane of my mother's life that while Doug was a pale, blond boy who never looked untidy, I was a grubby little thing with rosy cheeks and unruly dark hair. When would I remember I was a lady, she would ask me. Well, I remembered now.

The sign for the garage was a welcome sight. The metal shutter door was about three-quarters of the way closed, but by crouching down I could slip underneath. I stood up and looked around. The workshop smelt of petrol and oil, familiar smells that reminded me of my father's garage at home, as did the neatly stacked boxes on the high shelves that lined the walls. A large Chevrolet filled most of the space, and muffled sounds coming from behind it suggested that somebody was at work. As I stood there dripping, wondering if I should call out, a man appeared from a doorway in the far corner, looked at me, disappeared, then returned, holding out a towel.

'Good lordy! You've taken a proper soaking.'

He wore slacks and a leather jacket, a rumpled fedora pulled down over his forehead, and I wondered if he was the owner. The man who then popped his head out from the other side of the Chevrolet was younger, probably not much older than me, and wore dirty green overalls. He offered me a black hand to shake, then withdrew it, laughing. They both watched me as I politely blotted my clothes, trying not to notice the musty smell the towel left on my fingers.

'I'm sorry about this,' I blurted. 'We've got a puncture, and blow me, we don't have a spare. We knew we should get one, but we haven't had the car long. We were in Public Square – right beside a "No Stopping at All Times" sign – and it's chock-a-block there right now! My friends are waiting with Flatus – the car, I mean. I said I'd try to get help.'

The men looked at each other, amused. Neither of them spoke.

'It wasn't raining when we set off,' I added helplessly. I wished one of them would say something. It wasn't like Americans to be lost for words.

'It's just a puncture,' I continued. 'I know how to—'

The older man interrupted me. 'I think she's saying she's got a flat, Bill.'

I took off my jacket, wrung out a sleeve, and was mortified when I saw the torrent that flowed on to the floor. 'Oops, sorry! I'm making quite a puddle here.'

Bill tugged on his baseball cap and looked at me shyly. 'No problem, ma'am. We could listen to you talking all day. Don't get many accents like that round these parts, do we, Tom?'

Tom looked at me, nodding slowly. Then he jingled his keys in his pocket. 'You're busy. I'll take her over in the truck to fix things up.'

It had stopped raining when we went outside, and a pale sun was washing over the concrete, lighting up rainbows in the greasy puddles on the forecourt.

Tom drove with an arm on the window ledge, and I felt his gaze on me a few times. 'So you got a flat,' he said. He made a clicking sound with his tongue. 'Some place to get a flat!'

As we reached the street where I had left the others and I pointed out the car, he quipped, 'She sure seen better days!' and I felt a flash of indignation on behalf of Flatus.

'She's not that bad! We're going to Philadelphia for the weekend soon.' Then I added, a little more deferentially, 'Do you think she'll make it? We're taking a carload with us.'

He looked at me again. 'Let's see what we can do.'

He made us all sit in his van as he removed the wheel.

'Just stay there, right. No funny business.'

We laughed, but he looked serious. We did as we were told.

When the wheel was off, he came back to the van and popped his head inside. 'I'm gonna give you a new wheel, then I'll take this one back and get it patched up for you. Looks like you got yourself a spare. Can you come and pick it up one evening?'

We thanked him and said that would be no problem.

When he had finished, he beckoned us over, and we trooped obediently out of the van to admire our new tyre, and to pay him what seemed a very reasonable sum. Tom wiped his hands on a piece of rag and walked round Flatus, his eyes constantly shifting between us and the car. He lifted the bonnet – he called it the hood – and peered inside. He lay down on the ground and did something to the exhaust. He wiped his hands again, then opened the door and slipped inside, where he fiddled with the controls.

Pat folded her arms and muttered, 'I don't think we said we wanted a full body inspection.'

'He seems very nervous of us,' said Joan.

He opened a window. 'What'cha say you paid for this?' Then, without reacting to our reply, 'You ever met the Queen of England?'

Joan rolled her eyes. 'I was busy when she rang last night, but I'm thinking of popping up to Balmoral for the weekend. Fancy it, girls?'

Tom looked at her, slightly puzzled, then got out of the car and ran his fingers over the peeling paintwork, sighing to himself. Finally, he came towards us smiling. He did have a nice smile, I thought, I had to give him that.

'Not a bad little machine you got yourselves, but she could do with a bit of a tighten-up in places. When you come round for the spare, we'll sort her out for you.'

That was how we adopted 'our garage'. Tom and Bill turned out to be two of the nicest men we ever met, and we became good friends. Perhaps not friends in the usual sense – we didn't learn very much about their private lives, and they certainly didn't pry into ours. But they were good to us, and we did our best to return their kindness when we could. Sometimes Tom would have found something at the back of the store cupboard, gathering dust – or so he would tell us – that would suit us nicely: an old car radio, a new wiper, a prism that sat on the dashboard and reflected the traffic lights that soared over each junction. We paid for any new parts we needed, but not for these extras or, ever, for their labour. 'She's quite a novelty,' they would say, as if that explained their generosity. Pat and I joked that they treated Flatus like a child whom they enjoyed spoiling.

'What you say her name is?' asked Bill.

'And it means?'

They both chuckled.

'Are all English ladies like you two?'

'We're nurses. We're a special breed.'

When we found out from Bill that Tom's wife was feeling run down, we smuggled some vitamins and iron tablets from hospital supplies, and were embarrassed to see how grateful he was.

There was so much going on, it was hard to feel homesick. Working nights was grand. We slept until three or four in the afternoon, and there was still time to spend the evening with friends before going back on duty. On our weekends off we drove to Philadelphia, Washington DC, New York – wherever took our fancy – taking a carload of girls with us to share the cost. Even the nearest of these places was almost four hundred miles away, and we often left behind a cold and snowy Cleveland, arriving in a city where magnolia trees were already showing off their tulip-like flowers. We would pile Flatus with blankets and pillows so that we could sleep in the turnpike plazas for one night – making the most of their coffee shops and washing facilities – and treat ourselves to a cheap hotel on the other, returning just in time to get ready for work. I had bought a pair of slacks for travelling in, but I always had my skirt ready to change into so that I would look respectable at our destination.

I think our arrival in New York City was one of my most exciting arrivals anywhere, driving over the George Washington Bridge and seeing the lights of Manhattan floating before me. The next day we took a bus tour all over the city, from the Bronx to Brooklyn, climbed to the crown of the Statue of Liberty and went by high-speed lift up the Empire State Building, hardly able to believe how small all the other skyscrapers looked from the top. At Radio City we made an appearance on TV, which was shown in the next room, and saw how colour television was made. The quality was surprisingly good. The only low note was the squalor of the Bowery, which our tour guide seemed to find hilarious. 'Look at this guy with no shoes on, and this one here trying to sell his coat! You ever seen anything like it?' If we had driven there on our own, we would have thought a plague had hit the place and stopped to offer first aid.

We were also frequent visitors to Detroit, where Pat's Aunt Anne and Uncle Bill had emigrated many years before with their two children, now grown up and with families of their own. Their grandchildren were proper little Americans, and even Aunt Anne and Uncle Bill sounded American now, with just a hint of their old north-eastern accents discernible. Pat and I had looked at each other in horror when Aunt Anne asked the two-year-old if he wanted mustard or ketchup on his hot dog, until Uncle Bill told us that American mustard was far milder than ours.

In quieter moments, when no one came knocking on our doors suggesting a run out to the lake, or an evening listening to records in someone's apartment, there were always letters to write. We both wrote to our parents two or three times a week, as well as to friends and other family members, and had a reputation for receiving the biggest pile of post in the building. Hearing from home was a joy, and made us feel close to everyone without ever actually wishing we were there with them.

'I'm sure Mam is boring everyone to death about me,' Pat said, as we sat reading that day's post in the kitchen one evening. 'Aunt Edith says she went round for a cup of tea and the latest instalment. She'll be inviting the whole street in next.' She stopped and frowned at me over the top of the letter. 'Gwenda, you're not singing along to the advert, are you?'

I hadn't realized I was doing it. '"You'll wonder where the yellow went when you brush your teeth with Pepsodent,"' I trilled, along with the radio. I'd had the darn tune in my head all day. 'Sorry.'

'I think I miss the BBC more than anything, apart from people, of course,' mused Pat. 'Sometimes I just long for *Take It from Here* or *The Goons*. Those adverts drive me to distraction.'

We were invited to lunch one day by Margaret Falconer, a Scottish lady Pat had nursed, who worked as housekeeper for a wealthy widower in Shaker Heights, one of the smartest residential districts in the city.

We both felt like poor relations as we stepped inside. The house had fitted carpets, chandeliers and, Margaret told us, in an accent that could only be described as Scottish-American, three bathrooms.

'Tssk,' she said. 'As if anyone needs three bathrooms.' But we could tell she was proud of the fact, especially when she added, 'Actually, I have my own, with a pink bath and basin and everything matching.'

We stood in the kitchen, drinking Scotch on the rocks, while Margaret fried two-inch-thick steaks. It was hard not to gawp at the electrical gadgets that lined the work surfaces: a coffee-maker, an oversized toaster, an electric frying pan, a small device that Margaret said was for grilling sandwiches.

'I'll fix you one some time. Grilled cheese. They're delicious.'

A machine under the sink turned out to be a dishwasher. 'Och, you must have them at home by now? And look,' she chuckled, enjoying our admiration, 'you pop your laundry down this chute here and it ends up in the basement, right beside the washing machine. Go down and take a look.'

We were amazed to find part of the basement done out like a saloon in a Western, with swing doors, a bar and a polished wooden floor. Some old furniture and a stack of packing cases stood neglected in one corner, and in another, a deep-freeze hummed. 'Big enough to put a man inside,' said Pat. 'Who has enough food to fill one of these?'

We peeped inside. A few neatly labelled packages lined the bottom. We closed it quickly.

'My mother would love all this,' I said to Margaret, back in the kitchen. But even as I said it, I wondered if it was true. I could even hear my mother's voice, 'What's wrong with a pair of hands and a good bit of elbow grease?'

We drove back to Mount Sinai much later than intended. Lunch had been followed – with indecent haste – by dinner. Tomato juice, chicken, beans, baked potato and salad, followed by ice-cream cake. 'You nurses need feeding up. I've seen how hard you work.'

Now, Pat sat cradling her stomach. 'Too much,' she murmured.

We watched the palatial houses rolling by.

'Aren't they magnificent,' said Pat.

But I was looking in their driveways. A sweep of white down the side of one car gave the impression of a tucked-in wing that might at any moment unfurl and fly the vehicle away. The head-lights on another were like a pair of eyes, deep-set under heavy brows, while on its neighbour they protruded like the golf-ball eyes of a magnified insect.

America, I thought, land of the automobile. Every American I had met so far was a driver. When Lillie moaned about her old Studebaker not starting on a cold night, I would smile to myself, thinking how, at home, excuses for lateness usually involved buses, not cars.

In April we had an unexpected snowfall – seven inches in one night. It melted, came back again for a day, then suddenly it was spring. Buds sprouted from what had appeared to be dead branches, the grass was a bright, acid green, and flowers were blooming as if someone had come down and planted them all in the night. The temperature shot up to seventy degrees. Then seventy-five. Spring? It felt as if we had gone from winter to summer in one short hop. On the ward, patients cooled themselves with fans made of stiff paper.

'Aren't they lovely,' I enthused, picking one up by its wooden handle and admiring the flowery scene it depicted. I almost dropped it in disgust when I saw that the reverse bore the name of a local funeral home in bold, unmissable letters.

The air outside was smooth as butter. The British nurses spilled on to the streets in a sweep of colour, tipping their faces to the sun. I bought a pair of red shorts and practised wearing them in my room, wondering if I would dare venture out in such scanty apparel.

One balmy evening, we rushed off to an open-air swimming pool, but the car park was deserted and the pool empty, brown leaves rustling quietly into piles in its corners.

We called in at our garage on the way home, and found Bill on his own, sitting on an upturned crate, smoking a cigarette. He seemed a bit edgy and, when pressed, told us he had just done a job for the 'customer from hell'.

'I was tempted to use this,' he said, patting his leg.

'What?'

He stood up and took a revolver out of his pocket. It was as small and neat as a toy.

I flinched. 'Is it real?'

'Sure it's real. It won't help me if it fires water.'

He gave me a strange look, and said that surely I must have known that Tom had a gun with him when he drove me to Public Square that night.

'We don't take no risks, 'specially with English ladies who talk funny.'

We were both shocked, and Pat hurriedly told him about our abortive attempt to go swimming.

'Psshh. It ain't summer till Decoration Day. What were you thinking of?'

We moved into a hospital apartment, in a block on East 100th Street, on a steamy Thursday afternoon in May, just as the weekly tea-party was taking place.

'We've never been back,' said Pat guiltily, as we packed Flatus in full view of the gathering. 'Apparently they drink iced tea now. Did you ever!'

A few nurses left the party to give us a hand. One of them, an American girl called Barbara, insisted on accompanying us to the apartment, where she cheerfully carried several loads up the two flights of stairs. We promised to invite her to an English tea-party one day, and she made us laugh by telling us how, on a trip to the UK the year before, she had finally discovered the purpose of a wedding present her mother had received from British relatives.

'She'd had this tea cosy for thirty-five years, and nobody knew what it was.'

'What did she think it might be?' we asked her.

Barbara shrugged. 'She just thought it was real pretty. She still says it's too nice to use.'

The living room had a non-functional fireplace, a divan, a desk and a pair of lamps. At one end of it, an archway led to the bedroom, into which two single beds, a built-in wardrobe and two chests of drawers just fitted. A small passageway at the other end of the living room led to the bathroom and kitchen. It was perfect. We walked through it, touching everything with curious fingers.

'I can't wait to get this full,' I said, opening the door of a fridge far bigger than any fridge I had ever seen, except for the one at Margaret's. 'Then it will really feel like home.'

Pat was opening kitchen cupboards and drawers. 'We need some cutlery, some more plates and a couple of saucepans.' She sat down at the table. 'Which is it to be until we're paid again?'

'Food, of course. Silly question.'

We cooked some chicken and opened a tub of cole slaw, eating with a shared knife, fork and spoon.

'This is how Americans eat, anyway,' said Pat between mouthfuls. 'Have you noticed how they cut everything up first and then use a fork? It reminds me of being back on the children's ward.'

We rinsed out the frying pan to boil water for coffee and drank it sitting at the large windows on either side of the fireplace, which faced some of the other hospital apartments across a narrow alley.

'Yoo-hoo!' called a voice, and we looked up to see Joan hanging out of the window opposite, waving her hand madly.

'What's it like? Need to borrow a cup of sugar?'

'I think we've got sugar, but it would be handy if you could pass your vacuum cleaner over. In fact, you might as well come round.'

I hadn't been sure if Mitzi liked me and Pat at first. She seemed to prefer the company of the more sophisticated girls, who spent lots of time talking about which doctors they fancied and held their arms at a permanent ninety-degree angle to flaunt their burning cigarettes. I had smoked a bit at dances in my younger days, hoping that it made me look more grown-up, but I had no intention of wasting my money on cigarettes now.

'I told him, he's not walking over me no more,' I heard Mitzi say as I passed her desk one morning when I was still living in the nurses' home. She was invisible behind a group of admirers, whose heads bobbed fiercely in approval.

Then, one night, there was a message on the ward for me to call in at her office the next day. I found her smoking a cigarette with such savage pleasure, it might have been her last one ever. She got up when she saw me, all smiles, stubbed out the cigarette and asked me to follow her down the corridor. Her frock, tight at the bodice, with a wide belt and a billowing skirt, accentuated her curvy figure.

We stopped at an unmarked door. She chose a key from a large bunch and unlocked it. We were in what appeared to be a storeroom, filled with cardboard boxes and spilling carrier bags.

'There's a rummage sale tomorrow,' she explained in her girly voice. 'I thought you could use some of this for your apartment?' The last word was almost a squeak.

She opened one of the boxes. 'I've put aside two nice big dinner plates, a serving plate, four cups and saucers, a set of cutlery . . .' Her voice took on a sing-song quality as she listed it all. 'Oh, and this Dutch oven is just to die for. Is there anything else you need? I don't suppose Dr Gibbons left you anything worth having? Doctors!' and she rolled her eyes in mock exasperation.

I wondered if she was angling for more information about our apartment's previous occupant, but she carried on, not waiting for a reply. 'Well, I should be able to get all of this for you for a couple of dollars.'

I was almost struck dumb with gratitude, and surprise.

She even sent one of the porters to our apartment with the two boxloads she had procured, plus some mail that was still turning up at our old address. The poor boy looked ready to expire in the heat, and we had to revive him with a glass of lemonade and a slice of fruit cake.

I took Mitzi some home-made toffee a couple of days later, to say thank you. Stepping outside was like walking into the steam room at a Turkish bath.

'They say it's going to hit ninety,' she said, when I found her stocking one of her beloved vending machines. She fanned her face with her hand and pursed her lips, making a whistling sound. (Whoever said that the British were obsessed with the weather had obviously never been to America. I was convinced that they were even worse. Every ten minutes on the radio we were informed – with the enthusiasm only Americans could muster – of the current temperature in the city, the expected high of the afternoon and the expected low of the night.)

'Lord, you could fry an egg on me today!' she chirped, though to my eyes she looked as immaculate as ever. 'Hey, what's this? Aw, aren't you a doll! Most of my baking comes from Betty Crocker.'

The humidity continued to rise. We took a cold shower before we went to bed, and another when we awoke, slipping on shorts and sleeveless shirts, and not bothering with make-up. One night Joan and Tommy's fridge broke down, and all the food had gone bad by morning.

Pat was chuckling over the *Observer*, which her parents posted out each week.

'Everyone flocked to the coast last weekend. Guess how hot it was – sixty-five degrees!'

'It sounds blissful. I can't remember what sixty-five feels like.'

'Darn chilly.'

It was 3 July, and the radio gleefully informed us that five hundred and thirty-five people were expected to die in the celebrations the next day, four hundred of them on the roads. We agreed that we would stay in to catch up on letter-writing rather than risk life and limb.

That was the plan, but just before we went to bed the next morning we heard Joan calling at the window. She was inviting us to lunch with the International Students' Group, who were having an Independence Day party at a lakeside picnic ground. We'd been hearing about the ISG ever since we arrived, but never managed to find time to get ourselves to their meetings.

'It's the perfect chance to meet everyone,' she pleaded. 'They're all so friendly.'

We didn't need much convincing. Besides, it was too hot to sleep for long that day. Even the thin sheet I lay under felt heavy. We got up at around noon and took a cool shower. I put on a sleeveless cotton sundress that didn't cling anywhere, and a pair of open sandals which were little more than a sole and a single leather strap. Out on the street, the air seemed to hum with heat and trepidation. We could hear shouts in the distance, and the cracking of what might have been gunshots. Flatus sat there waiting, an oven on wheels.

It was a relief to arrive at the picnic ground, with its shady trees and cooling view of the water. A gentle wind puffed on our faces like warm breath. Behind us, the city trembled in the haze.

The party was well under way. Groups of men were expertly tending chicken on the barbecues. 'Herman Leggon!' said one of the chefs, an American, raising a hand that held a giant pair of tongs. Although we had already witnessed American barbecues on lazy days at the lakeside – we sometimes headed straight for the outdoors after coming off duty, to sleep under the trees or on our lilos – we were still enthralled by the sight of men cooking with such confidence. We introduced ourselves to Herman, who said he was working in a laboratory while he studied for his master's degree, and he showed us where the bottles of beer and soft drinks stood in cooler boxes under the trees. I spotted some familiar faces: Bunty and Agnes, both of whom we had met at the tea-party on the day of our arrival, and had continued to socialize with; an Irish girl called Josie, who had accompanied us on our trip to New York; Joan, who was deep in conversation with a tall, serious-looking man in browline glasses. But there were lots of new faces, too. The ISG was open to university students as well as hospital workers, and some of the American 'host' members didn't belong to either category.

Bunty introduced us to a neat, dapper man of slightly oriental appearance, with a smooth round face and lively eyes. He was wearing a pair of immaculate tailored shorts and a crisp white shirt. Enrique Kierulf had lived in America for several years, and worked for a shipping company on the Great Lakes. We were thrilled when we discovered that his father had been the director of a leper colony in the Philippines that we had read a lot about.

'How do you like the United States?' he asked. His voice had an American twang, though it was still heavily accented. 'You like the way they eat?' His eyes twinkled. 'They like their food, no?'

We laughed, remembering our very first picnic, when we had turned up at the lake one afternoon with our bathing suits, a sandwich each and a can of Coke. We had watched as parties of Americans drew up in their vast cars, unloading cooler boxes as big as coffins from the trunks, slamming cleavers down on whole chickens, dishing out cole slaw and potato salad from industrial-sized containers. One man had even taken a pile of logs from his car and proceeded to chop sticks for a fire, before donning a chef's hat and apron. We must have looked to them as if we were living on rations, for we quickly found ourselves the recipients of plates of salad, chicken legs and even pieces of choice steak.

(Now we were slowly becoming Americanized ourselves, stopping at the Ice-o-mat to fill our cooler bags, and realizing that what could be eaten inside could also be eaten outside.)

We had tried to attract Joan's attention a few times, and she finally looked over, bringing her companion with her.

'This is Olov, from Sweden.' She introduced us all, then carried on, excitedly. 'He says he knows someone who's selling a Plymouth '48. I'm seriously thinking of buying it. What do you say, Gwenda?'

'But Joan, you can't drive.'

'I know, I know.' She waved her hand, nonchalantly. 'But you can teach me, can't you? You taught Pat to drive.' She looked at me beseechingly. 'Just think. We can take two cars every time we go away. We can have twice as much fun.'

Our house was open house, and everyone knew it. Girls would pop by in the evenings, giving us time first to get up and showered. Our tuna casserole would serve two or half a dozen; a chicken – bought oven-ready for a dollar twenty from Benny in the drugstore – might last a day or a week, depending on the company. We had acquired a kettle – a gift from our Irish friend, Celia, when she came round for breakfast one morning – so making drinks was easier.

Now we had male visitors, too. Some of the boys from the ISG were students at the Western Reserve University or Case Institute of Technology, and lived in dormitories. They loved feeling part of a proper home. Tony Shibley – a slight, handsome boy from

Lebanon, with the enthusiasm and childish humour of a school-boy that could be both endearing and maddening – opened the fridge one evening to help himself to a beer and almost dropped his glass with surprise when he saw the amount of food inside.

'Can I come and live here?' he asked. But he and the others always behaved like gentlemen.

Enrique was soon one of our most regular visitors. Rarely did he turn up without a gift of some sort. If he had been out in the country that day he would arrive with a box of fragrant peaches, cherries or strawberries, or huge corn cobs encased in their silky wrappings. Once, he rang to ask us if we were hungry, and appeared at the door twenty minutes later with a chicken he had just cooked, along with a bottle of Scotch and another of ginger ale, to make us all highballs. He and his friend, Andy, an American of Russian parentage, often turned up with music for us all to listen to on the record-player that Pat had treated herself to. How we loved that record-player! No more having to endure those maddening commercial breaks on the radio. (Though I still went around singing the Pepsodent jingle.) I had brought with me to America my record of *Salad Days* – a musical about a magic piano that makes everyone who hears it dance – and we now knew every song by heart, as did Joan, who spent as much time in our apartment as she did in her own.

'Oh, look at me, I'm dancing!' I would cry, mimicking my favourite song, as I sprang from the passageway into the living room with a hot dog in each hand.

We were pleased that our new crowd seemed content to keep friendships platonic. While there was the inevitable romance in the ISG, the knowledge that most of us were not in Cleveland permanently, that we came from different backgrounds and cultures, was an unspoken barrier to romantic attachments, and a boyfriend was the last thing on my mind. Yes, I wanted love one day – just not yet. Pat, on the other hand, insisted that she would never marry, and would toss her head indignantly when I told her otherwise. But I liked the comfort of a friend like Enrique: I could sit beside him, as close as I would have done to Doug, and not worry about an arm slipping around my waist, or hot breath closing in on my ear. Enrique was a confirmed bachelor, and we felt safe with him.

My mother had often warned me about the dangers of the male sex. 'You don't know what men can do to you,' was one of her favourite sayings, frequently spouted when I told her about the boys I was going dancing with, or the ones Pat and I had met on one of our jaunts. She seemed unaware of the fact that, as a trained midwife who had delivered babies to fourteen-year-old girls in London's East End, I had a good idea by now of exactly what men were capable of, and I was also sufficiently confident to tell them when enough was enough.

Everyone liked Enrique. He took on a role between that of brother and favourite uncle, and, in truth, I had no idea how old he actually was. Late thirties? Early forties? It was Enrique who gently shifted our guests homeward when he could see we were tired or needed to get ready for work, but who stayed around to do the washing-up when everyone else had gone.

One night, as we sat playing records, he saw me struggling to mend the zip on my jeans. Owning a pair of jeans was quite a novelty. I'd barely worn trousers before we got here, except for an old pair of my father's when I went sledging as a child. But when it became clear that jeans and slacks were acceptable wear for women, that nobody was going to give us disapproving looks or refuse to serve us when we were out, I had decided to embrace this new culture – in the matter of dress, at least – and join the crowd. I'd already had to mend this zip once before, and had made a poor job of it. Enrique shook his head at my efforts, and took the jeans home with him, returning two nights later with a new zip that he had fitted himself. When we asked him where he had acquired these skills – there seemed to be little he could not turn his hand to – he gave a quiet smile that I hadn't seen before, and touched my arm lightly. Something had happened to him during the war, we learned later. But I knew, at that moment, there were things about Enrique we had no right to know.

When the heat and humidity began to wane, we decided to throw a party.

'But it's party day every day at your place!' said Joan when we told her.

Joan's flatmate, Tommy, was married now, and Maureen Houghton, a pretty blonde girl with a short boyish crop, from Feltham, West London, had moved in with her and become one of our crowd. She had arrived in Cleveland a couple of months before us, but when we first met her she had never left the city. When we invited her to New York with us, she had said no at first.

'My friend and I are saving up until we can stay in a four-star hotel. I don't really fancy roughing it.'

When the two of them did some sums they found they could easily afford the hotel now and opted to join us after all – until the friend saw how stuffed the car was and decided that she would be too uncomfortable in the back seat, leaving Maureen to come on her own. The prospect of a luxury hotel with no one to share it with was not quite so appealing and Maureen had ended up in the YWCA with the rest of us, where she was perfectly happy.

When we wrote a list, we realized to our surprise that most of our friends were Europeans, so we racked our brains to think of some Americans.

'Some of the new interns are quite friendly,' said Pat. 'No doubt they'll soon be as cocky as the last lot, but I can think of a few we could invite. And one of the registrars always asks how we're getting on with the car. I think he might be married, though.'

We ended up with a list of just over thirty guests, of several nationalities, and with a few more men than women.

On the day of the party, Enrique woke us in the early afternoon with a phone call and we began to tidy up. We made one hundred and sixty sandwiches, and threaded combinations of cherries, marshmallows, cocktail onions, pineapple pieces and wieners on to sticks. We prepared our own punch, but put a poster we had pinched from the park on the door as a joke – 'Absolutely no intoxicating liquor of any kind'. It caused lots of amusement, but we did have to rush out and grab two American doctors clutching a bottle of whisky, who thought they had come to the wrong apartment and were on their way back downstairs.

At 8 p.m., six men arrived and helped to move the furniture so that there was plenty of room for dancing. We set up a bar in the passageway, and laid out the food in the kitchen. Now we were ready for the rest of our guests. As they arrived, we couldn't help noticing that the European men wore suits and asked permission to remove their jackets, which we granted, while the Americans wore casual slacks with coloured sports shirts hanging over the top.

We were making a lot of noise and someone kept turning the music up, but living in a block full of hospital workers who were mainly young and kept irregular hours like ourselves, we thought that it might be overlooked for one night. However, somebody must have complained, for just after 11 p.m. the manager of the apartments, Mr Neppel, knocked on the door with his young sidekick. He had rarely spoken to us since we moved in, except for one occasion when he had presented us with a Stars and Stripes sticker to go on the car, along with our Union Jack. 'Looks kind of lonely on its own,' was all he had said.

Enrique greeted the men with a glass of punch, and ushered them inside before they had the opportunity to state their complaint. He showed them the collection of English postcards tacked to our wall – I saw them nodding their heads politely – introduced them to some of the other guests, then excused himself. I peeped out of the kitchen a couple of times and noticed them standing on their own, watching the dancers, their faces impassive, though the younger man began to tap his foot when 'Shake, Rattle and Roll' came on. Twenty minutes later, as I prepared hot dogs and burgers for the very hungry, a flush-faced Mr Neppel was serenading me to Frankie Laine, and declaring me the most beautiful woman he had ever seen. His mother's maiden name was Brady, he told me, so he'd always had a soft spot for me.

'Doncha just love it,' he said, opening another beer and nodding his head in the direction of the door. 'All these folks from all over the place, together enjoying themselves. That's what the world should be like. I wish I could show this to the politicians. I wish I could bring 'em all here and show 'em. Then we'd have no problems, then there'd be no more wars . . .'

I realized he was rather drunk, but he appeared to be genuinely moved. In the passageway outside, his friend was dancing cheek-to-cheek with our American friend Barbara.

Somebody changed the music, and the fruity voice of Elvis seemed to tremble off the walls.

'Let's dance!' Mr Neppel grabbed my hand. 'Hey, baby! Get down with me!' His grip was surprisingly tight for a man who had to be at least seventy. I left the hot dogs simmering on the stove and let him lead me into the living room. He clapped his hands and spun round. 'Hey, baby!' he cried again. 'Let's do it!'

Pat, who was dancing with Andy, raised her eyebrows at me across the room.

Half an hour later a banging on the door heralded the police, but when they saw how respectable everyone was they left us very politely, and even apologized for interrupting the evening.

'I'm surprised you didn't have the police up and dancing,' Pat said hours later, as we got ready for bed. The last guests had left at 3.30 a.m. Enrique, Andy, Herman and a couple of other boys had stayed behind to help tidy up. The furniture was back in place, most of the washing-up had been done, and we had a long lie-in to look forward to.

'Well, it wasn't me who got Mr Neppel going, I can assure you. I'd be surprised if I don't have a bruise where he grabbed me.' I looked indignantly at my fingers, as if expecting something to materialize before my eyes.

'A likely story,' said Pat, as she slipped into her baby-dolls. She changed the subject. 'I did wonder if the American girls would come in their bobby socks and flat shoes, especially as we've never seen some of them in anything else. But they all looked very nice, didn't they?'

When we first arrived, we had been surprised to find women of our age and older, and even doctors, wearing thick white ankle socks with blue and white shoes, as if it were a uniform, and even if they were wearing a skirt.

A couple of days later, Pat was home before me, setting the table for breakfast.

'Remember that patient I told you about, Pat, the one who . . . What is it?'

She was pointing at the radio. 'Haven't you heard about Sputnik?' She practically spat out the word.

When I didn't reply she went on, 'The Russians launched a satellite last night. The Yanks are trying to play it down, but I don't think they're too impressed at being beaten. Some of my patients are very put out about it. They think it's got sinister connotations.' She fluttered her hands in the air in a ghostly manner.

'No doubt because they didn't get there first. I wonder what Eisenhower has to say about it.'

'Oh, Ike's putting on a brave face. Listen, there it is again. I'm sick of hearing about it now.' She switched off the radio with a flourish. 'Let's have some *Salad Days* before we go to bed.'

3

Salad Days

Cleveland, Ohio, Autumn–Winter 1957–58

'Are we really going home next April, when there's still so much to see?' asked Pat.

We were in a car park at Niagara – Pat, Joan and me – waiting for our companions to return from their trip on the aero car over the rapids. It was our fourth visit to the falls so we had done most of the attractions by now, though we never tired of their splendour, or of seeing the water laced with rainbows. We had driven up the day before with Maureen, Barbara and Celia, who had never been out of Cleveland before. I think I got as much pleasure from watching Celia as I did from anything else. She was thrilled just to drive through three states, even though it was dull and rainy for much of the way, to eat her picnic lunch on the back seat, to stop at a Howard Johnson's for dinner and then to book into a tourist home, nestled between a pair of honeymoon motels, whose garish lights flickered across our curtains all night long. It was dark by the time we arrived and we had driven straight off to see the illuminated falls, which elicited further cries of delight.

'Forty-eight states,' Pat continued, dreamily. 'I bet there's a car here from all of them. Oh, look, South Dakota! Doesn't the name just make you want to be there!'

Joan said she had seen a car with a California number plate, and that the driver looked just like Gregory Peck.

I wound down my window. We had woken up to glorious sunshine. It was October now, but the sun could still be fierce. I had a couple of postcards on my lap that I intended writing, but in the warmth of the car I closed my eyes, wondering when I had last slept for more than a few hours. I had done a couple of back-to-back shifts recently, hoping to save up enough money for the mink stole I had promised my mother, but we always seemed to spend whatever we had, and when I had seen the price of the stoles, I wondered, despairingly, if I would ever be able to afford one.

Pat's voice made me start. 'Well? What do you think? Do you want to see more of the country or not?'

I had written to my brother, Doug, asking him if we might be able to travel on one of his Merchant Navy ships when the time came, but other than that we had not spoken about going home. One day, in some hazy future, we would return laden with gifts, and try not to turn up our noses at fruit cocktails for pudding (we were agreed that while English chocolate couldn't be beaten, our desserts were decidedly unadventurous) and our parents' old-fashioned attitudes.

'Well, I don't suppose we're ever likely to come back,' I replied, putting the postcards into my bag in defeat. 'So we might as well make the most if it. Perhaps we can take a carload and drive to the west coast?'

'Two carloads,' piped up Joan. 'We can cover the whole country. And Canada. And what about Mexico?'

'What about passing your test first?' I said. 'They're starting to ask after our families in the test centre. Not a good sign.'

Joan sighed. 'It was the parking last time. And I'd done it so perfectly with you.'

'What about Olov?' asked Pat, putting on her most innocent face. 'Will he be coming with us?'

Joan was silent for a few seconds. She and Olov had seen a lot of each other recently.

But when she spoke up she said, 'Don't be silly. I'm not tying myself down yet.'

The ISG organized more events than we could possibly attend, but we rarely missed ice-skating at the Winterhurst rink on the west side, usually followed by coffee and doughnuts at Enrique's, then a mad dash through Cleveland to get to work on time. I had asked for a pair of skates for Christmas every year since I was ten years old, but they had never materialized. As I was paying to hire a pair every visit, I decided that I could justify treating myself to my own at last. They were reduced from seventeen dollars to ten, had a Sheffield steel blade, a tartan lining and a fur tongue. I felt like Sonja Henie when I put them on.

One night, on a group expedition to the rink, Pat and I were already inside and about to take off our shoes when we heard the sound of raised voices. The woman on the door was saying firmly, 'I told you, it's policy. I'm not making no exceptions.'

We went back to join the others and see what was going on. Enrique had a strange expression on his face that I hadn't seen before – almost a smile, but one of utter disbelief. He shook his head. 'Ay, ay,' he said to himself under his breath, followed by some words of Spanish I couldn't catch. When he saw our puzzled faces, he said, 'This is not good. She won't let Herman in. Says no coloureds allowed.'

By now, twenty voices were raised in protest and a few of the men stepped forward to remonstrate with the woman, but Enrique held up his hand to stop them. He addressed her again himself.

'Well, lady, as you can see, my friends here don't like this one bit. We're members of a club, and we come from all over the world. My mother is Spanish and my father's family were Danish, and I grew up in the Philippines. This friend here is from Germany, and this one's from China. Look at us all real close. We all look different. We all talk different. And you tell me you're not admitting a fellow American?'

The pitch of his voice had gone up, but he sounded more perplexed than angry. 'It's very crazy.'

The woman looked back at him. I noticed her knuckles were clenched. When she spoke, she barely opened her lips. 'I don't make the rules.'

She looked at us all. She looked across at Herman, standing at the back of the crowd, then looked quickly away. Pat went up to Herman and slipped her arm through his.

'Don't worry, Herman. We'll all leave. There's plenty of other things we can do. I'm not sure I want to stay anyway.'

She, Herman and some of the others began heading for the exit.

'We all come in or none of us do,' said Enrique.

The woman puffed out her cheeks. She unclenched her hands now, and held them out in appeasement.

'I guess I can make exceptions. You look like a decent bunch. Go on, quickly.'

And she called out when we were all inside, as if in self-justification, 'And don't none of you give me no trouble.'

I couldn't help making more of a fuss of Herman than usual that evening, but he acted good-humouredly, as if nothing had happened.

It wasn't the first time we had come across segregation. I had noticed, particularly on our out-of-state journeys, that the toilets for coloured people were often hidden away in outbuildings, while everyone else had the use of modern indoor facilities. Although I had grown up in the white world of Newcastle, it had never occurred to me that people of a skin colour different to my own should be treated differently. My first proper contact with coloured people had been at the maternity hospital in London where I did my midwifery training, and where I was one of the few white members of staff. There I discovered that coloured people were as funny, infuriating and sensitive as the rest of us.

I felt a hot rush of indignation on Herman's behalf, but I also felt embarrassed and ashamed, as if I was just as much to blame as the woman on the door, as if every time I had benefited from a 'Whites Only' sign I had been snubbing my friend.

I thought about the vivacious coloured lady who had come to speak at the club one night and had us all singing Negro spirituals after just a few minutes, accompanied by much hand-clapping and stamping of feet. She told us of her own efforts to wipe out the colour bar in the town where she lived. She had asked the owner of the local store to put an 'Out of Order' notice on the water fountain for whites, so that everybody had to use the one signposted 'Coloureds'. In the baking heat, folk were desperate for a drink, and though they were reluctant at first, soon everybody was drinking from the same fountain. Then she asked the owner to remove both signs, encouraging people to use either fountain. And they did. It was a small but significant step towards overcoming segregation in that community.

'Hey, don't look so serious!' Herman laughed and took my hand as we skated, telling me that as the weather got colder, the lake in the park opposite the hospital would freeze over.

'It's like having a private ice-rink,' he grinned. 'But wait till you see how cold it gets.'

Walking to work one night, two skeletons jumped out from a doorway and I nearly died of fright.

'Jeez, sorry, but it *is* Hallowe'en,' said one of the culprits when I could finally breathe again. 'You all right, miss?'

On the ward, a plastic witch and her cat sat on my desk, and some bats with luminous eyes hung upside down on the walls.

Lillie came towards me, stopped suddenly and clutched at her chest, where a bright red stain appeared to be spreading.

'Aaargh, they got me. I'm a goner.' She staggered forward, clutching the desk for support, but before I had time to react, a strange snorting sound made her shoulders shake and she folded over, convulsed with laughter.

'Oh, you shoulda seen your face! Happy Hallowe'en, Miss Brady!' She peeled the red patch from her dress and held it out for inspection. 'It was my kid's. Looks real, huh?'

I was determined to get my own back on Lillie, even if I was a day late.

'Well,' I said to Pat over breakfast the next morning, 'in Britain we don't need a special day to play tricks, do we. We've got a sense of humour all year round.'

'Listen to you, Mrs High Horse.'

Lillie was a little late in getting to work, which suited me perfectly. I was buried deep in my report as she approached. 'Patient looks blue but gives no reason,' someone had written on one of the charts. A few months ago I'd have gone rushing over to the bed to deliver oxygen, but now I knew that 'blue' was most likely to refer to the patient's mood.

'What time do you call this, Lillie?' I said, without looking up.

She must have noticed the change in my voice. I sounded as if I had a couple of gobstoppers jammed in my mouth. I could almost hear her tense up, unsure what to make of this new me.

'Oh, Miss Brady, that old Studebaker of mine. Do you know—'

'It won't do, Lillie. It just won't do.'

I put down my pen with a flourish. A shudder of laughter threatened to overwhelm me, but I managed to hold it in. I straightened up, looked her in the eye and gave a massive grin – more of a leer really – my huge joke-shop teeth sticking out at an alarming angle. She jumped back with her hand to her mouth.

'Oh, oh!' Then she joined in my laughter.

I told Lillie how I had worn the teeth once for a particularly dry nursing lecture. I could tell that the poor tutor could hardly bear to look at me, thinking I had some terrible deformity, yet was compulsively drawn to do so.

The following week, I took Joan to sit her driving test for the ninth time.

'Hi, Joan!' said the girl at the desk.

Two of the examiners walked out of an office together talking, and waved in recognition as they passed.

I tried not to laugh. 'Well, at least they like you. Good luck.' I gave her arm a squeeze.

I was sitting writing a letter when she bounded over.

'You've passed!' I cried.

'No. Failed on the parking. Again. But the girl at the desk gave me a tip. Says there's another centre and to try that one next time. She says it often does the trick.'

By mid-November the shops were decorated for Christmas, and the lake had frozen. There were two small islands we could skate around, and we had great fun pretending to be in the Ice Follies, resulting in a swollen knee for Joan and a lovely black and blue bottom for Pat. The air was so cold, it was painful to breathe. The inside of our noses crystallized. Our faces stung. Every time we went out I would don a pair of knee-length socks under long johns, another pair of socks, ski pants, a blouse, three jumpers and a windcheater. We had some of our best times on that lake, and afterwards everyone usually ended up back at our place for hot dogs and coffee before we had to shoo them away to get ready for work.

One evening, we were warming up after a lengthy session with Joan and Maureen. We had been joined by a bubbly little nurse called Molly Adams, from Hamilton, near Glasgow, who was always beautifully dressed. The road trip had become a serious topic of conversation now whenever Pat and I and our two neighbours got together, and Celia, too, had expressed an interest, asking us to put her name down for whatever we were planning. Now Molly's eyes lit up.

'It sounds super! Are you going to Hollywood?'

We assured her that while we certainly hoped to visit, we didn't expect to be staying with film stars.

'Wait till I tell my wee sisters,' she exclaimed.

'If you come with us, you won't be able to bring your whole wardrobe,' warned Pat.

Molly pulled a sad face, then she perked up. 'I've got an aunt and uncle in Los Angeles and they're desperate for me to go. We can all stay with them.'

That would be grand, we agreed.

She looked thoughtful for a second. 'I'm going to need a new bathing costume before we get there. I need to diet, too.' She patted her stomach.

'Molly, there's nothing of you,' said Pat. 'Anyway, we'll probably all need fattening up by the time we get to Los Angeles if we don't find work along the way. You'd better warn your aunt to start cooking now.'

Christmas is a special time in hospitals, and I had spent some memorable ones in the past. The previous year, Pat and I had been at London's Hospital for Tropical Diseases, where Sister had decided that out of all the nurses we should be the ones to work on Christmas Day. We had been appalled at first, knowing that we were leaving for America soon after, but we decided to make the most of it. We turned our ward into a jungle, with large-fronded plants and brightly coloured flowers, monkeys swinging from nets, and even a giant mosquito with eyes made out of ping-pong balls hovering above the doorway. It dropped down to greet you when the door was opened, and took ages to get right. But our *pièce de résistance* was a stuffed lion we borrowed from a taxidermist, which we sat on Sister's desk, waiting for her arrival. Her screams could be heard all over the hospital, before, 'Beadle! Brady! I'll get you for this!'

This year we were off on Christmas Eve and working on Christmas night, but as that gave us two free days we felt that we were in the best position to cook dinner for everyone. We decided to invite all of our ISG and nursing friends who had nowhere to go, and planned a two-shift sitting to accommodate everyone. The list came to twenty-nine.

On Christmas Eve we got up early to start cooking the first of our two turkeys. Tony, our Lebanese friend, rang to see if he could come round, and we gave him the job of decorating the tree. He turned out to be a dab hand at it, and it looked beautiful when he had finished, standing on a snow blanket and decorated with the baubles and lights that our friend Margaret from Shaker Heights had lent us. He then hid in its branches the thirty-five tiny little presents we had wrapped.

'Gee, I think I need to get myself a new job,' he said, admiring his own handiwork.

The tree lights were like glass candles, with coloured liquid inside that bubbled when they were switched on. We were transfixed by them. Our Christmas cards – many of them from nursing friends and sisters from our old hospitals – hung on the walls, and the overall effect was very festive.

We invited the postman up for a highball, a piece of my Christmas cake and a small present from the tree, and he was tickled pink (though I thought the cake was rather dry compared to my mother's). A decent chap, he had once carried two loads of shopping up the stairs for us.

Friends arrived to leave presents under the tree while we were busy making mince pies, chocolate crunchies, coffee kisses and bunty creams, and cakes were disappearing under our noses as fast as we were producing them. Enrique and Andy helped to move some furniture. We borrowed Joan and Maureen's table, and all of their chairs. A doctor and his wife on the ground floor who were going away for Christmas lent us half a dozen smart dining chairs, though they looked too good to sit on.

Enrique had brought two large but differently shaped parcels with him, and Pat and I had to draw lots to see who had which gift. Pat won the bigger of the two – a box measuring about two by three feet – and we were scratching our heads wondering what they both could be. He also decorated our front door, which we thought a bit over-the-top, but all our neighbours had done the same so it was obviously the right thing to do.

We had already made a Christmas pudding, which I had taken on duty with me earlier in the week so that it could steam all night. Nobody had seen one before, and all the night staff kept popping into the kitchen to take a look. Mrs Remenyi, my supervisor and a great help to me at times, had begged me to save her a piece. She had tasted my toffee, and now thought that all English food was 'real special'. Knowing that Christmas pudding could divide people, I hoped it would live up to her expectations.

On Christmas Day we got up at 6.30 a.m., made coffee, put some light classics on the record-player and opened all our presents from home. An hour later we were surrounded by a mountain of gifts that included ski pyjamas, Dairy Box and Brazil nut chocolates, long-playing records, Yardley gift sets, jars of mincemeat, handkerchiefs, jewellery, aprons, Christmas cakes, underwear and packets of liquorice. I felt rather guilty that we had so much. Enrique had insisted we open his presents early, and we found an electric frying pan for Pat and an electric hand-mixer for me, just like the one I had sent my mother. Doug's present to me had been a phone call home the night before, when Mum told me she had a cold and Dad said that Doug would be helping them to insulate the loft when he got back from his current tour of duty. It was funny, I mused, the banal things that came up in conversation when we had been looking forward to speaking to each other for so long. Pat said her parents were just the same, and that in her call her mother had spent half the time reading out her father's chest and collar measurements that Pat had asked for but would have happily received in a letter.

We went to church, then came back and cooked ourselves breakfast in the new frying pan. Then we popped over to Bunty's, where one of the girls had a short-wave radio, and heard the Queen's speech at 10 a.m. our time.

'Let's have a toast to all our family and friends back in good old Blighty,' said Bunty, handing round some plastic cups of warmish fizz, and a couple of the girls got tearful.

'My granny will be up and doing the hokey-cokey now after too much sweet white wine,' said one of her room-mates, and that got everyone laughing.

Once we got back to the apartment, it was all go. The first guests arrived at 11.30, twelve of them who were going on duty that afternoon, so we concentrated on getting them fed.

We had two further sittings after that. Enrique spent a whole hour carving the turkeys, and it looked as if we had enough meat to serve twice as many people.

It was quite an exercise in logistics. We had borrowed all of Joan and Maureen's crockery and cutlery, but we still had to improvise. We served gravy in coffee pots and milk jugs, cranberry sauce in yogurt tubs. The roast potatoes were balanced on the Christmas pudding, and the plate of meat was on the floor. If anyone so much as put down a spoon or fork, Josie would have it washed up and given to someone else. Our twenty-nine had grown to thirty-three, though we weren't quite sure how.

Squashed at the far end of the table for our final sitting, I looked round at our guests. Faces were flushed and happy, everyone was looking after everyone else. They had all dressed up for the occasion. Molly looked beautiful in a silver scoop-necked off-the-shoulder gown with a pale pattern of roses, as did Celia, in a dress of dusky pink with a high neck, three-quarter-length sleeves and nipped-in waist. The men were just as fetching in their suits and ties. There were few nicer things in life, I thought, than seeing other people enjoying themselves.

After lunch was finally over, and the Christmas pudding deemed a success, we sang carols and dished out the gifts from under the tree. Everybody had bought and wrapped a small four-dollar present – pocket diaries, memo pads, biros, make-up bags, mini tool-kits – and it was pot luck who got what.

Then most of the party went for a walk in the park, except for Josie and Agnes and a man called Rafael, a Mexican doctor from the clinic whom we hardly knew, who helped us wash up.

We served tea when they all returned: turkey sandwiches, mince pies and our cakes.

'No Christmas will ever be like this one,' said Andy, looking quite emotional, as they were all leaving. As he was normally quite a reserved man, we took this as high praise.

'Hear hear!' said Herman. 'When we're all older and have children of our own, let's tell them that all you need for a good Christmas is to be with friends.'

'Friends and good food!' shouted someone else.

'And English Christmas pudding!' added another.

Later that night, Bunty and her gang threw a party, and we went there for a couple of hours before it was time to go on duty.

It felt strange arriving on the ward. The day's events already had a mythical feel to them, as if they belonged to a story I would relate one day. There was no sign of Christmas anywhere – not a card or decoration – which only added to that feeling of strangeness. Lillie had the night off, but I had brought a little gift for the aide I would be working with.

'Gee, thanks,' she said, turning the handkerchief over in her hands before thrusting it into her pocket. 'It's neat.'

I asked a sixteen-year-old girl who was admitted that night what she had been given for Christmas, and she replied, quick as a flash, 'A sixty-dollar coat.'

'Oh, how super. Is it nice and warm?'

'I guess. It cost sixty dollars, ya know.'

Everything felt a bit flat once Christmas was over. Boxing Day was not a holiday, and the word 'Christmas' disappeared from everyone's vocabulary except ours. Chez Beadle and Brady, the decorations stayed up until Twelfth Night, and the Christmas spirit carried on well into the new year as we continued to delight in our gifts and eat up our turkey, chocolates and home-made cakes. We even discovered a ham at the back of the fridge that we had bought to accompany the turkey, then forgotten about.

On the Friday after Christmas, we popped to the club as usual, and were immediately roped in to help with their new year party. We were given the task of buying paper hats and noise-makers from club funds.

'Noise-makers?'

'You know, horns, things to blow and make a noise.' The girl giving us our orders hooted through her cupped hands by way of demonstration.

'Ha ha, very funny. What do you really need?'

But they were serious, and we found ourselves buying items

that we had thought were only bought by parents organizing parties for six-year-olds.

At least we didn't have to worry about the catering, which was being done by the Chicago Sausage Company.

We both had new year off, and everyone was coming back to our apartment after the party. Enrique and Andy arrived early to collect us, and just before we left, the phone rang. I picked it up and immediately wished I hadn't. It was the hospital, wanting me to come in. My replacement had called in sick. It wasn't the first time we had been asked to work on our days off.

'You know why, don't you,' Lillie had said. 'The girls are entitled to two sick days a month, and some of 'em just take it. Try saying no some time.'

Pat was mouthing that very word at me now.

I felt torn, not knowing which side I was letting down the most. The extra money was always attractive, of course, though I really wasn't thinking of that tonight. In the end, I agreed to work, but not until 12.30 a.m., so that I could see the new year in with all the others.

The party was fabulous – a word Americans used a lot – and Pat and I blew our horns along with everyone else. An Indian boy made a delightful toast to us all, then, after at least fifty kisses – some of the boys came back for seconds – Andy whisked me off to work.

I drove Joan to Fairfield for her driving test, steering her Plymouth like a great barge. She seemed more nervous than usual.

'Oh Gwenda, I'm not sure I can do this. Look at my hand, it's shaking.'

'Well, you don't know what to expect here. It's probably better that way.' I pulled up at the test centre. 'Go on, you know you're capable.'

She sat very still, looking straight ahead. I wondered if she was going to get out of the car.

'Think of California,' I suggested, opening the driver's door. 'Let's go.'

'Oh, the pressure!' she moaned, putting a hand to her forehead.

We had started to plan our trip seriously, talking about it at every opportunity. Joan would take her car, with Maureen and Molly as her passengers. Pat and I would take Celia. One evening we had finally managed to get all six of us together to discuss it and plan our route. We would drive west, stopping off at a few places on the way to Denver, Colorado, where we hoped to nurse for a while. From Denver we would travel north to Yellowstone National Park, south to the Grand Canyon, and on to San Francisco to work once again, probably via Yosemite. If we had time – and enough money – we would take a slow route home across the southern states, and perhaps even go to Canada first. We needed to be back in Cleveland before the end of the year, and home for Christmas 1958. Spending Christmas with our families again was a must, and we had assured them we would return by then. Pat and I were lucky that both sets of parents were very understanding about our changes of plan – in their letters, at least.

I was flicking through a magazine in the waiting area, reading about the latest antics at the Mocambo on Sunset Strip, when Joan came and sat down quietly beside me.

'Well?'

'Oh, you've been so patient with me, and I hate to keep on letting you down.'

'Don't be silly. We'll come back another time.' I put down the magazine. 'What was it then?'

'Nothing. I've passed.' And she jumped up and down like a child. I grabbed her hands and we swung each other round, to the amusement of the woman on the desk.

'Come on then, you can drive me back. Don't spare the horses.'

As we drove through University Circle, I thought I recognized some of the boys from the club in a group at the side of the road. I reached over and tooted the horn a few times, then hurriedly opened my window and yelled, 'She's passed!'

They waved enthusiastically, though I could see now that I didn't know them.

Pat and I went to see Miss Harrison to tell her that we were leaving. With six of us going all at once, it seemed only polite to give her as much notice as possible. We both went rather pink as we heard how we were 'reliable, steadfast, pleasant and accommodating – as well as being excellent nurses'. She told us how much she would miss us, that she would write references for us, and that we would be welcomed back on our return.

The mercury continued to fall, and it was all that anyone talked about. They said it was the coldest winter for seven years, and that Mardi Gras in New Orleans was in danger of being cancelled because of the cold. A carload of girls from Mount Sinai were going down there, so we hoped that there would be something for them to see. Benny in the drugstore told me that Lake Erie was frozen all the way to Canada, and that some hare-brained folk were trying to drive across it. I shook my head at their stupidity, then mentioned the idea to Pat, who looked at me as if I'd lost my mind.

We worked extra shifts to save up as much money as possible before leaving. The plan was for each girl to put one hundred dollars in the kitty to start off. Flatus was to have a thorough overhaul from Tom and Bill, so we had that to pay for, too. We did some private nursing at the Women's Hospital, where Matron always welcomed us with open arms (though I did feel guilty, knowing that my pay was coming straight from the patients themselves). With its laundry chutes, dirty-dressing chutes, hatches for clean dishes and hatches for dirty dishes, hatches to and hatches from the central supply room, working at the Women's Hospital was always a smooth operation, if a slightly surreal one. I went to find another nurse to borrow a stethoscope one day, and found her and her patient watching *Queen for a Day* together. She was even sitting on the patient's bed – a cardinal sin at home. She whispered to me that her patient was a very nervous lady who liked to have somebody with her at all times. I couldn't help thinking that I would be rather bored sitting doing nothing for the greater part of eight hours. And to spend it watching American television would be sheer torture, especially if that programme happened to be *Queen for a Day*, which was a favourite of Pat's Aunt Anne. 'Would *you* like to be queen for a day?' host Jack Bailey asked the audience of women, before the show's contestants shared their personal tragedies, interspersed with advertising for laxatives, shampoo and pet food. We had watched it the first time with an appalled fascination, all the way through to the weeping winner – usually the one judged by the audience to have suffered the most – being crowned and robed while her list of prizes was read out. Now it just made me cringe.

We usually refused invitations to pop round and watch television, which seemed to be a popular activity here. Doug and I had withdrawn our savings – twenty-five pounds each – to buy my parents a small set for their silver wedding anniversary in 1954, but

I had never seen so many until I came here. If British television ever moved closer to the American model, Pat and I agreed, we would rather not have it at all.

One night, just after we had finished eating, there was a series of rhythmic raps on the door, which could only mean Joan. When we opened it, she was standing there with Maureen, her eyes big and anxious behind her spectacles.

'Can we come in?' Joan had a peculiar expression on her face, her lips stretched into what looked more like a grimace than a smile.

She normally walked straight inside, so the formality bothered me too. I ushered them both into the living room and sat them down, while Pat and I exchanged a worried glance over their heads. When Joan grinned sheepishly at Maureen, I relaxed a little.

'Come on, I'm on tenterhooks,' said Pat.

'Gosh, I'm sorry to scare you,' Joan began. 'It's not that bad. I mean, it's not at all bad, not for me, anyway. Oh, what am I talking about . . .'

'Spit it out,' I said.

'I'm getting married,' she said in a sudden rush. 'So I won't be able to come with you.' And with that, she burst into tears.

Joan, not coming on our trip! We could hardly imagine it without her.

'And we assume this man is Olov,' said Pat, wiping her own eyes, for we were all crying now.

'Olov? Oh no, didn't I tell you . . . Yes, of course it's Olov. Dear Olov. I couldn't leave him for so long, and when he proposed, well . . .'

'This calls for a drink, not tears,' I declared, and went into the kitchen to prepare highballs.

After we had all toasted Joan, who had now composed herself, she began to look more like a radiant bride-to-be.

'We're going to live in California – Olov's got a job there – so I'll get there after all.'

'California! We can come and visit you!'

'And is there a date for the wedding?'

'Yes, the day before you leave. I couldn't not have you all there. It'll just be a small affair, of course. Now, before you ask any more questions,' she stopped, and wagged a finger at us both, 'there won't be anyone from England, my parents that is. I haven't told them yet. It's just not possible to bring them out here. And I don't want to cry again.'

'Perhaps your parents could come out for a holiday one day?' said Pat helpfully.

Joan nodded glumly.

'But at least we'll see you again. Oh Joan, it's not so bad after all.' I put my hand to my forehead. 'Oh, I'm as bad as you now. It's wonderful news. And we're all delighted for you. But it won't be the same without you.'

We had over fifty guests at our farewell party, and it went on all night. We bought one hundred and ten long bread rolls, cut them into four, and with the help of Joan, Maureen and Celia, made them into sandwiches. Every single one of them was eaten. Though the party started at 8 p.m. prompt and the first guests did not leave until 4 a.m., not a single person was the worse for wear. At five-thirty, twenty of us had some champagne that Herman had brought. We gave him the honour of opening the bottle, but the cork came out before he was ready and went straight for his eye, breaking his glasses. He was fine, but we were most upset on his behalf. At around seven, Enrique, Andy, Herman and Tony joined us for a proper English breakfast.

While the party was a happy occasion, if you were to scratch the surface of any of us, you would have found a layer of sadness not too far below. Some of the university students we had met through the ISG were returning to Europe soon, and we knew that we were unlikely to see them again. In fact, it was anyone's guess who would still be in Cleveland when we returned later in the year. Enrique, certainly, Herman and Andy, too, but many of the others were part of a constantly shifting population of students and doctors who gained their qualifications then returned to their home countries. One of the boys proposed that we all meet in Rome in 1960, and everyone agreed a little too loudly and enthusiastically.

The apartment was in chaos as we emptied drawers and cupboards and tried to decide what to take with us, what to leave behind – and where to leave it. Luckily Enrique had a spare room he said we could use, and Mr Waldman, Margaret's boss, whose clients clearly included a set that we didn't move in, offered to clean and store our furs for us, which we thought was a hoot. We did, however, leave our tweed coats and suits with him, the latter unworn since our arrival.

Every night somebody different invited us for a 'last' dinner, and we gave some tea-parties of our own, including one for the hospital bigwigs who had been kind to us. Sadly, Miss Harrison, our special guest, had to decline at the last minute due to illness. We said goodbye to Tom and Bill, who had pronounced Flatus

ready to hit the road. Tom fitted the windscreen washer I'd
bought out of the kitty – a marvellous device which squirted
water over the glass when I pressed a button. As he admired his
handiwork, he said that if we returned in the same car six months
later, Flatus ought to go into the Ford Museum. We hadn't even
left, but I was already anticipating the look on their faces when
we drove back to see them.

We received so many parting gifts, it was quite embarrassing.
Bunty gave us travelling vanity cases; three of the newer arrivals
we had taken under our wing (one of whom I had been teach-
ing to drive as she planned to buy Joan's car) gave us a tartan
travelling rug; Lillie gave me a white nylon waist slip with a lace
trim at the bottom. At the club on our last night, we had to open
a big box in front of everyone. When we got to the bottom, we
found the spectacles Herman had broken. 'A souvenir!' said the
card with it.

One day there was a hand-delivered envelope in our mail box,
and inside it a short note from Mitzi, wishing us good luck and
enclosing a sticker for the car. It depicted a curvaceous blonde –
not unlike Mitzi herself in stature – wearing a bikini, and the
words, 'Watch it, Mister – Soft Shoulders' under the picture, a ref-
erence to the sides of the roads that one had to be careful not to
drift on to when driving.

We made some purchases ourselves – a roof-rack (now that
five of us would be piled into one car, space was going to be in
short supply), and a super little camping stove with two burners,
a cylinder for petrol and a shield on three sides.

Joan was married on a bright day in early April, amid smiles and
tears. She wore a white broderie anglaise dress and carried a

bunch of spring flowers. Tommy, her old room-mate, was her matron of honour, and we all mucked in to help at the reception afterwards.

I wore my coral coat and dress and white hat, and the boys were tickled pink to see us all dressed up and made quite a fuss of us, which we lapped up.

After helping to serve coffee to the guests, I popped into the ladies' room to powder my nose and heard someone crying in one of the cubicles. I was horrified when Joan came out, wiping her eyes. But she batted away my concern with a shake of her head.

'I'm just being silly. I'm missing my mother. It's not right, is it?'

I offered her a clean handkerchief and looked at her anxiously, not feeling able to reply. Pat and I had agreed that we could never even contemplate marrying overseas, away from our families, yet we had already attended the wedding of Tommy and Ralph, while two of our ISG friends, Kari and Jadran, were engaged. We could only conclude that love must do strange things to you.

Pat and I popped in to see Margaret in Shaker Heights after the wedding, while we were still in all our finery. She had roasted three guinea hens, and made soup, spaghetti and meatballs for us to take away with us.

'Och, I'm sure gonna miss you two,' she said, picking a piece of lint from her dress.

We promised to write. We felt bad about leaving her. Though she always showered us with gifts, we sometimes felt that she needed us more than we needed her.

The day before our departure, Enrique, Herman, Andy and a couple of other boys helped us clear out and pack Flatus, making four return journeys to Enrique's apartment. It was 2 a.m. before they left and we were all a bit weepy, wondering when we would see our good friends again.

I was the last one up. Celia, Maureen and Molly had already collapsed in the bedroom. Pat's sleeping bag was stretched out on the settee, with just a clump of dark hair proving that she was in it. I looked around the strangely bare room. I thought of the number of times the phone had rung, or someone had banged on the door. Of the laughter that had rung out. Of Enrique's mysterious smile. Of Andy's quiet charm. Of the cheeky salesman who had woken me with his banging one afternoon, and told me that I had been chosen to win one thousand dollars, and could he come in and explain it all, and – gee! – didn't I have a swell accent. Of the day we heard about the Manchester United air crash on the radio, and how we felt as if it affected us personally. Of the night when a little mouse had run over my foot at dinner, and Pat had been on the table before you could say 'Jack Robinson'. Of Fritz, a German doctor, who had suddenly pointed at one of our postcards and cried, 'The town of my birth!' with such affection in his voice, we had all been moved.

I wondered if it might feel lonely moving from place to place, even in such close proximity to four others. We had a good life in Cleveland, and we were wilfully abandoning it.

For a few seconds, I felt almost weak with the horror of what we were doing. I might have woken the others and cried, 'No! No, we can't do this! We're throwing too much away.'

Then the feeling vanished as quickly as it had arrived. I rolled out my sleeping bag on a spare bit of floor and lay down.

We had set our alarms for five o'clock, and we were ready to leave at seven. To our surprise, Herman turned up with his camera and took pictures of us leaving East 100th Street in a thunderstorm. But we were so heavily laden that the silencer broke before we had gone very far, and we had to crawl back to Tom and Bill's before we could even get out of the city.

4

Wandering Girls

Ohio to Colorado, April–May 1958

We drove all day – five hundred miles non-stop – through Ohio, Indiana and Illinois. Flatus went like a bird. Coming off the turnpike at Chicago into the worst of the traffic, one man drove his car into the one in front while staring at us open-mouthed. Luckily, both drivers found it funny. We treated ourselves to a motel for our first night. 'Three guests maximum per room', read the sign, so we smuggled Molly and Maureen inside amidst the chaos of unpacking. As we were all dressed in jeans and blue shirts, topped with my trademark short haircuts (a last-minute job performed the night before), it was probably hard to tell the difference between us anyway, though we did wonder if we might give the game away by flushing the lavatory so many times.

The next day we carried on into Wisconsin, where we whiled away the afternoon looking for a lost canyon that didn't want to be found. The weather had brightened since the menacing departure from East 100th Street, and we drove in glorious sunshine for much of the way, the countryside sparkling in the intense light.

At about 4 p.m. we decided to stop at the next farmhouse and ask if we could put up my tent, but changed our minds quickly when we saw dirty washing hanging on the line. A few miles further on, hordes of noisy children were running riot in the farmyard, but the one after that looked clean and prosperous so we drove cheekily up the drive and knocked on the door.

The farmer and his wife were horrified at the idea of us sleeping in the open and gave us the keys to an empty building a mile and a half down the road, pointing out a red gable just visible across the fields. We pulled up in front of a picture-book white-clapboard farmhouse, with red window frames and a colonnaded porch, even if it did all need a coat of paint. Black pigs were snoring happily in a shed, and cattle were munching in the large barn next door. Inside, the house was dim and dusty, but an electric bulb fizzed into life in the main downstairs room, where we decided to make our camp. The room was spacious, with furniture covered in dustsheets pushed to the edges and a piano standing in one corner. The narrow kitchen was almost totally bare, apart from an oversized sink with a cold-water tap. At the foot of the stairs, what appeared to be a cupboard was, in fact, a lavatory – in working order, but with no light.

After unpacking the stove and some of our cooler boxes, we soon had a meal ready. We kept looking at each other, our faces breaking into broad grins, not quite able to believe our luck. We decided on an early night, and as we were getting undressed, a loud banging on the door gave us the fright of our lives and the farmer let himself in. Pat and Maureen, who were already in their nightwear, ran into the kitchen to hide.

'Just came to see how you girls were doing,' he said. 'And Mary has sent you an apple pie.'

We thanked him profusely, then Celia asked him why the house was empty.

'Oh, there's some stupid talk in town that it's haunted. Someone starts up some hokum and next thing I know, I can't rent the place.' He shook his head in annoyance. 'Well, if you want some breakfast tomorrow, just come back to the farm and we'll fix you up.'

We thanked him again, but assured him that we had enough provisions to last us till Christmas, and that we'd be making an early start.

When he had gone, Molly folded her arms. 'Just our luck. Probably the only haunted house in the whole of America, and we have to find it.'

'I'm sleeping in the middle,' said Maureen, reappearing from the kitchen. She had swept the floor earlier and now began to lay out our sleeping bags in a neat row.

'Oh, you don't believe that nonsense, do you?' said Pat. 'He said himself it was rubbish.'

'Hokum, actually,' I corrected her.

'Well, he would say that, wouldn't he,' said Maureen. 'Now, who's coming with me to brush their teeth?'

Dusk was overtaken by the swift fall of darkness that seemed to envelop the house like a fog. 'You can't see a single thing out there,' said Molly, her face pressed close to one of the windows. By eight o'clock we were all in bed.

'What if the ghost starts to play the piano in the night?' said Maureen, from her position of safety.

'Well, we'll see if we like the tune and if not we'll tell him to shut up,' said Pat.

'Who says it's a "he"?' I asked.

'Does anyone here play the piano?' asked Maureen.

'Are we about to have a sing-song?'

'I just need to know it could be one of us if I do hear it.'

'Who said that ghosts can even play pianos?' said Celia.

'Yes, I thought they went in for carrying their heads under their arms and parading along parapets. I didn't think they were known for their music-hall acts,' I said.

'Let's all just go to sleep,' said Pat.

'No, I don't want it to be too quiet,' insisted Maureen. 'Let's talk until we all drop off. I can't bear the silence.'

'Are we going to have this every night? It's not a very good start,' said Celia.

'Did we think we'd ever sleep in a haunted house?'

At some point in the blackness I heard a cry, and woke with a jolt.

'What was that? Was that you, Maureen?'

'The piano. Just a couple of notes. Did you hear it?'

Celia spoke up beside me. 'Yes, I heard something.'

I reached for my torch and switched it on. Maureen, Celia and Molly were sitting up, clutching their knees to their chests. The four of us threw wild-eyed looks at each other and laughed nervously.

'Where's Pat? She's not here.'

Pat's sleeping bag was empty. I shone my torch around the room. The piano lurked silently in the shadows, but the lid was up. Had we left it like that? The furniture looked ghostly under its white shrouds.

'Don't shine your torch on the piano.'

'Why not?'

'We might—'

'Oh, there's something coming!'

A light flickered in the doorway, then a fuzzy shape moved in behind it. Molly and Maureen screamed.

'What's going on? I only went to spend a penny. Do you mind not blinding me?' Pat put a hand up to her eyes. 'I didn't expect a welcoming committee when I got back.'

'Did you play the piano on the way?'

'Don't be silly.'

'You honestly didn't?'

'I'd just like to get back to sleep. 'Night, everyone.'

We all said goodnight, then, after a pause, Celia said, with a hint of mischief, 'Were you all waiting for a sixth voice to say goodnight?'

'I'm glad I'm in the middle,' said Maureen.

If Alex and Betty Neil were surprised to find five girls turn up on their doorstep in Ames, Iowa, at breakfast time a day later, they didn't show it. Betty was an old schoolfriend of Molly's from Hamilton, and she and her husband had moved to the prairie town a year earlier.

'Make yourselves at home,' said Betty, and we took her at her word. Before long, bras, pants, socks and blouses were snapping on the washing line in the backyard; the smell of shampoo drifted down the stairs as we took our turns in the bathroom. Whoever wasn't washing clothes or soaking in the tub was cooing over the three-month-old baby, or clacking away at Pat's typewriter on the dining-room table.

In the two days we spent in Ames we were taken out for breakfast, out for lunch and out for dinner. We were interviewed by Connie Walter, a reporter from the *Tribune*, and we had a party held in our honour at which we heard so many Scottish accents we might have been in Hamilton itself.

'If we stay any longer, we won't want to leave this little thing,' said Celia, changing the baby's nappy after the party guests had gone. She rubbed her nose on the baby's tummy, making him laugh. 'Do you want five new mothers? Do you? Do you?'

'That wee laddie is going to be spoilt rotten if we don't get away soon,' said Molly. 'Poor Betty is going to have a dreadful time with him.'

Betty, sitting with her feet up for the first time that day, smiled across at us. 'It's been super! Stay as long as you want.'

We left, reluctantly, the next morning, driving through the town to a fanfare of tooting horns and waves of recognition, as the front page of the local paper cried out:

Where Are Our Wandering Girls Tonight?
Traveling Cross-Country In '49 Car

'It sounds rather romantic, doesn't it?' said Molly, reading the article out to us all. 'Or does "wandering girls" make us sound a bit flighty? Och, I keep getting toilet rolls banging my head. Will you please stay in place?' She wedged the offending items back against the rear window. 'Now, where was I? "*The car is filled to overflowing with various and sundry items.*" Don't I know it.'

Flatus was flying along, in spite of her load. My right elbow kept catching on the boxes piled up on the front seat between me and Pat. I would nudge them away, but they kept sliding back. Pat sat with her typewriter on her lap, more boxes between her and the passenger door, and a collection of bucket bags and other containers at her feet. On the roof-rack were our cooler bags and six suitcases – piled high and fastened with an ingenious elastic strap called an octopus – and the boot was tightly packed with tins of food, pans, cooking utensils, the stove, a table and chair, the barbecue, a coffee percolator, two sleeping bags, the tent and five pairs of ice-skates. Maureen, Molly and Celia were somewhere in the back of the car, wedged in amongst blankets, pillows and the rest of the sleeping bags, their feet resting on yet more boxes. My view from the rear window was non-existent most of the time.

The miles and miles of cornfields gradually gave way to cattle country and the landscape of Westerns. Low hills rose in the distance and creatures dotted the vast plains, some of them no more than pinpricks on the horizon. We were in Nebraska, and it felt like the real West. We even passed a cowboy on his horse. We saw few cars and people, but when we did, heads would turn and gaze after us.

Though we had seen a signpost heralding their proximity, nothing prepared us for our arrival in the Badlands of South Dakota. A lonely landscape of rocky hills and deeply carved valleys rippled into the distance. Some of the rocks were flat-topped, others pointed. In the light of the lowering sun, the colours of the rock were constantly changing – yellow, pale pink, amber, purple. We stopped to take photos and to film ourselves. Short stumpy grass was poking through on some of the flatter surfaces, giving the impression of a ruined city slowly being covered over by mother nature. We didn't see another car for hours, and felt as if we were all alone in a lost world.

We took Flatus to a garage in Rapid City for a grease and oil-change, and made use of the facilities there. Maureen and Molly changed into their baby-dolls in the restroom and came back to the car to find that I had accepted the garage owner's offer of a trip to Dinosaur Park. They were horrified, and rushed back to cover up.

He drove us in his truck up a steep hill, then along Skyline Drive, where we had a terrific view of Rapid City by night. The park had life-size reproductions of prehistoric animals and was quite eerie in the dark. The man told us he only wished his wife was at home so that he could take us back for a meal, but she was away, nursing her sick mother.

We left Rapid City early the next morning, bound for Mount Rushmore in the Black Hills. After a steep climb, which was almost too much for Flatus – the water boiled over when we reached the top – we found ourselves face to face with the huge memorial to presidents Washington, Lincoln, Jefferson and Theodore Roosevelt, their faces blasted out of solid granite on the mountainside. The sun was shining brightly, and after taking photographs, we sat down on the steps to write cards. Time wore on so we prepared lunch – spaghetti au gratin followed by fruit and cream. The sun grew hotter, and we were in no hurry to leave. A handful of visitors arrived and left, but we had the place to ourselves for much of the time. We got talking to a couple from Ohio, who laughed at our overloaded car and to see us cooking for five on a tiny stove. At last we said goodbye to the imperious faces and followed the road over the mountain, round some very sharp bends. The view was magnificent – miles and miles of mountaintops were spread out before us, some capped with snow, their slopes densely wooded. A sign, HORSETHIEF LAKE CAMP GROUND, caught our eye, so we stopped to investigate. It was too early in the season for visitors, but the stone shelter had a deep fireplace and a plentiful supply of logs, and even a corner labelled THE WASHROOM, equipped with soap and a clean towel. Below the shelter lay the dried-up lake bed – now a round green meadow with a rocky shoreline. The whole site was encircled by mountains, a view that gave me a shiver of delight. This was what I had come to America for.

After we had eaten, it was dark. We toasted marshmallows in

the fire, then got ready for bed. The shelter was too cold to sleep in so we put our sleeping bags on some flat ground near the car. The night brought strange animal noises – something howling, something chattering – which sounded suspiciously near, but I was too tired to lie awake for long.

I got up at five in the morning and prepared pancakes for breakfast, then we spent the day inspecting our new environment. We followed tiny streams to their sources, passing mysterious-looking caves in which we imagined a bear or a wolf might be sleeping. Once, a deer skipped out from behind a tree right in front of us, and little creatures, striped from their heads to their tails, began to appear everywhere. This felt like real Indian country. Sometimes I would turn at the snapping of a twig or a rustle in the bushes, half expecting to find one stalking me. You could almost see the smoke signals rising from the hills.

The days drifted by most pleasantly. We soon had a little routine: up early to watch the sunrise, breakfast at 6 a.m., all the jobs such as gathering wood, washing up, sweeping the floor and fetching water from the pump done by 7.30, mid-morning break at 8.30. The rest of the morning would be spent sunbathing and writing letters. We braved the ice-cold water from the pump to wash our hair, and the screams echoed round the mountains. Molly insisted she always used two lots of shampoo, but changed her mind after the first.

We would have a good lunch, followed by a walk, then supper, and bed at sunset around 7.30 p.m. Maureen wanted to stay up late for a change one night, but found sitting on her own in the dark rather spooky and soon snuggled down with everyone else.

It was the most peaceful place I had ever been to, but it was never quiet: frogs croaked, birds twittered, and the wind made queer yowling sounds in the trees. As soon as the sun set, a constant chattering would start up, the howling would begin, and we would burrow deep into our sleeping bags. We preferred not to think about these noises too much, ever since I had consulted my book and identified the howling as coming from coyotes. 'Attacks on humans do occur occasionally, but are very rare,' it stated, alarming us more than it had probably intended.

Pat was always careful to turn her shoes upside down while we were sleeping to prevent creepy-crawlies from getting inside them. One night, I heard a rustle beside my ear and was convinced that a huge animal was about to eat me. When I shone my torch, I saw that a little mouse had knocked over Pat's shoe and was sitting inside it. The small stripy creatures turned out to be chipmunks, and they were becoming braver by the day. One of them ran over Molly's sleeping bag while she was just dozing off and the sound she made would have roused any Indian tribe to war.

Molly stood in her baby-dolls and twirled around like a ballerina, her arms outstretched. 'I could stay here all summer. I'm going to apply for a job picking up litter on horseback.'

'What would you use?'

'A harpoon, of course.'

Since arriving at Horsethief Lake, we hadn't seen another car, or a person, apart from on quick trips to Keystone to pick up fresh groceries. We had begun to feel like part of the landscape ourselves. We were strong, fit and suntanned. We had forgotten what day it was. How will we sleep in a bed again, we wondered. Or manage to work again? Cleveland and Mount Sinai seemed almost as long ago as England.

'This really has to be the most incredible place I've ever been to,' said Maureen, sipping her coffee as she perched on a warm rock. 'Americans are right when they boast about their country. Molly, are you not getting dressed today?' She shook her head at Molly, who was now doing some exercises, and chuckled. 'I think we'll have to leave her behind. She's going to get us arrested if she behaves like this when we reach town.'

'I used to think people were dreadful show-offs when we first arrived, but I understand them better now,' said Pat, hanging some dripping shirts on the line. 'They're just proud of what they've got, and they don't mind who knows it. Perhaps we should take a leaf from their book.'

'Yes, we probably seem awfully modest,' said Maureen. 'My mother always told me not to blow my own trumpet. Some Americans practically have their own orchestras.'

One day we woke up and saw a solitary black cloud in the sky. As we hadn't seen a cloud for days, it seemed an ominous sign, and knowing that some of the roads were little more than dirt tracks, we decided that it was time to move on. It was sad packing up and leaving our camp, dismantling the washing line, raking out the ashes on the fire, and putting the sooty kettle back on to the stone ledge that had been our kitchen table. We had even made friends with the chipmunks. Molly had surprised us one morning by crying out, 'Here's Hamish! Don't you recognize him? He's the one who ate those crumbs yesterday, the wee rascal.'

We stopped at Deadwood and Lead, mining towns from the Gold Rush days, where we saw old-style saloons and the graves of Wild Bill Hickok and Calamity Jane. But now that we were moving, we all wanted to get to Denver as quickly as possible.

Letters would be waiting for us there. We also hoped to find work.

We were outside Denver's main post office before it opened, and straight through the doors at nine o'clock. We spent ages sitting in the car reading our mail. It was all being sent to Enrique, and forwarded by him as soon as we had told him where we would be. Enrique had written his own letter, too, and said that the crowd were all missing us and that it was strange not being able to pop to the apartment on East 100th Street to finish off the evening.

The next stop was the employment agency, where we discovered that the best of plans don't always work out. We would not be allowed to nurse in the state of Colorado until we had been registered, a process that would take about six weeks. It was a bitter blow, and infuriating, particularly when we heard that they were desperately short of nurses.

'Would you consider anything else?' they asked, and sent us to a cinema to be usherettes, but the manager took one look at us and shooed us away, deciding that we wouldn't stay long. Pat and I went to see a man about selling carving knives door to door, but changed our minds when we saw the size of the suitcases we were expected to carry. Maureen went to see a doctor's wife about a cleaning job, but the lady was horrified at the idea of having a nurse doing her housework for her, and invited her in for coffee instead.

Petrol, food, film for our cameras (we all had a movie camera as well as an ordinary one) . . . Our funds were disappearing fast. In desperation, I bought a bottle of red nail varnish and wrote on the back of Flatus: 'FIVE BRITISH NURSES TOURING COUNTRY

REQUIRE TEMPORARY WORK – ANYTHING CONSIDERED'. I didn't know if it would attract the right sort of attention, but it seemed worth a try. However, before we had any response to it, the agency offered us work as practical nurses – a stage below registered nurses – in an old people's home. The work was basic – helping the residents to get up and washed and dressed, preparing meals, keeping them amused – but the old folk were delightful, and amused us as much as we did them. When Aunt Mary, who was ninety-seven, discovered that one of the men had a birthday, I had to help her to her drawer to choose a card. Inside was an Easter card, a postcard of a building and a card with a robin on it. She looked at each one for ages, her hand trembling between them.

'I couldn't bear to give that one away,' she sighed, pointing at the robin. 'He makes me smile whenever I look at him, and Robin is my grandson's name. And that one's not good enough.' She pushed the postcard to one side. So Pete was given the Easter card, which he subsequently put up with pride of place on his dressing table, next to his battered cowboy hat.

We grew quite attached to the owners and the residents of our new place of work during the week we were with them. And while we thought back wistfully to our days at Horsethief Lake, where we had no one to please but ourselves, we liked Denver, with its friendly people and mountain backdrop. The weather shuddered between heat and cold – we even had snow one day – but we had found a cosy apartment in a nice part of town. It was only meant for two, but with a little persuasion the owner agreed to rent it to all five of us, and it ended up cheaper than staying at the YMCA.

Now that we were familiar faces, the post office staff went to fetch our mail as soon as they saw us coming. The staff at the employment agency knew which jobs to hold on to until we had called in. We even knew the men at the fire station, ever since they had invited us to sleep there when they saw us bedding down in a car park on our first night in the city. Sensing that this could get them into trouble, we had refused, but we had accepted later invitations to breakfast, coffee, a TV evening and for a demonstration of what happened when the alarm went off.

One day there was a small fire in the block opposite ours, and we watched our new friends from the window.

'Don't put them off,' said Maureen, giggling.

'Look at Ted, he's seen us. He's trying not to smile.'

'I don't think it's too serious. Looks like they've finished.'

'There's Jimmy. Yoo-hoo! See – he's waving. Shall we invite them in?'

'Don't be silly. They're still on duty.'

'They're all tickled pink, though. In fact, I think Rick's blushing.'

Geena at the employment bureau waved a piece of paper at me.

'I've got the ideal job for all five of you. Waitresses at a big hotel in the mountains for a convention next weekend. Pay's not great, but just think of the tips. Folk say they really know how to throw a party there.'

'I don't think any of us have been waitresses before. It sounds rather frightening.'

'Don't be an ass. You're nurses. You've practically got the job already. The owner, his name is . . .' she looked down at her notes, 'Mr Hanson. He sounds terrific. If the weekend works out well, he'd like you to stay all summer.'

'Oh no, not all summer. We're not staying anywhere that long. We want—'

Geena waved her hand at me dismissively. 'Just go along for the weekend. He and his wife are dying to meet you all.'

The Hotel Colorado in Glenwood Springs looked like a renaissance palace, with its grand columns of warm stone glowing in the sun. A steep rocky slope, dotted with misshapen pine trees, shot up vertiginously behind it into the hard blue sky. We were probably fortunate that the majority of our guests that weekend were the Optimists of Colorado, a good-natured crowd who seemed to overlook our inexperience. Still, it was nerve-racking being set loose in the dining room in a white nylon dress and tiny apron, looking every inch the waitress while feeling anything but. There were three dining rooms and we rushed between all of them, as well as the patio, where another party were having a barbecue. Molly had been whisked off to the Bamboo Cocktail Lounge to be a waitress there.

I hoped that the guests couldn't see my hands shaking as I took my first orders. I was thankful not to be Pat, who was serving Mr and Mrs Hanson. We were expected to carry huge trays backwards and forwards between the dining room and the kitchen, but I could barely lift mine. I had to put my tray on the sideboard and rush between there and the table with a plate in each hand while watching a more experienced waitress balance her tray on one arm and serve straight from it. It was going to be a slow service, I thought.

While I was dishing out little pats of butter with a pair of tweezers, I managed to drop one into a lady's ample bosom. But taken aback by her sharp masculine haircut, I made matters worse by saying, 'Oops, sorry, sir. I mean, madam.' I received a frosty stare. Oh well, even optimists can't be jolly all the time, I thought.

Then, at some point in the evening, something changed and I began to enjoy myself. When I smiled at the guests, it was a genuine smile and not the frozen one I had forced my lips into earlier. It helped that the hotel staff were all pleasant folk, from the talented head chef, who carved swans and baskets from blocks of ice and filled them with gardenias, right down to the Mexican boys who helped to clear the tables.

But it was a long, long day. At eleven o'clock on Saturday night we were setting breakfast tables for the next day, despite having been up since five-thirty that morning. We were exhausted.

'My feet are just waiting for the rest of me to die,' said Theda, one of the regular waitresses, and though we had never heard that expression before, we knew just what she meant.

I could see the advantage of carrying the trays at shoulder height in the jostling dining room, but I hadn't quite dared to try it. At least, by the second night, I could negotiate the heavy door between there and the kitchen without being knocked flying. The trick was to kick it with one foot, turn sideways and slip out deftly before it banged shut.

I was feeling more like a proper waitress by the minute, when one of the local girls hissed over my shoulder, 'What's the matter with your tip? You don't wannit?'

I caught the whiff of fruity chewing gum on her breath. 'But that's his change,' I replied, confused.

She shook her head and took me by the arm. 'Here's what you do. You give him his change, if he don't pick it up right away, you say, "Thank you, sir," and you take it right back. You've earned it, girl.'

That seemed far too presumptuous to me, and I wondered if I had the makings of a waitress after all.

However, by the end of the weekend we had each made around twenty dollars in tips, and Molly had made over thirty in the cocktail lounge. We were almost sorry to be packing for Denver so soon, but the convention was over and there were only a few other guests in the hotel. It felt sad to see the swimming pool empty, the courtyard and patios that had been alive with conversation so quiet.

'I'm just glad we didn't show ourselves up too much,' said Pat, as we were packing Flatus. 'Good job we weren't chambermaids. We'd probably have greeted our guests with, "Morning, sir. Bowels opened?" Oh, hello, Mrs Hanson.'

Our employer waited to get her breath back. 'Phew! Everyone said you were in the pool. I thought I'd missed you. Mr Hanson and I hope that you'll consider staying for the summer.' She saw us look at each other. 'A few weeks even? We'd love to have you on board. You're good for business.'

'We are?'

'Oh yes, the Optimists were crazy about the cute accents they heard at dinner. One of the ladies was asking me if Mr Hanson went to pick you up from Great Britain. She seemed to think it's somewhere in Canada.'

When she promised us a room on the top floor of the hotel instead of the rather insalubrious staff quarters we had been stabled in, and said she'd put us on the payroll immediately, we all nodded as one.

We returned to Denver to collect our belongings and say goodbye to our friends the firemen and the old folk. One old boy I had shared a few jokes with shuffled off to his room with his walking frame, and came back with a pair of antlers balanced on the front. He dipped his head towards them, and I realized they were a gift.

I picked them up, embarrassed, wondering what on earth we were going to do with them. I imagined one of us impaling ourselves on one of the lethal-looking prongs if I were to brake suddenly, and had to swallow a sudden urge to laugh.

'We'll tie them to the roof-rack,' said Celia brightly. 'We can't get any stranger looks than we do already.'

And so Flatus was adorned with a pair of stag antlers. We tried to stand them up, but they kept slipping, so in the end we fastened them horizontally, pointing the way ahead.

We also bought ourselves a cowboy hat each, to go with the Levi jeans and Western-style belts we had already treated ourselves to. Most people in Colorado dressed like that. You didn't know if you were talking to a millionaire or a beggar.

We had told Mrs Hanson we would return to the hotel on Thursday, a day before the next convention was due to start, but first we decided to go skiing, and drove to a resort high in the mountains.

Flatus struggled with the heat and the altitude, boiling over several times on the ascent. We had to keep stopping and packing the radiator with ice and snow. It was a relief to see the sign for the ski lodge, and a spacious, empty car park where we could spend the night, knowing that we couldn't afford to both ski and pay for a room.

Maureen and Celia went inside to fill our water containers, and came out with a tall, dark-haired man in a red sweater, who introduced himself as Dennis. He told us that the season was over and the lodge empty, apart from a honeymoon couple staying one last night, and he wouldn't hear of ladies sleeping in a car. If we would help him with some light duties, he would even let us use the equipment for free the next day. We did some cleaning, and polished the bar, then spent the evening chatting to the honeymooners, as Dennis showed us how to make hot buttered rum and Glühwein, and allowed us to drink whatever we wanted. We didn't have much – none of us was used to a lot of alcohol – but it was nice to try drinks that would have been out of our price range. Dennis also showed us how to work the jukebox without putting in a dime. His own favourite was 'Good Golly Miss Molly', which he played so often it drove us all mad.

It felt like the middle of the night when I woke to the sound of the dormitory door opening and light streaming into the room. My heart thudded as a tall shape walked past my bunk. I almost stopped breathing. Something clinked, and I saw Dennis put down a tray on the table.

'I've gotcha all some tea.'

I looked at my watch. It was just after midnight. We had gone to bed early, and I, for one, had fallen asleep almost immediately. 'But we don't want it now, Dennis. Tomorrow morning would be lovely. Eight-thirty please,' I laughed, before adding more quietly, 'The others are all asleep.' As I spoke, I could sense some of them stirring.

Dennis lowered himself on to an empty bunk, as if he hadn't heard a word I'd been saying.

Pat sat up suddenly. 'What on earth . . .? It can't be—' I heard her give a little gasp of annoyance. 'What's going on?'

Celia and Molly were both pulling themselves up now, rubbing their eyes.

Dennis had been drinking with us earlier, though not excessively. Now, the whole room reeked of alcohol. Suddenly he stood up and reached for the gun in his belt. He had already shown us his shooting prowess when he had lined up our cowboy hats on the ground outside and put a gunshot through each of them in turn, insisting that we would never be proper cowgirls without this badge of honour. Perhaps we had encouraged him, humoured him too much. But he had been pleasant company, and had given us no cause for concern.

I froze. Somebody whimpered. I watched as he slipped his fingers round the grip, as if checking it for size, tossed the gun in the air and deftly caught it. We had laughed when he did this earlier, but no one was laughing now. He turned to face me and pointed the gun at my head, a cruel smile on his face.

'You drink your tea now,' he said. 'I made it special. You're all English, right? You all drink tea.'

It didn't seem the right moment to point out that one of us was Scottish and another was Irish, nor was there a requirement that we all like tea.

My heart was hammering so hard, I thought that everyone would be able to hear it. I wondered if my dry mouth would be capable of forming any words. I tried anyway, and was surprised at the false breeziness I managed to project. 'Oh, lovely, Dennis, how kind of you. We'll just have a quick mouthful, then we must get back to sleep. Busy day tomorrow! I'll pass them round for you.'

I unzipped my sleeping bag with fingers that had turned to jelly and got out of my bunk, forgetting any thoughts of modesty. I only hoped that I wouldn't spill the tea.

'What about her?' Dennis was pointing his gun at Maureen, who was still lying down, apparently asleep. I went closer to wake her, but I could see she was shaking.

'We should leave her, Dennis, she's such a heavy sleeper. She'll sleep through anything.'

'She needs to drink her tea. I made one for all of you.' He walked across to her bunk and tugged the edge of her sleeping bag, slightly awkwardly. I heard her give a little sob.

'Please, Dennis. Leave her alone. She needs her sleep more than the rest of us. We'll drink hers too.'

'She don't sound like she's sleeping to me.' He was fingering his pistol again.

'Dennis, please put down your gun. We can hardly enjoy our tea with that pointing at us.' This time I could hear an edge of hysteria in my voice.

He looked as if he was about to say something, then sat back down on the spare bed, obediently placing the gun beside him.

'Humour him,' I whispered as I passed a cup to the others. Before I took my own, I offered Maureen's to Dennis. 'Would you like this one?' He didn't answer, but I pulled the table closer to where he was sitting and left it there for him anyway.

I glanced across at the gun. If this were a film, I thought, I would be grabbing it now and forcing him to leave the room. But the idea was too preposterous, and it could all go horribly wrong. I imagined him lunging for it . . . it going off accidentally. It made me feel cold just thinking about it. I picked up my cup and went back to bed to drink it.

Dennis took a deep swig from Maureen's cup, pulled a face and put it down. He wiped his mouth with his sleeve, then picked up the gun again and pointed it at each of us in turn, laughing at the horrified expressions on our faces.

'I thought you was all cowgirls,' he said. 'Don't look much like cowgirls now. Hey, where are those hats?'

Most of them were visible, and he picked them up, one at a time, and placed them on our heads. I ended up with Molly's red one, which felt as if it might topple off until I tucked the string under my chin.

I tried not to look at the others, nervously sipping tea in baby-dolls and cowboy hats. The tea might have been anything, its taste and temperature (stone cold, actually) barely registered. When I had drunk most of mine, I got out of bed once more and collected the cups from the others. Molly's was still quite full, and I frowned at her until she had managed a few more gulps.

'That was delicious, Dennis,' said Pat. 'I think we'd better all get some sleep now.'

He appeared to be in no hurry to leave.

'Whaddya all think about American men?' he asked suddenly.

Nobody spoke, until Molly piped up, 'Och, they're so friendly. And generous.'

He liked that. 'Yep, they sure are those things. *We* sure are those things. What else?'

'It's simply marvellous the way they do the grocery shopping here,' said Pat. 'You'd never see that at home.'

'You wouldn't?'

'No, nor the cooking. I don't think British men know one end of a carrot from the other.'

Dennis put his head back and laughed, as if it was the funniest thing he had heard.

Then Celia spoke impatiently. 'This is all fascinating, but we really need a decent sleep if we're going to ski tomorrow, Dennis, so if you don't mind, can we continue this conversation in the morning?'

I flashed her a look that said, 'Don't antagonize him,' but she stared back defiantly.

Dennis seemed surprised, then he stood up quickly, and for a second my heart froze. But he spoke lightly. 'Guess our little tea-party's come to an end. I'll see you all for breakfast. Sweet dreams.' He left the room, leaving the tray of half-empty cups behind.

There was no sign of Dennis in the morning, and we were all relieved about that. We cooked ourselves breakfast, then said goodbye to the honeymoon couple, who asked us to call on them if we were ever in St Louis, Missouri. The ski instructor turned up to collect his gear, but said that he wasn't in a rush and he'd be happy to give us some lessons. It was a perfect day for skiing – cold and blue-skied – but when I held my face to the sun, I could feel a heat that suggested summer was not far off at these heights, and the snow was wet and slushy in places. We had the slopes to ourselves. Bud gave us lessons all morning, and left us to practise in the afternoon. When he offered to do the same the following day, we accepted immediately.

'I think I like this almost as much as ice-skating,' I said to the others.

'Do you know how much these lessons cost?' said Maureen, after pulling herself back up the slope on the T-bar. 'Two dollars fifty an hour. Aren't we the luckiest girls in the world!'

I don't know if anyone gave a thought to Dennis while we were on the slopes. I was certainly enjoying myself far too much to dwell on our ordeal. But as we made our way back to the lodge, I think we were all a bit anxious about how the evening would progress.

'Howdy, cowgirls!' said Dennis, as we entered the bar, and soon 'Good Golly Miss Molly' was on the jukebox and he was making us laugh with his funny dancing.

The evening passed pleasantly. Some of Dennis's friends dropped in, and he let me serve them like a proper barmaid, but once again we were ready for bed early.

'Perhaps he sleepwalks,' suggested Celia as we got undressed. 'He certainly seems charm itself now.'

'Sleepwalking with a tray of tea? Sounds unlikely,' said Molly.

'People do silly things when they're drunk. My mother calls it "the demon drink",' said Pat. 'He probably doesn't even remember.'

'Let's put something in front of the door, just in case,' said Maureen. 'We could move that spare bed.'

We decided that was a good idea and, giggling with the effort, managed to manoeuvre it to the other side of the room. Then Pat wanted to go to the lavatory, so we had to move it again. I thought that I might stay awake longer than usual, but the fresh air had exhausted me and I fell asleep with the voices of the others in my ears.

The next morning, we opened the bedroom door to find a tray of tea on the floor right in front of us. A brownish film had settled on the top of each cup – it had clearly been there a long time. No one had heard anything in the night.

We skied all morning, and were sorry to have to stop. Bud asked us to stay for longer and help him prepare the lodge for the summer season. It was almost tempting, but we had promised to get back to the Hotel Colorado that day.

It was late afternoon by the time we were packed and ready to leave. Dennis and Bud both came out to see us off. They looked sad figures, standing waving goodbye. We had driven only a few yards when a cloud of grey smoke appeared from the front wheels. It seemed that the brakes had frozen, then burned out from our sudden start. We needed to get to a garage, and the nearest one was in the next valley.

'There's no point in all of us dying if we go over the edge,' I said to the others. 'Pat and I can take the car, if you three don't mind waiting here.'

We took out most of the luggage, but when Pat and I tried to leave, Dennis had other ideas. Bud almost had to physically restrain him from holding us back. 'You can't go now! It'll be dark soon. You don't know these roads. Wait till morning.'

As the car slipped away, he cried out in defeat, 'If you must go, be sure to say I sent you.'

We drove in first gear all the way down the pass without too much difficulty. 'Dennis sent us,' blurted Pat, after I had explained the problem to the mechanic. When I tried to pay him, he shook his head and said something about 'friends of Dennis'. 'Great guy,' he added, and we nodded vigorously.

It was getting dark as we began the climb back to the lodge. Stars in the sky were so numerous, they seemed to bleed into each other. About halfway up there was a tremendous clatter, as if the bottom of the car had fallen out. I stopped, and Pat got out to see what was wrong. I heard a little shriek, the sound of tumbling stones, and she disappeared. Shooting out of Flatus, I realized to my horror that I had parked far closer to the road's edge than I had thought.

'Pat!' I cried. I couldn't see her. How far had she fallen? I felt sick with fear. I peered down into the blackness. The twisting road and dark cathedral shapes had instantly become malevolent. A few seconds later, on the point of tears and wondering what to do next, I heard a little scrabbling noise, and a puffing and panting Pat was clambering back on to the road.

'I'm OK, I landed on a ledge. It's a steep drop, though. Good job you didn't stop just a bit further up.'

I helped haul her to her feet. 'Let me get my breath back, then I'll be OK.' We were both laughing, but it was verging on the hysterical.

We needed to get back to the garage, but there was no room to turn the car round. The only solution was to reverse back down the pass with Pat hanging out of the window, guiding me with a flashlight. One misjudged bend, and . . . Well, it didn't bear thinking about. I don't know what would have happened if we had met another car. My nerves were shattered by the time we reached the bottom.

The problem turned out to be the fan belt, and after a quick repair we had an uneventful drive back to the lodge for the others. All I wanted to do now was set off for the hotel, but first there was another argument with Dennis, who said we were not to go until morning. Bud, too, pleaded with us to stay.

'I can't let you go in this light. I'll never forgive myself if anything happens to you.'

We were close to relenting, and the thought of our comfy bunk beds was quite appealing. I barely had the strength to protest. Then Celia suddenly 'remembered' that we had to work the next morning, and that if we didn't turn up we might lose our jobs. The men reluctantly helped us reload the car.

Dennis walked alongside us as we pulled away, one hand resting proprietorially on the side of Flatus. Then, as I tooted the horn and we picked up speed, he finally let go, and raised it in a sad farewell. We all waved madly as we left the lodge behind.

'Good job he didn't shoot our tyres out,' said Maureen cheerfully. 'We might have been stranded up here for evermore. Has anyone seen that film . . .?'

'Poor man, he's just very lonely,' said Celia.

'I hope he doesn't stay up there all summer,' said Pat. 'What will he be like at the end of it?'

We arrived back at the hotel at 4.30 a.m. It was freezing in the car so we put our sleeping bags down in one of the lounges, not knowing where else to go. We were woken what seemed like only minutes later by a maid polishing the floor, who gave a little gasp and rushed off, returning with Mrs Hanson.

'Thank the Lord!' cried the owner when she saw us. 'Mr Hanson was talking about calling the police. I told him you'd turn up sooner or later, but he's such a worrier. One minute he was thinking you hadn't liked it here, next he had you stranded somewhere in the mountains with a lunatic. Mountain folk can be mighty strange, you know.'

We nodded solemnly.

'But you're here at last! And we sure are happy to have you back!' She rubbed her hands together. 'We've got one hundred and fifty restaurant owners from Colorado and Wyoming coming this weekend. It's going to be a riot.'

5

A Biscuit Tin of Dollars

Glenwood Springs, Colorado, May–June 1958

About halfway through our spell at the Hotel Colorado, I took Pat to sit her American driving test. Although she was less comfortable behind the wheel than I was, she did take over when I needed her to, though in truth it was hard to get me out of the driver's seat, and I often felt carsick as a passenger.

I had taught Pat to drive after we bought our first Flatus, back when we were trainee nurses in Newcastle. (My mother was horrified at me for buying a car, and decided that Pat must be to blame as, at twenty-two, she was three years older and should have had more sense.) We kept the car in a neglected corner of the hospital beside the piggeries – part of the old workhouse that the General had once been. The path was on a slight incline, which was helpful, as we had to crank Flatus up to start if we were on the level. As Pat switched on the ignition and pushed the starter button, I would give her a push, run alongside until the engine had sputtered into life, then jump in quickly, hoping that we wouldn't meet any obstacles on the way out. The steep roads that swept down to the Tyne, dark with the shadows of office buildings, were ideal for testing the brakes and practising hill starts.

Pat was the first in a long list of my driving-school pupils. Once, when she was changing gear on a sharp corner, the gear lever came away in her hands. We were both helpless with laughter. I took over and we crawled through town to Billy Robinson's garage in Byker. Billy's life had been saved by staff at the General, and he would put everything on hold to help a nurse or a doctor. We sat drinking tea in his office while he and his boys got to work. I don't know what we would have done without him.

Pat passed her American test, so at last we had two legal drivers. Whether our overstuffed car satisfied legal requirements, with its gravity-defying load on top and limited driver vision, I don't know, but we were never stopped by the police.

Life at the Hotel Colorado was a non-stop round of work and partying. For most of the time we spent there, the hotel was playing host to weekend conventions and from Monday to Thursday there was little to do. When Friday arrived, the calm would lift, people would move faster and shout more (though I never heard Mr and Mrs Hanson raise their voices) and the temperature always seemed to rise.

Parties of restaurant owners, credit-company managers, lawyers, bankers – they all came to the hotel to let their hair down, and keep us on our feet from dawn to late at night (on Friday and Saturday, we would be lucky to snatch more than three or four hours' sleep). It was a huge task for all involved to place three hundred main courses in front of three hundred guests in the dining room at the same time as another hundred guests needed serving in the Palomino Room or on the patio.

There was only one job I hated – chipping chewing gum from the undersides of the tables. Don, the maître d', gave me a bucket and a paint-scraper and set me to work in the dining rooms and the bar. I felt quite sick after I had finished.

The bankers were the nicest crowd, and the most generous. They gave us exotic-smelling corsages to wear as we waited on table, and one day decorated the dining room with more roses than I had ever seen. In the evenings they held lavish cocktail parties, yet rose early for milk punch and silver fizz at breakfast banquets.

Serving them at the pool one lunchtime, balancing one hundred and fifty glasses of tomato juice on my shoulder, I felt the tray slipping forward and just managed to catch it before it crashed to the ground. I discovered that two of the guests were standing behind me removing glasses. They thought it was a hoot, but made up for it by taking me into the mountains on the chair-lift the next day, where they pointed out twenty-seven peaks, all over fourteen thousand feet high.

We also had parties of high-school students at their junior or senior prom, and others on something called a 'sneak day', chaperoned by two couples.

'Have you seen those girls?' I whispered to Maureen, who was on the lunch shift with me as we served a noisy party from a school in Grand Junction, the next town. 'Marilyn Monroe has nothing on them.'

'They've already asked me how many dates I've had since I got here,' said Maureen, rolling her eyes.

The girls looked older than we did, with their disturbingly revealing dresses, styled hair and heavy make-up. It was a relief to see them later that afternoon, frolicking in the gardens wearing cropped trousers and bobby socks, and looking like children once more.

When Sunday came, the convention guests would gradually

slip away, and our own social lives could begin. Sunday was barbecue night for the staff, and if we weren't invited to the home
of Betty, Ruth or Theda, the three regular waitresses, a group of
us would go into the mountains with crates of beer and Coke and
fry fish or roast wieners on the fire. Sometimes we hired horses
from the ranch and followed rocky trails in the moonlight, feeling more like cowgirls every day.

Crystal River, Hanging Lake, No Name Creek. The names of
the places our new friends took us to were as magical as the places
themselves.

Molly had continued working as a cocktail waitress since our
arrival, and one night I was asked to join her, which meant dressing up and wearing high heels. I was baffled by some of the
orders, and practically ran to Al, the bartender, for help in deci-
phering what might as well have been a foreign language. I
expected to be back in the dining room the next day, but to my
surprise they asked me to stay, and as the work was easier and the
tips were larger I couldn't refuse.

The atmosphere in the bar was more relaxed, and mistakes just
laughed over. I must have gained a reputation for clearing away
unfinished glasses, for one night there was a printed card placed
on top of one:

GONE TO

P

LEAVE MY DRINK ALONE

'Gwenda, darling, say "tomato juice" for me, just once, in that
cute accent of yours,' someone would bellow across the room, or,

'Scotland, aren't you going to bring me another drink?' But if anyone got too fresh with me or Molly, Al would stride in and put them in their place.

Al kept an expensive cocktail for us both behind the counter, and when customers offered to buy us a drink we'd pick up the glass and toast them, then Al would give us the money. We felt as if we were rolling in it, and the biscuit tin under the bed into which all five of us put our tips was filling up nicely. But I was still far too polite, as far as Al was concerned. A lot of the men were a bit tipsy, and it felt wrong to take advantage of them.

'Jeez!' said Mr Hanson, when I confided that I had felt guilty about accepting a big tip for serving a man only one drink. 'It's good for his ego. Lets him think he's a big shot. Besides,' he added more seriously, 'it makes up for the small salary I'm paying you.'

On another occasion, a man who was slightly the worse for wear handed over what he thought were three dollar bills to pay me two dollars twenty-five for some drinks. However, only the top one was a dollar, the others were five- and ten-dollar bills. Of course I told him of his mistake and took the correct amount. Al rolled his eyes and asked why I had to be so honest. But I could never have taken it all; I would have thought about it for evermore.

The staff were all larger-than-life personalities. Don, who had taken us all under his wing from the start, was also a rodeo rider, though it was hard to picture him on a bucking bronco when you saw him in his dark suit, charming the diners. Al told us he had been married and divorced three times – 'Like a film star!' said Molly, admiringly. Another fellow had supposedly been a millionaire three or four times and lost or spent it all, but seemed not to care. Cleo, the receptionist, whose gentle charm won over even the most difficult guests, was quieter than the other men, but just as much part of our crowd.

I went to the Goofy Gal for a burger with Cleo after work one night. Just the two of us, for a change. Molly had the night off and had gone on a date, and the other three had decided to go to bed early. I was starving. Working in the cocktail bar, I missed the exotic restaurant food, the shrimp curry and butterscotch sundaes, and seemed to live on meatballs and spaghetti.

Cleo asked me about my family and friends in Newcastle, and whether I was ever homesick. A lot of people asked us that, and I had rehearsed my answer so many times I barely considered what I was saying. But I felt I had to be more honest with Cleo.

'You know, every new place I go to, I think of someone from home I'd like to share it with. Sometimes it's my parents, or my brother, but other times a certain friend. I'll say to myself, "Barbie would love this!" or, "I wish Kathleen could see that!" But I don't want to *be* home. Not yet. There's still far too much I want to see and do here.'

I told him that Kathleen and Barbie and my cousin Beryl were like sisters to me. 'My mother and Aunty Kitty – that's Kathleen's mother – meet every Saturday morning in Tilley's tea-room, or Fenwick's. They always dress up for the occasion. Well, my mother *always* looks smart. She was one of the first people in our part of town to wear the New Look. She'd be horrified to see the sort of clothes I'm wearing now.'

I saw Cleo glance at the dress I had borrowed from Maureen (I was working my way through all of our wardrobes now that I was a cocktail waitress).

'Oh, not this, I mean when we're in shorts and shirts. You know, we were most surprised when we saw women our mothers' ages wearing shorts here, and some of them a little . . . well, on the large side. You'd never see that generation wearing shorts at home. Times are changing and it's hard for our parents to accept it, especially after all they've been through. A lot of them still think that it's a woman's job to marry young and spend the rest of her life at her husband's beck and call. Perish the thought!'

I looked at Cleo, who seemed to be concentrating hard. 'Sorry, I'm talking too much. And too quickly! How did I get on to this? Your turn – tell me about your family.'

Cleo was laughing now. Then he pushed his empty plate to the side of the table and spoke more seriously. 'I grew up like that, too, with good values and good folks. You know who my best friend is? My mom. And after that it's my younger sister, Roberta. She's got herself married now, got a boy of her own. They're all back in El Dorado, Kansas. You been to El Dorado on your travels?'

'No, but it's a beautiful name.'

'Stupid question. Nothing much to see in El Dorado. But your Newcastle, it's a big place, right?'

I nodded. I told him about the coal mines, about the shipyards on the grey river, the colourful bridges, the vast empty beaches, and the castles that seemed to grow out of the rocks they stood on. My own words surprised me. North-east England sprang into a place of mystery and magic.

'It sounds like you miss it a lot.'

I shook my head. 'No, but it's always with me. Once, an old miner said to me when I was little, "Scratch my skin, hinny, and I'll bleed coal dust." I was terrified. But now I know just what he meant.'

I smiled at his puzzled expression. 'Tell me more about El Dorado.'

One day, a reporter from the paper in Grand Junction came to interview us round the pool. We were so used to telling the guests about ourselves – that, yes, we really had driven all the way from Ohio, and yes, we really were qualified nurses, even if we were waiting on tables – that it was starting to feel normal to be the centre of attention. But our reporter had other questions, too. She wanted to know about our National Health Service, and what we thought of it. We had been surprised how suspicious Americans were about the NHS; sometimes, the more we extolled its virtues, the more doubtful they became.

'So the patients like socialized medicine,' said our interrogator, in a statement that sounded rather like a question. She wrinkled her brow and scribbled something on her pad. 'But it must encourage them to run to the doctor for even a minor ailment?' That bewildered tone was more pronounced this time.

'Some people will always do that. I've met lots of Americans who do,' said Molly.

The reporter looked at her, frowned again, and carried on writing.

A couple of days later, Don was leaning on the reception desk, reading the *Daily Sentinel* as Pat, Molly and I were on our way out.

'Hey, charming lassies!' he called as we walked through the lobby. When we looked back, bemused, he said, 'That's what they're calling you here, but you sound more like savages to me.'

We rushed up to him and he held the paper in the air, laughing. 'Hey, I haven't finished it yet. Scat! Oh, go on.' He spread it out on the desk and we gathered round him.

'Oh, the picture!' I groaned. I had been hoping they wouldn't use it. We had been caught out by the photographer, who had arrived after the reporter had left, just as some of us had got changed to go swimming. I was standing on the edge of the group, unsmiling, looking awkward in my bathing costume, while Pat was protecting her modesty by standing behind the chair on which Molly was reclining. Yet Maureen, also in a swimsuit, was posing most fetchingly. I wished I could look more natural in photos, like she did, but I had always been happier on the other side of the camera.

'You're fine,' said Molly. 'Look at me – I'm like the old granny lying back there.'

'Will you two stop worrying about the picture and read this rubbish!' scolded Pat, who was already halfway through the story. 'I think that woman fancies herself as a novelist, making all this up.'

The article claimed that we had been practically starving in the Black Hills, surviving on a diet of canned tuna and sardines, and living in the car – renamed Lizzie – due to inclement weather. Apparently we had considered begging, but had been saved from this indignity by scrubbing floors.

Don shook his head, laughing, and moved away so that Cleo could read it. 'I guess we might get some extra customers from this. You may be a bunch of wild women, but it sure is a fetching photo of you all. I'd better warn the boss to expect an influx over the next few days.'

'That's the last time I talk to the press,' said Pat. When the rest of us laughed, she added, 'Well, I mean it.'

A couple of days later, someone turned up from the *Rocky Mountain News* in Denver and it seemed churlish not to speak to them. But we had to turn down a request to travel to Cheyenne, Wyoming, to be interviewed on a local radio station.

A group of us from the hotel set off on a fishing trip one morning. It was 4.30 a.m. and not fully light as our two vehicles
followed the mountain road. I was in Al's car with Molly and
Celia, the others in the hotel jeep with Don at the wheel, but
when the road deteriorated we abandoned Al's car and all piled
into the jeep. There was no room on the back seat, whose occupants already shared the space with fishing rods and baskets of
food, so Molly and I sat on the bonnet, shouting out instructions
to Don. By now the road was just a rubble-strewn track, with a
sheer drop on one side and a scree-covered slope, studded with
low bushes and spindly trees, on the other. The slope looked as if
it might give way at any time and take us with it over the
precipice.

We were high in the mountains. Glenwood Springs was close
to six thousand feet above sea level, and most of the journeys we
made from there involved climbing further. A large bird, soaring
on an air current, was barely higher than we were. Snow lingered
on some of the mountain slopes, and on top of one peak sat a
neat white cloud, like a puff of smoke. I wished I had brought my
movie camera to film it all, though in truth I needed both hands
to hang on.

We reached our destination, and the men busied themselves
setting up the lines while the girls made a fire and prepared breakfast. Fires burnt quickly here, as there had been no rain for several
weeks. We had brought with us four pounds of bacon, three
dozen eggs, a pound of coffee, four loaves of bread and the cases
of beer that accompanied us on all our picnics with this group of
friends – some of whom we rarely saw without a glass in their
hands. By now, it was very hot. We wore jeans rather than shorts

to avoid getting burnt, and our cowboy hats kept the sun from our eyes. After breakfast, we were all given the task of looking for big juicy worms, and Pat surprised herself by becoming the champion worm-catcher, despite being the most squeamish person I knew.

It was beautiful, standing at the river's edge, watching the water lapping over smooth brown rocks. The fast-flowing water in the centre glinted as if it were studded with diamonds. We had to share the rods. I didn't catch anything but Pat caught two trout, and we had about twenty fish by the time everyone had finished.

'There's an old mining town further up here, if you'd like to take a look,' said Don later that morning. He was lying back on the grass, his hat covering his face. He had given his rod to Celia, who was still fishing, hidden from view behind the trees.

Mr Schlegel, the head chef and the only person we addressed formally (apart from Mr and Mrs Hanson), was snoozing in the shade, having already filleted the fish in readiness for lunch. It was rare to see him resting, and even rarer to see him in jeans and cowboy hat like everyone else.

The rest of the party were relaxing, too, and for a while all was silent, apart from the rushing of the river, birds calling from the trees, and the whistling sound of Mr Schlegel's breathing. The air smelt of woodsmoke and pine needles, and everything was perfect in the world.

Molly and Maureen had made coffee for the five of us, and were handing it round (the men had moved on to the beer by now), when we heard the sound of a vehicle approaching and a jeep pulled up behind ours.

Don looked up and swore under his breath. He kicked Al, who sat up quickly and also swore. It was the game warden.

He wished us all a good morning, then asked to see our licence. Nobody had one. He reminded us of the law, which apparently stated that anyone found with a baited rod was guilty, whether caught fishing or not. We didn't really stand a chance.

'This is mighty serious,' I heard Don say to Mr Schlegel.

Meanwhile, Al was turning on the charm. 'Listen, pal, we didn't mean to break no law. We're from the Hotel Colorado in Glenwood, our friends have come all the way from England, Scotland and Ireland. Show us a little leniency, please, and you have my word it won't happen again.'

The warden seemed unimpressed, and was already taking down names and addresses.

'Aw, come on. We didn't mean no trouble. You drag this whole thing out and it's our boss at the hotel who's going to suffer. And he doesn't deserve it. Be decent.'

Don and Mr Schlegel were talking quietly, looking worried and shuffling their feet.

'Come on, pal, let's just say, just this one time, that you found us before we got started, you warned us, and we learned our lesson.' Al held out a hand. The warden ignored it.

Then I heard Don groan quietly, and saw him waving his right arm. He could see what the warden – now inspecting the jeep and making notes as he did so – hadn't yet seen. Celia had appeared through the trees and was walking towards us, swinging her rod happily and waving back at Don with her free hand.

I flapped an arm at her, too, and mouthed, 'Go back.' But it was all too late. She frowned for a second, mouthed 'What?' back at me, then grinned again, and pointed to the rod.

'Look what I've got! It's only a minnow – but what terrific fun! Oh, have we got visitors?'

The game warden looked up, and I could swear he had a look of satisfaction on his face.

We were all a lot quieter on the journey back. Pat and Maureen were taking their turn on the bonnet. I was squashed on the back seat with Celia on one side of me and Molly on the other. Mr Schlegel took up almost half of the seat on his own.

'We'll all laugh about this one day,' I said cheerfully, but Molly nudged me and shook her head. She pointed to Al and Don in the front, and we tried to listen to what they were saying.

We caught parts of it. '. . . bad publicity for the hotel . . . Mr Hanson . . . real bad . . . lose our jobs.'

Suddenly Al turned round and looked at us. 'What kind of visas have you got? They could kick you out of the country if they wanted to.'

Now I felt alarmed. Such a consequence had never occurred to me. I couldn't bear the thought of leaving America yet, and to do so in disgrace . . . to come home a criminal . . . I would feel as if I had let so many people down, not least myself. I felt a knot of worry tighten in my chest. Then I thought, don't be silly, they wouldn't do that to us, not for one unintended offence. And we were permanent residents. Surely we were safe.

Nobody spoke for a while. The jeep clung to the narrow track, whipping up little dust storms as it went. Far below us, the mountain stream was frothing silently. Oh, why did this have to spoil our grand day out? Well, I wasn't going to allow that to happen, and I blurted out, 'I won't regret it if they do deport us. I really won't. We've had the time of our lives.'

'Hear hear!' said Celia, and Al turned and flashed us a grateful smile, though it was still a more serious Al than we were used to seeing.

The jeep bumped violently, and Pat and Maureen bounced up

high, then turned to each other, laughing. Pat swivelled round to share the moment with Al and Don, but they must have been looking grim for she turned away quickly.

As we unloaded back at the hotel, Don cried out suddenly, 'No goddam fish, either. That son-of-a-bitch warden's going to have himself a mighty fine barbecue,' and he kicked at the ground, sending a shower of pebbles into the air.

Two nights later, after coming off duty, Al took Molly and me to the Red Steer for burgers and milkshakes. The rest of the crowd, who finished earlier in the dining room, were already there. The men usually managed to eat two burgers, though I didn't know how. They were huge, served on a plate stacked with chips and salad.

A young man was playing the piano. We hadn't taken much notice of him at first. In fact, he must have despaired of our table, which was producing more noise and laughter than any other in the room. Don was telling Cleo, for the fifth time, about Celia's dramatic appearance from the river bank – in which she was now holding a large trout in her hands – and was laughing almost as much as he had been the first time he told it. Of course his rendering of the tale had changed now that it had a happy ending. Someone at the hotel knew someone who knew the District Attorney in Grand Junction, and after several telephone calls backwards and forwards all charges had been dropped. But Mr Hanson had given the men of the party a severe talking-to, and made it clear that he held them responsible, and that no matter how indispensable they thought they were to him, they'd be out the door if it happened again. Cleo, who had overheard part of it, told me he had never known him so angry.

Suddenly Maureen's eyes lit up. 'It's one of our songs! If you'd just stop talking for a minute! It's "A Wonderful Guy" from *South Pacific*.'

We all started to sing.

'I saw Mary Martin play Nellie Forbush on the London stage,' Maureen told the boys, breaking off for a second. 'My sister Betty and I went. We were both teenagers at the time. It was such a thrill.'

We were all singing along now, even the men, and we clapped loudly at the end.

'Perhaps he knows *Salad Days*,' I said to the others, shrugging my shoulders.

'I doubt it,' said Pat.

'What you call it? *Salad Days*?' asked Al. 'Hey, pal, you heard of *Salad Days*?'

The man at the piano – he must have been about our age, with brown curly hair and a high forehead – acknowledged our applause with a grin. Then he began to play again. 'Will this do?'

The plinking notes of the musical that we loved so much seemed to be suspended in the air.

Al frowned. 'That ain't Jerome Kern, that's for sure.'

When he had finished, the pianist came over to join us. His name was Robert Loewe and he was a teacher, earning some extra money so that he could travel to England in August.

We left the men to talk amongst themselves while we suggested places that Robert absolutely had to visit, then Don butted in to ask if we had told our new friend how we almost ended up in the can over a fishing trip.

Robert turned up at the hotel one afternoon a couple of days later, right at the end of lunch. I'd been asked to step in, and was setting tables for dinner when he came into the dining room.

'You free later?'

I nodded. I was off for the rest of the day.

The room was empty, apart from a few stragglers finishing their desserts, but there was still another ten minutes of service to go. I put a finger to my lips and went over to the big clock on the wall, stood on a chair, and moved the hands to half past one.

Two minutes later, a young couple appeared in the doorway.

Robert, sitting at a corner table, looked pointedly at the clock. 'Dang, I think you missed it,' he said.

'Aw, I was sure we had time,' said the woman. 'And it's getting late to go anywhere else. Oh, Stanley, what'll we do?'

I was too soft-hearted not to serve them.

'Do you fancy a little boating?' asked Robert, when I had finally escaped. It felt like the hottest day of the summer so far, and the idea of being on the water was appealing. Maureen and Celia were on duty later, but Pat, Molly and I quickly changed into our costumes and joined him. A small inflatable dinghy was strapped to the roof of his jeep, and I expected to be heading for one of the mountain streams. Instead, we drove to a spot on the shoreline of the mighty Colorado.

'Golly, are you sure about this?'

'Trust me. This will be one of the best times of your life.'

I felt a mixture of panic and excitement as I put on the life-jacket Robert insisted we all wear. 'Just as a precaution,' he added. 'I don't take any risks.'

We pushed the dinghy out into the shallow water, then got carefully inside. There was only room for three of us in it at one time. The fourth person would have to drive the jeep downriver and take their turn later.

We started off smoothly, gliding past meadows, the water

slapping delightfully against the sides of the boat. Then Robert cried, 'White water ahead!' and we were being swept along so quickly, I doubted if we had any control at all over our direction. I tried to follow Robert's commands, but felt as if I was wasting my efforts. A wave washed straight over us, dumping half the river at our feet.

'Bale her out!' yelled Robert, and Pat spent the rest of the voyage scooping out the water like a madwoman, while I tried to copy his actions with the paddle, wondering why we hadn't thought to practise somewhere a little calmer first.

The river was raging, the noise so loud that we could barely hear Robert as he shouted instructions at us.

'Stay with it!' he called, as another wave slammed into us and we were flipped sideways.

Well, I don't exactly have any other plans, I thought. I might have been starting to feel as if I was trapped in one of those new automatic washing machines, but I certainly didn't fancy my chances in the water, lifejacket or not. Thankfully we righted ourselves.

I went through every feeling, from terror to exhilaration, and just as I was thinking I had never had such fun in my life and was sure we weren't going to drown, Robert indicated that we were to paddle to the side.

'You fancy taking it on your own?' he asked, after we had all had a turn. Feeling like experts now, the three of us agreed, and took the dinghy further downstream. We shot along, soaked to the skin, grinning widely whenever we looked at each other. All was going well until we heard what sounded like Niagara Falls ahead, and paddled furiously to reach the bank. The current was stronger here, and a wind had picked up that kept pushing us back to the centre of the river. The sound of crashing water was becoming louder, and we started to panic. We spotted a patch of still, dark water ahead, trees forming a canopy over it, and as we got close, Pat grabbed an overhanging branch and Molly and I paddled like mad. We were able to pull ourselves in, but we had landed in a mosquito swamp. In seconds, our arms and legs were black with biting insects.

Robert took us back to the hotel, and a couple of hours later I had a raging fever. I treated my bites, and the pain slowly began to ease. Niagara, incidentally, turned out to be just a few feet high, but we were still relieved not to have gone over it.

One day a large parcel with a Cleveland postmark arrived for me and Pat. It was the biggest box of chocolates we had ever seen and it came from Margaret, who wrote that the humidity in Cleveland was unbearable and she wished she was in the mountains with us all. Reading between the lines, we guessed that she was feeling unsettled; her employer had recently married again and she felt that her position was under threat.

We all ate a few chocolates, apart from Molly, who had just started a diet, then I went looking for our friends to share the rest with them. Cleo wasn't at the desk, so I popped into the kitchen and dining room, then returned to the lobby, expecting to see him there. After a while, I approached the girl who was standing in Cleo's usual spot.

'Haven't you heard?' she said. 'There's been a tornado in Kansas, and his family are dead.'

I gripped the edge of the desk. I think my legs would have given way if I hadn't.

'His family?'

'His mom and his pop, his sister. I think a little kid, too. Twelve deaths in the town. Isn't it a tragedy. And such a nice guy. Mr

Hanson had to break the news. Cleo was in pieces when he left. Hey, you look like you seen a ghost. Let me get you a glass of water.'

While we continued to smile and joke with our guests, there was a sombre mood amongst the staff those next few days. Cleo was a popular man, and everybody felt his loss keenly. Mr Hanson had told him to take as long as he needed, but I wondered if he would come back to Glenwood at all, and felt sad to think that I might not see him again.

It was a relief to us all when Bunty from Cleveland came to stay for a few days. As soon as she set foot in the place, every-one began to make a terrific fuss of her. Mr Hanson would have given her a room of her own, he said, but the hotel was full, so she came in with us. Al and Don wanted to know when the rest of the Mount Sinai nurses were arriving, and if, perhaps, we were turning the Hotel Colorado into the Hospital Colorado. It was fine by them, they said, as long as they could stay on the staff.

Late that night, when we were all off duty at last, we pestered Bunty for news of Cleveland as we shifted cases and bags to make room for her. (The chambermaid had long given up trying to sweep the bedroom floor, as there was so little visible floor to sweep.)

'Well, the most amazing thing is that your old friend from the Newcastle General moved into your apartment. Did you know that?' Bunty was looking through her suitcase as she spoke, trying to find some letters that Enrique had given her to bring.

'Which friend?'

'Sheila Mack. Oh, where are those letters? I hope I didn't leave them.' She rummaged around a bit more, before pulling them out triumphantly. 'Now, where was I? Oh yes, nobody could believe that Sheila knew you both. Nor could she. She kept saying, "You mean this was *Gwenda Brady*'s and *Pat Beadle*'s apartment. Really? From *Newcastle*?" Fancy missing her by just a month. Anyway, it's been just like old times hearing northern accents there again. Eeh by gum!'

'Bunty, we do not talk like that!'

'Of course you do. Now, what else . . . Well, you know that Alex and I are still courting. That's old hat. Enrique still talks about you all the time. Miss Harrison is back at work. You know she was ill, don't you? But she doesn't look at all well, poor love. Honestly, though, it's just the same. Oh, two of the doctors have been taking bets on whether old Flatus makes it back. They reckon you'll end up stuck in the Mojave Desert with some big rescue operation to get you back to civilization. But apart from that . . . Now, is there anywhere I can hang this dress?'

Bunty's visit coincided with our last week at the hotel, now full of summer visitors, and we were working more or less solidly up until our departure. This meant that Bunty had to take care of herself, but with the rest of the staff fussing round her she was rarely on her own. Mr Hanson allowed her to eat her meals in the restaurant, she was quite happy lazing by the pool – if she was left in peace for long enough – and she spent her evenings in the cocktail bar with Molly and me, while a queue of men waited to dance with her. Then, to everyone's surprise, Cleo came back, looking thinner than we'd remembered him, and as Mr Hanson insisted he take some more time off, he busied himself showing Bunty round.

Robert was playing all of our favourites in the Red Steer when we dropped by with Bunty one night. When he came over to chat, he told us that he had another outing planned.

'Are you wanting to drown us again, or is it death by blood-sucker?' asked Celia. She and Maureen had gone out with him in the dinghy a few days later, and their experience had a familiar ring about it. Mr Hanson had been horrified, telling us that three people had drowned the previous year in the same spot. Maureen had also managed to lose a shoe in the swamp and had to buy a new pair, but at least that meant we all got ten dollars to spend from the kitty, too. That was one of our rules – what one got, the others got.

Robert's latest idea sounded tame in comparison – a drive into the mountains to where his friend lived in the middle of nowhere, a night camping there, then on to see some of the most unspoilt land in the American West.

'Now, who's up for it?' He rubbed his hands together, his boyish enthusiasm reminding me of Tony in Cleveland.

'What do you say, Bunty?' asked Maureen. 'We'll still be back in time to put you on your train.'

Bunty grimaced. 'You know, darlings, that I'm one for hotels.'

'Believe me, love,' said Maureen, 'an experience with Robert is worth a thousand hotels.'

We set off for the home of Tex two days later, before the sun had risen. It was a hair-raising drive in places, over rocky roads and passes, up alarmingly steep inclines. I looked across at Bunty a few times, but could see that she was enthralled with the view.

'Isn't this terrific!' she kept saying. 'It's not like this in the east, you know.'

'We know that,' we laughed. 'We were there with you, remember.'

Tex lived with his wife, two children and two husky dogs in a ramshackle house, without the television, dishwasher and waste-disposal unit we had become accustomed to in the other American homes we had visited. Pairs of skis of all sizes were propped up on the front deck, and on a piece of grass at the side of the building stood a boat and a small aeroplane. We were warmly welcomed, and we girls were given a bunk-house to sleep in, with a mattress each.

'A luxury!' said Celia.

When Bunty saw me remove a large spider from Pat's back just as we were about to settle down, she said, 'If this is your idea of luxury, I think you're all barmy.'

We were up at dawn the next morning and set off in two cars, three of us with Robert and three with Tex, plus a husky in each.

'I wonder what Tex's wife thinks of her husband jetting off all over the place while she's stuck with the children,' I whispered to Maureen, who nodded in sympathy.

The milky light of early morning gave the surroundings a magical air. Deer scattered before us in all directions, and a creature Tex called a whistle-pig clawed at the ground. There were no proper roads, and we drove on tracks that had seen little traffic. I don't think we had ever imagined it was possible to be in America and yet so far away from society, where it might be the eighteenth and not the twentieth century, with no telegraph poles, no vehicles apart from our own, no billboards advertising the next diner or Goodyear tyres. The men told us that this part of Colorado had been used for the filming of a number of Westerns.

We had lunch beside a stream – hamburgers wrapped in foil and thrown into the fire – then swam in the icy mountain water, and had a snowball fight when we came out. On our return, we stopped to take a dip in a natural hot-spring pool. Robert said we should come back when we were old ladies, as the waters were said to cure rheumatism and arthritis.

I went for a walk with Cleo on my last afternoon in Glenwood Springs. We had dropped Bunty at the station the previous day. We were all sorry to see her go.

'For such a hot-house plant, you've done remarkably well,' Pat told her. 'Wait till you tell the others in Cleveland what you've been up to.'

'Better not tell Alex about all those dances,' said Maureen.

'Believe me, I won't,' she said, hugging us all. 'And I'm going to miss all those jazzy shirts and cowboy hats. Eastern men are going to seem very tame from now on.'

Cleo and I followed a stony track that rose behind the hotel, but it was too hot to walk very far. We found a spot of shade under a dusty conifer and sat down. The building that had been my home for the past few weeks looked as familiar to my eyes now as the General, or Mount Sinai. I told Cleo about our trip with Robert and Tex, and he said that we had seen more of America than most Americans had.

Then he grew more thoughtful, and said quietly, 'I've been doing a lot of thinking lately, Gwenda, all those big things, you know . . . life . . . death . . . kids. You never know what's round the corner, do you? Probably just as well.' He sighed and I looked at him anxiously. It brought tears to my eyes just thinking of his family, and especially his one-year-old nephew, the youngest victim. The tornado had appeared to pass El Dorado before making a deadly turn, demolishing a large part of the south-west neighbourhood where Cleo's family lived.

He carried on. 'But what I realized was, I'd like to marry you, Gwenda. And I hope that you'd like to marry me.'

His words were so sudden, so unexpected, that I thought I must be mishearing him. I felt hot and cold all at once. My heart pounded against my ribcage. Was he joking? But no, his face looked calm and serious. I wished I could rewind those seconds. Perhaps if we hadn't sat down, if I hadn't let the mood turn sombre. If I hadn't gone walking with him on my own . . . How could I have let this happen? It was all my fault.

I wished the ground would swallow me up, so that I didn't have to answer. Cleo was looking at me, gently but seriously.

'Oh, Cleo. I . . . I couldn't. I mean, I'm so . . . You don't mean it, do you? No, I can't get married yet, Cleo. I just can't.'

'Oh, I understand you've got your travelling to do, and I don't want to get in the way. But you come back here when you're done with all that, and I'll be waiting.'

'Cleo, I'm flattered, and, um, well I'm surprised, because I like you so much, and we're great friends, aren't we, you and me, but I just didn't expect this.'

He pulled his hat down over his eyes. Then he touched my arm. 'Like I said, I'll wait for you.'

Cleo's proposal rather spoilt my last day at the Hotel Colorado. I would have liked to feel flattered, but I felt more troubled by it, and guilty, too. I couldn't bear the thought that I might be the cause of yet more unhappiness for him. But should I have known it was coming? I honestly felt that he had given me no indication that he felt that way about me. Nor did I feel that I had given him reason to do so. We had lived and worked in close proximity to our new friends for several weeks, and I liked to think that the

friendships that had developed amongst us were just that – friendships. If there had been any flirting, it was always done in jest. I
even began to feel slightly angry with poor Cleo, though I hated
myself for such sentiments.

I was almost afraid to tell the girls later, and relieved when I
saw the surprise on their faces.

'Jiminy Cricket!' said Maureen.

'Oh, the poor man,' said Celia, looking quite tearful. 'He's very
confused. Who knows what he's feeling now.' She patted my hand.
'I'm not saying that you won't make a lovely wife for someone
one day, but for Cleo? I don't think so.'

We'd been here six weeks, it felt like home, and we were loath to
leave.

'How is it we keep saying goodbye to people and places just
as we settle down?' I said to the girls as we closed the bedroom
door behind us. A grey line of dust formed a perfect rectangle
where a pile of cases had been standing.

Don helped us squeeze the final box on the roof. 'Just look at
that old jalopy,' he said, standing back. 'You are *not* all going to fit
in there.'

Mr Hanson hoisted the Union Jack beside the Stars and
Stripes, and told us that he would fly it for three months in our
honour.

'Now, I mean this, if you're ever stuck somewhere and want to
come back, I'll take care of it, wherever you are.' He patted his
pocket.

'How about Hawaii?' asked Molly, and he said he might have
to draw the line at flying us, but we would still be welcome.

We promised to write to everyone. It really felt as if we were

leaving a family. Ruth, Theda and Betty had brought some of
their children to wave us off. We had spent happy times with
them, playing in the swimming pool and making them laugh with
some of our expressions. 'Cheerio!' called two of the girls. Al was
there, and our regular chambermaid, even though she said we
were the bane of her life. Chef, too, appeared briefly at the door,
before being called back to the kitchen. Cleo had bought us all
a leaving gift. The other four had a small box of candy each, but
when I opened mine I found a dainty pair of gold earrings that
I knew must have cost a small fortune.

'I know we'll meet again,' he said quietly, as I kissed him goodbye.

We had said goodbye to Robert the night before, at the Red
Steer, and given him our home addresses as he planned to drop
in on our parents later that summer.

'Remember, Robert, we censor our letters, so no worrying
them with too much detail.'

He promised to be discreet. 'At least I can change my repertoire now,' he said. 'I'll be glad to see the back of you.'

We had just left the hotel grounds when Pat said, 'Let's count
our money now.'

That was when we realized that we had left the biscuit tin
under the bed. I turned Flatus round with a screeching of tyres,
and Pat and Maureen rushed back inside, much to the amusement
of the folk still hanging around. Cleo, leaning back against the
wall, smiled at them both as they dashed past. Then he straightened up and went to help a young family who had just arrived.

6

It's a bum's life!

Colorado to Montana, July–August 1958

On 2 July we arrived in Sun Valley, Idaho, and set up camp just a few miles out of town. Sun Valley! We felt as if we knew it already from *Sun Valley Serenade* with Sonja Henie, though the slopes that had been covered with snow in the film were now scattered with wild flowers.

We went to look at the lodge, with its swimming pools and all-year-round skating rink. Two female employees, standing together talking, stopped their conversation and regarded us rather snootily. I suppose we didn't look like the sort of people who could afford to stay there.

'I feel rather put out that we're back to being nobodies again,' said Pat, as we hurried past them, pretending not to notice. 'After all the attention we got at the Hotel Colorado, I'm rather expecting everyone to know who we are and to make a big fuss of us. Isn't it silly?'

'And for Mr Hanson to appear, saying, "I just love all five of you!"' added Molly, doing a passable imitation of our previous employer.

We had driven for days after leaving Glenwood Springs, stopping off briefly to see the Garden of the Gods, Mesa Verde National Park and Salt Lake City. Sometimes the heat was one hundred degrees in the shade. Stuck for hour after hour in the baking interior of Flatus, we had all begun to resemble boiled beetroot.

A family were playing noisily in the pool together, and I smiled to myself as I thought of the children of Theda, Ruth and Betty, who had been so delighted when Mr Hanson had allowed the staff and their families to use the Hotel Colorado pool. We had fallen on our feet there, no doubt about it.

We arrived at the camp before all the holiday visitors and picked the best spot, cut off from the other sites by the river. But still, the newly arrived campers found plenty of excuses to walk past our tiny tent to take a good look at it, and us. Their own tents were the size of small bungalows, with garden chairs and tables arranged neatly at the front, and pans, washing-up bowls and other paraphernalia stacked on metal racks in open-sided extensions. They sat outside having breakfast wearing dressing gowns and slippers, as if they had been transplanted from their kitchens at home. We thought they were far more amusing than we were. But they were kind, and we were grateful for the watermelons and potato salads they thrust upon us.

The biggest 4 July event in the area was the rodeo in Hailey. As we arrived, an old water truck was being driven around the ring in a vain attempt to keep the dust down. The lumpy hills in the distance were the same colour as the earth that was being dampened.

Some of the cowboys sat on the fence, chewing tobacco, and

we felt quite scruffy in our jeans and cowboy hats when we saw how smart and colourful they managed to look in theirs.

'I told you I wouldn't be the only person in the world with a red hat,' said Molly, looking round at the spectators and adjusting the string under her chin.

Even the children were kitted out like miniature cowboys, despite the sizzling heat.

We took our seat in the bleachers beside a young couple with a large, angry baby, who was squirming underneath his layer of denim and leather.

'He just don't know where to put himself,' said the mother, passing him to me. She was a thin, anxious-looking girl of about twenty, with wispy hair that she kept tucking behind her ears, and so tiny, it was hard to believe she was the mother of such a solid child.

'He's got his hat right here, but look what happens when I put it on him.'

A fat fist grabbed the scaled-down Stetson and hurled it to the ground with surprising defiance. The child opened his mouth, ready to bawl.

'La-di-dah-di-dah,' I sang, not being able to think of anything more melodic, as I jiggled him around. He cheered up almost instantly, and even began to chuckle.

Celia picked up the hat. 'Isn't that just the cat's whiskers? I didn't think they'd make them in this size.'

'Mah wife's brother's one of the riders,' drawled the boy's father. 'We just hadda come see him. It's his first time.'

I saw a blind man struggling up the steps, and passed the baby to Pat so that I could help him to his seat. He sat down in the row in front, assuring us that we would just love the entertainment. The announcer's voice rose and crackled over the loudspeaker and the crowd became nervy and excited.

A cheer went up as the Sheriff's Mounted Posse, all dressed in green and white and carrying flags, opened the show with a grand parade. When the first bronco rider came on, we were already yelling along with the rest of the crowd. The cowboys were allowed to hold on to the horse with one hand only, and if they managed to stay on long enough a bell would ring and another rider would draw up alongside so that they could leap on to that horse, leaving the bucking one to find its way back to the corral. Most of them, though, didn't last that long.

'There's Vernon!' shouted the baby's mother, as the next bronco appeared. The man looked as young and as tiny as she was, and didn't last more than a few seconds. He lay on the ground, like a pantomime dead man, face down, arms and legs stuck out at dramatic angles.

'Vernon! Git yoursel' up!' cried his sister. But he just lay there. 'Vernon! You all right?'

The crowd was yelling, the first-aid workers were preparing to run on, when Vernon suddenly leapt to his feet, looked at each arm and leg in turn, gave them a little shake, then thrust his right arm victoriously into the air. Everyone laughed, and his sister looked at her husband, breathing a loud sigh of relief.

'Darn show-off,' muttered his brother-in-law, scowling. 'He'll go gittin' hisself hurt.'

The blind man appeared to be enjoying the show as much as anyone. He explained to us that the rodeo was a showcase for the skills that cowboys needed to do their job.

'This here's the calf-roping,' he announced, when the next event started. 'A cowboy gotta catch his calves to brand 'em.'

'Oh look, he's hurt him!' yelped Maureen, her face in her hands.

The blind man tensed slightly, craned his neck, as if to get a better view, then seemed satisfied that all was well.

He turned round. 'No, missy, don't you worry. He's just fine. This part ain't so dangerous.' He was looking at a point just above Maureen's head as he spoke. 'A cowboy is just as skilled as a doctor or an engineer in my book. As fine a profession as can be.'

'I think it's the calf she's worried about,' I laughed.

'About the animal? Ah well . . .' The man chuckled and sucked his teeth. 'Up here we live for our animals, but we don't go getting sentimental 'bout 'em.'

One cowboy wrestled his calf to the ground in just fourteen seconds. The judges inspected the knots then released the animal, which scampered away on frisky legs.

I asked the blind man if he was a cowboy, too, and he gave a whinnying laugh. 'A cowboy? Good lordy, no. I was a school-teacher. But Idaho born and raised.'

Next up was the bull-dogging, similar to the calf-roping except that the bull was turned on to its back. What strength was needed! But the most thrilling event of all was the bull-riding. The cowboy mounted the creature in a small enclosure, the door opened, and out it thundered, tossing and writhing as it attempted to unseat the rider. Just the sound of its feet on the dirt, of its contemptuous snorting, sent a frisson of glorious terror right through me. One bull discarded his cowboy swiftly, then walked round the perimeter fence, eyeing up the crowd, before suddenly stopping, lowering his huge head and preparing to charge. Two rodeo clowns used red cloaks to distract him. The bull glared at them both, but barely altered its stance. A few seconds ticked by and the crowd seemed to hold its breath as one. Then the bull picked up its head, lowered it again almost immediately, and made a dive for one of the clowns. The clown took to his heels and shot towards the fence. Meanwhile, the announcer was telling everyone to keep calm, but his pleas only served to increase our hysteria.

'Run!' I screamed. 'Oh no, he's going to . . . oh . . .'

Pat and Maureen had hidden their eyes and were making whimpering sounds.

'Uh-oh, he's real ornery, that one,' said the blind man.

'That bull's got to weigh a good ton. That clown weighs next to nothing,' exclaimed Celia, clasping her hands together.

The clown reached the fence, the bull at his heels.

'He could smash that fence down if he wanted to,' said Celia. 'I wonder how often that's happened.'

'It's a terrific show, for sure,' said the blind man, tapping his stick and nodding his head in the direction of the ring. 'Terrific.'

'Keep calm, folks. Stay in your seats. You're all quite safe. And . . . he's made it!' shouted the announcer.

The clown had leapfrogged the fence as dextrously as any gymnast, the bull missing him by inches. The crowd breathed out, then cheered. The bull retreated, looking bored, and snorted at us all.

After this drama, the rodeo queen was chosen, but we were talking too much to pay any attention. The baby had fallen asleep long ago, and Molly, who had been holding him for some time, passed him to Maureen.

'That head of his is a dead weight,' she said, shaking her left arm.

We looked longingly at his fat cheeks, and the perfect pout of his sleeping mouth.

Striking camp was a big undertaking, with everything having to be cleaned and stacked securely back in Flatus – and the usual problem of wondering how it had ever all fitted in the first place. The night before we left anywhere was always spent sewing on buttons, and taking stock of our wardrobes. Molly offered to sell me a pair of Jantzen Bermuda shorts that were brand new, and I tried them on.

'I'm so small, Bermudas just don't suit me,' she moaned. 'I only bought them because they were in the sale. Oh, they do look nice on you!'

Maureen, trying to fix a broken strap on a sandal, nodded her agreement.

'You can have them for two dollars, if you like. Oh, look at you, Maureen! What have things come to when we have to cobble our own shoes!'

We set off in a land devoid of colour, as if the sun had withered and destroyed anything that was lush and green. The hot air settled over us like a second skin. The girls in the back had drifted off to sleep, heads lolling on each other's shoulders, when we shuddered to a halt. I cursed silently and looked across at Pat, but she, too, had dropped off.

I cleared my throat. 'Um, I'm afraid, ladies, that we've run out of petrol.'

It wasn't really such a surprise. We had been pushing our luck since the petrol gauge stopped working several states ago, trying to remember to fill up every hundred miles or so. The other four sighed and yawned, and got out of the car, reluctantly, to begin pushing. I couldn't help laughing to myself as I listened to their efforts. There were definitely some compensations to being the driver. However, it wasn't long before they were giggling about something.

'Molly, really!' I heard Celia say.

A few minutes after that, a car overtook us and pulled up ahead. A man got out and began to walk towards us, squinting into the sun. He looked like a tourist, in his shorts and checked shirt, sandals and white knee-length socks.

He came to my window and the girls gathered round.

'My wife says to me, "Looks like they run out of gas. You got any spare?" Well, darn it, my can's empty, but I said to her, "I'll go get them some on one condition." Now, don't go getting strange ideas about me, I'm a respectable fellow, that's my wife and kids in there . . .'

Sure enough, I could see children's heads bobbing in the back seat of his car, and make out another figure in the front.

'If I could take some movie film of these girls pushing . . . It'll be the highlight of my vacation movie.'

There was a short silence. 'I didn't mean to offend you.'

Then we all burst out laughing. It was true, with their yellow, green, red and blue backsides, the four of them must have made a colourful splash in the brown landscape.

'How could we be offended? It's quite a compliment,' said Pat.

We drove all day and into the night, and parked on top of one of the Grand Teton passes to sleep. We woke early to the view of Jackson Hole below us, an oasis of green emerging from the bluey light of dawn.

Now that the holiday season had arrived, campsites were beginning to fill up, but we found room at the third one and it was perfect. There was a marked spot for every tent, a crate of logs and a picnic table. There was a brand new toilet block, and a washroom and laundry with an electric socket that we could plug our iron into.

One of our neighbours went fishing that afternoon, and stopped by later with five trout. I wasn't too sure what to do with them, but I decapitated them first because I didn't like them looking at me, then set to work with a rather blunt knife and removed all the sloppy bits inside. I thought about boning them, but doubted I would have any fish left if I did, so I stopped there.

Just as I was finishing, the man came back and said apologetically, 'I've made a booboo.'

None of us had heard that expression before, and we stood there grinning at him like idiots while he grinned back.

'Sorry,' he said at last, 'I meant to fillet them for you first.'

I assured him it had been no trouble, we were just grateful for the fish.

We got up early the next morning to climb Signal Mountain, from where we had been promised a sweeping view of the Teton range. The mountains were greyish purple in the pale light, streaked with snow in places. As we were taking photos, a tall man strode up to us and, in a voice brimming with bonhomie and self-confidence, introduced himself as the fire ranger.

'Bob Jones,' he said, almost crushing my hand in his. 'And I couldn't help overhearing those fine accents.' He chuckled to himself. 'My wife and I were in the British Isles two summers ago. You must come and meet her. Are you ready for coffee, or is it time to put the kettle on for a cup of English tea?' He laughed again.

Bob ushered us to the lookout, a large cabin with windows all the way round, where his wife, Mary Ann, tall and dark-haired like her husband, greeted us, a blonde baby in a type of rucksack on her back.

'We're both teachers,' she said as she made the coffee. 'We live in California, but we like the outdoor life.' She spoke in a sweet, girlish drawl that made you want to curl up and listen to it all day. She complimented Celia and Pat on their colourful sweaters – it had been cold when we got up – and pronounced them 'real neat'.

We took our drinks outside. Bob was talking to some other

visitors now, and his loud voice and hearty laughter were like a heckling backdrop to our conversation.

'We were expecting to be camping,' said Mary Ann, 'but we've got all mod cons in our cabin, and we can drive into Jackson real easy. But what about you folk? Tell me all about this trip!'

We told her that our plans were changing all the time, but the current idea was to go from Yellowstone to Vancouver, possibly via Calgary, then follow the coast down to California where we were hoping to meet up with Joan and Olov in Los Angeles.

When she heard that we had one tiny tent between five of us, Mary Ann gasped and said, 'But you must take ours! We don't need it this summer. You can return it when you get to California.' We insisted that we couldn't possibly, but Bob, who was back in our circle now, was just as adamant.

'We want to repay the British people for the kindness they showed us.'

He told us about the overseas trip they had made in the summer of 1956. 'We travelled round Europe first, isn't that right, Mary Ann? Then we finished up in Great Britain. Ah, we had some times there, didn't we, Mary Ann? We were cycling—'

He broke off when he saw our surprise. 'Oh yes, we cycled everywhere that summer, and one day we came across a cricket match. Of course we knew about cricket, but we'd never seen it played before, or understood the rules, so we stopped and sat down and watched.'

'We still didn't understand it,' said Mary Ann, laughing.

'No, we didn't,' agreed Bob. 'But the most surprising thing was when some ladies appeared with long tables, and play stopped while both teams had a small feast together. We'd never seen any-thing like it before. What did we say, Mary Ann? It was just like something from a story book.'

Mary Ann took up the tale. 'There was a couple sitting beside us, middle-aged, I guess, and we got talking, and they invited us to their house for tea after the match.'

Bob began to laugh at the memory, a laugh that seemed to rise up from his stout walking boots and shake the air around us. Baby Laura began to giggle. He sat down on the ground and stretched his long legs out in front of him, then he looked across at his wife, who carried on with the story.

'We accepted, of course, and we were sitting in their very nice parlour – is that what you call it? – talking to the husband while his wife was making the tea. We talked, and we talked, and we kept looking at each other and thinking, how can it take so long to make a pot of tea?'

'She'd been in the kitchen on her own for at least an hour,' interjected Bob.

'Well, perhaps not—'

'Oh, at least an hour,' Bob repeated, 'then, at last, the door opened, and she came into the room wheeling a cart laden with delicious little sandwiches, the things you call scones, butter and home-made jelly, cakes and cookies. We couldn't move after we'd eaten, could we, Mary Ann?'

'And now we know what you British mean when you ask folk for tea,' smiled his wife.

The Grand Teton National Park had only been intended as a brief stopping-off point en route to Yellowstone, but we had all fallen in love with it. Lake, shore and mountain, each seemed so perfect in its place, and we enjoyed the evening talks given by the rangers, where we would gather round, sitting on logs, to hear about the history and wildlife of the park. In the afternoons we swam in icy Jackson Lake, floating for hours on our lilos in a sheltered bay.

Sometimes we went for walks, though it was hard work in the heat, and one day we treated ourselves to a climbing lesson with a marvellous instructor, Bill Byrd from Oregon, a high-school teacher like the Joneses who shared their passion for the wilds. One night he invited us to join him and his wife, Jo Ann, at the guides' camp-fire. Two of the men had guitars, and they all had excellent voices, so we spent most of the time listening, just joining in with the choruses. We learned the proper version of 'I've Been Working on the Railroad', and hoped that they wouldn't ask us to teach *them* anything. Of course they did, and though when we were all together we sang the songs from *Salad Days* and *My Fair Lady* with gusto, we felt a little shyer with strangers.

I remembered some of my old Girl Guide camp-fire songs, thankfully the sort that others could pick up quickly, as I hated singing on my own. One of them seemed particularly appropriate, and we had sung it together in the car many times.

Oh you'll never get to heaven (Oh you'll never get to heaven)
In an old Ford car (In an old Ford car)
Cos an old Ford car (Cos an old Ford car)
Won't go that far (Won't go that far)

Everyone loved it, and soon they were making up verses about a ranger's knee, Bill Byrd's rope and Jackson Hole.

Bob and Mary Ann joined us for hot dogs at our camp-fire the night before we left. The pine logs smoked a bit, but they gave off a pleasant heat. Baby Laura was put to bed in the car, and settled down without a murmur. We all agreed that she was the best baby we had ever met.

'So, how long until we see you in Woodland?' asked Bob. 'Hey,' he laughed suddenly, 'don't suppose you ever have trouble spotting *your* car in a car park!'

'You should see her when she's loaded. There's even less danger of missing her then,' said Celia, giving Flatus an affectionate glance.

We told the Joneses that it might be a month or so before we got to them. We had looked at the map earlier that evening and decided that after Yellowstone we would need to find jobs in Helena, the capital of Montana, if we were to fulfil our wish of travelling to Canada, where we would not be allowed to work. 'Otherwise, are you home next week?'

After we had eaten, and listened to more of Bob's funny stories, he rubbed his hands together and looked at our rosy faces. 'Who would like to start the singing? I think, as our English hosts are more numerous, it really ought to be them.'

We all groaned, though we had been half expecting it.

But Bob had already begun with one of his own songs.

'*Have you seen the ghost of John?*' he boomed, sending us all into hysterics. 'Now you join in, come on, we can sing it in a round. *Long white bones and the rest all go-o-o-o-one.* Come on, guys!'

The elderly couple from the next tent came over to see what all the commotion was.

'*Ooooh wouldn't it be chilly with no skin on,*' sang Mr Ted Heaton from Charleston, West Virginia, as he sat down beside us.

We set up camp a few miles from the centre of Helena, at the end of a dusty track by the creek. It was blissfully quiet after Yellowstone, the only sounds being the wind in the trees, the calling of the birds and the gentle lapping of the water.

'It's just like camping in an apartment building at this time of year,' the Tetons guides had said of Yellowstone. 'You won't be able to move. And bears wandering round like they own the place.'

They hadn't been wrong, and we had stayed only long enough to admire Old Faithful and some of the hot springs.

When we were clean, Pat and I put on dresses for the first time in ages, feeling as if we were rehearsing for roles we hadn't played for a while, and went to St Peter's Hospital, where we were told to report back the next day to see the supervisor.

Twenty-four hours later we both had jobs, working daily shifts from 7 a.m. until 3 p.m. There was nothing for the others yet, but everyone in the hospital seemed eager to help, and promised to listen out for any opportunities. Getting up at five in the morning, when it was still dark and the air felt damp and cold on our skin, was the least favourite part of our new routine. As we washed under the icy tap and shook our heads like dogs, the other three lay still as corpses in their sleeping bags. I felt like a ghost, slipping between tent and tap and car in my gleaming white uniform. However, once we were at work, it all seemed worthwhile. We were back doing what felt natural to us, and any rustiness soon vanished. We had a good laugh in the car on the way home that first day when we both confessed that we had carried our trays at shoulder height through the wards.

Helena wasn't a big place, and word of our arrival soon got around.

There were three others? Did they talk like we did?

We were living on a campsite? How did we manage to wash our uniforms?

What a healthy colour we were! England must have a mighty fine climate!

'So, you're the two bums,' said a smiling doctor as Pat and I were leaving on our second afternoon, and I had to compose myself quickly before remembering that I had heard the term before and that no offence was intended. Looking at Pat's reddening face, I could see that she was just as confused.

Molly, Maureen and Celia kept house for us at the camp. They fetched firewood and made seats out of logs. They washed our clothes in the creek and strung them out to dry on lines tied to the trees. Most days they didn't see a soul until we returned, apart from the occasional picnicker. We half expected them to run away into the woods like savages when they heard anyone coming.

On my third day at St Peter's, I was told there was a phone call for me. It was the neighbouring hospital, St John's, wanting to employ the other three as soon as possible. The problem now was getting everybody to and from work, with only one car and two licences between us (not that we had ever let a small legal matter deter us before). The only solution was for Molly to drive when necessary, but it was still a logistical nightmare at times. One morning, Molly had to get up early with me and Pat so that she would have the car to bring her to work at 3 p.m. I drove it back when Pat and I had finished our shifts, took Celia to work at St John's that night, and collected Molly at the same time. Celia slept in the nurses' home and we took her back to the camp when we came off duty at 3 p.m. the next day. There was a shower in the nurses' home that we gratefully slipped into when we were passing. Although we bathed at the camp-fire every night, and our drip-dry dresses were no bother to keep clean, I'm sure we still smelt of woodsmoke all the time.

Our circle of friends was growing, and in the evenings car head-lights would bounce in and out between the trees, announcing our visitors. It might be Mrs Reid, the director of nursing, who was English and had trained at Guy's Hospital. How pleased she had been, she told us, to come back from her holiday to find us working there! Or Mrs Michaelson, known to her friends as Mike, the head nurse and a former rodeo queen. Or Mrs Hamel, the 71-year-old weekend relief nurse, who had invited all five of us to her house for dinner one day and given us even more food to take home – three dozen rolls, a lemon meringue pie, an angel cake, a jar of apple butter and sufficient fried chicken, potatoes and gravy for us all for the next night.

The day-trippers and picnickers were also becoming more numerous. Maureen started telling one woman who we were, and she laughed and said, 'Oh, we know all about you. My daughter works at the hospital. You're the biggest thing to hit Helena since the Gold Rush.'

The only disadvantage of our new-found fame was lack of privacy when we needed it. Molly had devised an exercise routine for us – so that we would look good in our bathing costumes when we got to California, she said. (I'm not sure what she thought we'd be getting up to in California, but it seemed to involve a lot of parading around in our next-to-nothings.) But now we were constantly interrupted as we performed our stretches. And no matter how quiet it might be as we heated the water over the fire, stripping off for a wash was always accompanied by the sudden splash of a headlight, and the screams of whoever had been caught in its glare as they ran for one of the tents.

One day, I nursed a man who had unwittingly walked between a mother bear and her cub. As well as sporting some cracked ribs and internal injuries, his torso and arms bore the imprint of a perfect set of claw marks that I couldn't help admiring. I asked him where it had happened, and realized that it was barely a mile up the creek from our camp. I decided not to tell the others, especially as one of us occasionally had to be left on her own there, and it could be creepy in the woods, anyway, when the wind sighed through the trees and every sound started to seem sinister. One night Celia and Molly were both at work, and Pat and I had been invited to dinner by one of the St Peter's nurses, leaving Maureen by herself. It was getting late and had been dark for some time, and she had just been making herself comfortable with a book, enjoying the luxury of our new 500-candle-power lamp, when she heard the sound of twigs being snapped underfoot. This was followed by someone – or some-thing – scratching on the tent, and strange moaning noises. She had been too terrified to look outside, and sat with her fingers stuffed in her ears until Pat and I got back half an hour later. Our minds all went back to Yellowstone, where our neigh-bouring tent had a huge hole in one side – the result of a bear searching for food. Fortunately, its occupants had been out at the time. It didn't help that many tourists in the park fed the bears from the safety of their cars, as if they were merely a bigger ver-sion of a pet dog.

In the reasonable light of morning, we went through all the possibilities. There was no obvious damage to the tent, no sign of large animals, so a bear seemed unlikely. Not far away in the woods were some holiday cabins, and Pat and Celia suspected that

Maureen's visitors had been children messing around, though Molly and I thought that a wild apeman, on the lookout for a sweet English girl to cater to his every need, was the most likely explanation.

But to be on the safe side, we decided on an emergency drill: Pat would blow a whistle, I would grab a knife, Molly and Maureen would pick up sticks, and Celia the pan.

Mrs Reid brought steaks to the camp one night, which we cooked in tinfoil over the fire. She soon had us laughing over tales of her arrival in America. They sounded remarkably like our own experiences at Mount Sinai.

'I always remember that my nurses have been trained differently, and I have to respect that. But the patient comes first in my hospital – that's something I won't compromise on.'

Pat looked across at me. We each knew what the other was thinking. The shadow of Sister Gunn was never far away. That woman must have had the longest shadow in the world.

'Tell them about last offices,' I said to Pat. 'I don't think the others have heard it either.'

Pat, who was poking the fire back into life, sat down on her log, which she had padded with an old rug. 'It was the last lecture of our preliminary course, the big one. We'd been told all the way through that it would be "last offices" – whatever they were. I don't think anybody had a clue; I certainly didn't. The great day arrived, and the lecture was from Sister Gunn herself, and it was all about dealing with the death of a patient. We had been told so many times to put ourselves in the position of the patient that when she began, "I'd like you to put yourself in the place of . . ." I had already imagined myself as a corpse, and I couldn't help smiling just a little. Of course, it wasn't the patient this time – the first time ever – it was the relative we had to think of. Well, we were having coffee later that morning and someone came to tell me that Sister wanted to see me immediately. When I got to her office she looked so serious, I thought that one of my parents was ill or dead. I was trembling so much I could hardly stand. But all she said was, "Nurse Beadle, you smiled during my lecture on last offices. Do you think death is a laughing matter?" I was so relieved, it was all I could do to stop myself beaming at her.' Pat shook her head slowly. 'Oh, she was hard work, that one. But at least Gwenda got her own back on her.'

I choked on my coffee. 'Oh, it wasn't deliberate, I wouldn't have dared.'

'A likely story,' laughed Maureen.

'Honestly, it wasn't. I was qualified by then, and, blow me, guess who ended up on the nurses' wing when she came in to have her bunions done. She refused to use a bedpan like everyone else, so I had to wheel her to the lavatory whenever she needed to go. And on one occasion, I forgot all about her. I don't know how, I just—'

'You didn't forget,' hooted Maureen. 'We all know you by now.' The others were laughing too, and I could hardly complete the story.

'I did. I plain forgot. I got busy doing something else and when I realized – with that awful hot feeling that makes you tingle all over – almost an hour had gone by. I wanted the hospital to collapse on top of me. I went flying back and found her struggling to manoeuvre her chair through the door. I thought my career was over there and then, and I spluttered out my apologies, but she didn't say a word. She wouldn't even look at me.'

'She didn't say anything at all? Not even later?' said Celia.

'It was never mentioned.'

'Yep, they don't make them like that any more,' said Mrs Reid, sipping her coffee and pulling her coat around her shoulders. Heat disappeared quickly under the high Montana sky, and most mornings now, the windscreen was frozen.

'But it's a great life, isn't it?' said Maureen, her cheeks flushed from the fire. 'Where else do you get to see the whole of humanity, the rich and the poor, the best and the worst of them, all of them—'

'With a thermometer up their backside?' I offered.

'Exactly,' she laughed.

'Did you always want to be a nurse, Maureen?' Pat asked her.

'As far as I can remember. When I left school, I started off working for the Fifty Shilling Tailors. Then I went to Mr Kirby's dental practice until I was eighteen, and old enough to start nursing school.' She laughed. 'Actually, it was the only way to get a room of my own after sharing with Betty and Margaret all those years.'

'The advantages of being an only child . . .' mused Pat, before adding, 'My mother put me off applying when I was eighteen. She thought I'd miss my friends and my social life with all the irregular hours. But by the time I was twenty-one, I knew it was what I wanted to do more than anything.'

'Some people thought I would be a nun!' said Maureen, making us gasp. 'I was always keeping everyone else happy – looking after my younger brothers and sisters, helping Mum and Dad. Going into nursing was freedom after all of that.'

'Yes, I'm with you there,' said Celia. 'I was on my own with my parents after my older siblings had scattered. Then my father died, and two of my brothers came back to the farm. I decided it was *my* time then, time to see a bit more of life. I applied to the Miller General in Greenwich, where one of my sisters had trained.'

Mrs Reid nodded in recognition.

'Later, I decided to spread my wings further. It was a choice between Paris and Cleveland. I suppose you could say the rest is history.'

Nobody spoke, and we all sat and stared into the fire. Nursing was a grand life, there was no doubt about it.

The senior doctor at St Peter's, Dr Cashmore, had taken an interest in us from the start. He and his family had a cabin in the woods, not far from our camp, and asked if they might come to see us one night.

'We're just real curious about your set-up.'

Mrs Cashmore, who always referred to her husband as 'the doctor', was as delightful as he was, and after spending an evening as our guests, insisted on returning the favour the following night. Celia was working, and Molly had been feeling under the weather all day but decided she was well enough to come along, so four of us turned up there, just as the wind picked up and a large black cloud settled over the woods. The cabin turned out to be a handsome wooden house, with porches at the front and back, dotted with rocking-chairs and children's playthings, and attractive rustic furniture inside. We were supposed to be eating in the garden but it looked too unsettled, so we all gathered around a huge wooden table, the lamps throwing a rosy glow over our faces. Pat was just explaining the origin of our antlers when Molly burst into tears and excused herself. We explained that she had been unwell that day, and when Dr Cashmore took her temperature, he found that it was a hundred and one and diagnosed severe tonsillitis. Despite Molly's protests, Mrs Cashmore gave her a dose of 'the doctor's special cure-all' and put her to bed.

The next day, Maureen woke up with a fever. We felt that we couldn't possibly impose on the Cashmores again, and cautiously asked Mrs Reid if she might be able to stay in the nurses' home at St Peter's, wondering if it was too much of an imposition. She readily agreed to let both her and Molly stay there, and arranged for their meals to be sent over from the hospital, while Dr Cashmore popped in twice a day to check up on them. Then Celia came down with the bug too – we decided that they must have picked up something at the other hospital – and there was just Pat and me left at our camp.

Falling ill in America was something we had all dreaded. At Mount Sinai, we had all paid our medical insurance, but I for one had let the payments lapse since leaving. Few people, anyway – American or alien – could afford to cover every eventuality. Jadran, our Yugoslavian friend from the ISG, had needed a serious operation while he was in Cleveland, and Pat and I had taken it in turns to 'special' him, as we called it at home, coming straight off duty and rushing to his bedside. When he left hospital he had been presented with a bill for five hundred dollars, despite having taken out insurance. We had also given blood for him afterwards, for he had to pay twenty-five dollars for every pint he had received, or replace each pint with donated blood – two pints for the first one and a pint for every one thereafter.

I suppose we had grown rather sceptical about the motives of American doctors after working in this environment, thinking many of them were out for what they could get, so it was heartwarming to see people we barely knew caring for our friends so generously.

It was peculiar being just the two of us again. It had never seemed so quiet. After work, we caught up on letter-writing at the fire. Pat's typewriter must have sounded like an industrious creature of the forest to anyone approaching.

'Any chance of a turn? Who have you written to tonight?'

'I've owed one to Cousin Dorothy for ages, and I've written to Sheila, too. Dorothy's baby supposedly looks like me, though I can't see it myself. You can have it in two ticks.'

'Not getting broody?'

'Heavens, no!'

The sun had dipped behind a mountain long ago, and a little later we retired to the tent.

'Hoo-oooo.'

We both looked at each other.

'Was that an owl?'

The noise was followed by a hissing, then what sounded like muffled giggles. Pat looked at me and whispered, 'Our mysterious visitors?' I put a finger to my lips and turned off the lamp. I untied the door and crawled out. I waited for a while until my eyes had adjusted to the dark. The hooting had stopped, and all I could hear when I listened hard was the bubbling of the creek. I could make out the glimmer of some last red embers on the fire, but otherwise all was thick blackness, apart from the sky, a few shades lighter against the tops of the trees. I crouched down behind the tent and shivered. What was that? A flashing light appeared at the edge of the woods. The light went off, and some figures emerged. As they got closer, I thought I recognized at least one of the teenage Cashmore children. They continued to walk towards the tent, whispering to each other. When they were about twenty feet away, I leapt to my feet and made the most blood-curdling sound I could muster.

'Eeeeeeeoooowwwww!'

If I say so myself, it sounded quite good, like a cross between the foxes I sometimes heard from my bedroom in my parents' house and the coyotes we had become used to in America.

The children screamed, clutched each other and ran back to the trees. Pat came shooting out of the tent at the same time.

'What on earth was that?'

'It was only me.'

'Well you'd frighten the devil away with that noise. Did you see who it was?'

'Just the Cashmore kids and their friends. Little devils.'

'I knew it was kids. Tssk. I'm glad *they* think it's funny. Poor Maureen – no wonder she was terrified.'

Then we both started laughing. 'It's the sort of thing Doug would do. You know what he's like. Oh well, no harm done. I don't think we need to tell their parents, do we?'

Mike, the head nurse, often talked about going home to exercise the horses, and when she learned that Pat and I were both keen riders, she arranged for us to accompany her after our last shift. The others were still in the nurses' home, recuperating, and we were due to pick them up the next day, and to leave Helena a day or so after that. Mrs Reid had begged us to stay longer, but it felt like time to move on. We now had enough money to visit Canada, though we were relying on finding work in California straight after.

We had both learned to ride at Danny's Riding School on the Town Moor in Newcastle. A small, round, immaculately dressed woman, who looked as if she was about to take part in a dressage competition, had seated us on our horses, showed us how to hold the reins, then mounted her own horse, and with a plummy

'Giddyup, Augustus,' had trotted ahead, the rest of us straggling behind her. There had been no further instruction, but nor had there been any mishap. Perhaps we were natural riders.

Mike was a championship rider for Montana, and owned three horses. They were beautiful, haughty-looking beasts who eyed us disdainfully, as if they knew already that we were not good enough for them. Mike was very patient with us, and soon we were off, cantering across the sun-bleached plains, a hot wind blowing at our faces. When that went fairly smoothly, she asked if we would like to ride bareback.

'Oh yes!' I said, though I was terrified at the thought. Pat looked at me uncertainly, but Mike said that we would both be fine.

It was thrilling, and I wondered if I had missed my vocation. Perhaps I had been born to be a cowgirl? Blow those plans to open a milk bar that Pat and I sometimes talked about! I would marry a farmer, I thought, and live like this, riding every day. The others had already told me they had my future mapped out; on one of the long journeys, when we talked about everything under the sun, one of them had come up with the bright idea that I would marry a vicar and serve tea and cucumber sandwiches on the vicarage lawn, dressed in my jeans and cowboy hat. They all thought this was hilarious.

Mike indicated that we should head for home, and it seemed to arouse a passion in our previously well-behaved horses. They shot off on a wild gallop and all we could do was cling to their necks, praying that we wouldn't fall. When Pat pulled up behind me back at Mike's, her look of sheer terror must have mirrored my own.

The next afternoon we went to pick up the girls. We thought they might be reluctant to say goodbye to their cotton sheets and hot water, as well as the special attention they had been receiving, but all three of them were hot and cross, and desperate to get back to camp. Though Dr Cashmore had made it clear that he was not charging us for his services, we still expected a bill from the hospital to pay for the room and the food – especially as Molly, Maureen and Celia were not even St Peter's Hospital nurses. But Mrs Reid had a surprise for us. She had put our position to the committee for special cases, and they had agreed to take care of everything. We stammered our thanks, embarrassed but grateful. Mrs Reid admitted that she, too, had been surprised that they had accepted. We drove back to camp, buzzing with our good fortune and believing that Americans had to be the most generous race of people anywhere. I had hardly parked Flatus before the three recovered invalids had shot out and scampered down to the creek to cool off, professing themselves happy to be home.

Most of our friends came to the camp on our last night – Mrs Reid, the Cashmore family, Mike, Helen the theatre nurse, even two of the elderly cleaners, who brought their grandchildren with them.

'Honey,' said Mrs Cashmore to her husband, 'we are coming here tomorrow to lend these girls a hand with their packing.'

Dr Cashmore winked at us. 'She just wants to see how you manage to get it all in the car.'

'The doctor's right,' smiled his wife.

We had spent the morning at their house in town doing our washing. The basement was a fully equipped laundry, with a washing machine, dryer and a large electric presser, the like of which we had never seen. We sat before this contraption and fed our clothes through two large rollers – rather like a mangle except that they were heated – stopping and starting the process with knee-operated controls. It saved hours of standing at the ironing-board.

The Cashmore children were chasing each other in the woods with the cleaners' grandchildren. When we heard some familiar animal-type sounds amid lots of laughter, the five of us exchanged meaningful glances.

Mike said she was recommending me and Pat for the next rodeo. 'How about the bronco riding?' she suggested. 'Oh, Pat, I'll never forget the look on your face when Calamity Jane turned for home and started to gallop.'

'If I'd known she was called Calamity Jane!'

'I really wish you weren't going, and my offer to you all still stands, but I've somewhat reluctantly brought you something to help you on your way,' said Mrs Reid, handing over a small package.

It was a book of road maps of North America and Mexico. The first page I turned to showed the whole of Canada, most of it a great swathe of white. In the top left-hand corner, stuck out on its own like an afterthought, was Alaska, a territory we had heard was to become the forty-ninth state. It looked so remote, so impossible to reach, that it tugged at something deep inside me. The road that snaked up to it, through Alberta, British Columbia and the Yukon, left the red and black lines and loops of populated Canada behind and wound through bare white space, where the only names were those of lakes or rivers, because there were no towns.

I looked at the others, who were busy talking, and wondered if I dare suggest to them that we try to get there.

Another Time, Another Place

The Alaska Highway, August–September 1958

It was lovely to be in Canada, with the Union Jack flying and English sweets and biscuits for sale in the shops. We gazed in wonder at Bird's Custard Powder, and couldn't resist a few bars of Aero chocolate and a slab of Mackintosh toffee, eating most of it in one go. Molly said that now she, Maureen and Celia were fit and well again, there was no excuse for us not to get back to our exercise routine. She led the way with some windmill swings and scissor kicks, then, after about half a dozen of each, complained of feeling sick.

'Let's start tomorrow instead,' she suggested. 'We'll finish these sweets first, so that we don't undo the good work afterwards.'

We had left Helena much later than planned, partly due to the promised visit from the Cashmore family, which had turned into lunch, then an invitation to use a friend's swimming pool. When we finally tore ourselves away it was six in the evening, and we managed only a few hours' driving before stopping to sleep in a field. The land was very flat, and the sunset that night seemed to fill the whole sky. After spending the next day and night in Glacier National Park, we crossed the US–Canadian border.

In the late afternoon we came to a tiny, deserted station somewhere outside Calgary, and stopped to cook our evening meal. We had intended to move on for the night, to find somewhere to pitch our tents, but when we discovered hot water in the restroom – the luxury of it! – we decided it was as good a place as any to stay, and took it in turns to strip down at the sink and to wash our drip-dry blouses. A sign announced that a train was due to pass through at 10.37 p.m. and to stop it two lanterns, one green and one white, had to be lit and placed on the platform. We all thought it was a hoot.

The air was hot and heavy, even now that it was dark, but it was pleasant in the waiting room, sitting on the cool stone floor under an orangey light, cushioned by our sleeping bags, which were strewn with writing paper, letters and books. Celia remarked that it didn't take us long to make ourselves at home wherever we were.

We sat in silence, the only sound being the fizzing light bulb and the rustle of paper. I looked up once, and saw an insect with a long, almost transparent body feel its way up the window pane outside, then topple down to the sill, saving itself by opening a pair of enormous wings. I thought it best not to point it out to the others, especially Pat and Maureen, whose reactions were unpredictable, to say the least, when large or unusual creepy-crawlies got too close.

'I vote we add Dr Cashmore to our list of ideal husbands,' said Molly suddenly, looking up from her letter.

'What brought that on?' asked Pat.

'I'm just telling everyone at home how kind he was.'

It was a list we had begun compiling earlier in the trip, though it was a pitifully short one. Bob Jones and Bill Byrd from the Grand Tetons had been the only men so far to have made the grade. However, Dr Cashmore was quickly admitted to this select group.

'Some of us didn't have the pleasure of being nursed by him,' said Pat, her eyes still on her book. 'I did wonder why you two fell ill so quickly after Molly.'

Celia exchanged a look of mock horror with Maureen, who pretended to aim her pillow at Pat, before adding, 'What about your friend Enrique? Don't you think we should include him?'

'He's not the marrying kind, unfortunately,' said Pat.

'You mean—' Maureen broke off.

'I don't mean anything. Just that he's a confirmed bachelor.'

'Most definitely,' I agreed. 'Yet he's so capable, he'd make a lovely husband. How many men do you know who cook and sew, as well as know how to treat a lady?'

'I didn't think men like that existed,' said Celia. 'What a waste.'

In Calgary, we found a campsite right in the centre of town. Pat wanted to contact a cousin who had married and gone out there during the war, but couldn't remember her address. She was sure her mother had sent it in a recent letter, and spent ages looking for it, before finding her listed in the telephone directory. I dropped her off there that evening.

Ethel and her husband were delighted to see her, but not as surprised as she had expected. Bud had seen a 'beaten-up old jalopy' in town that day 'that looked as if it had been round the world once or twice', and knowing that Pat was travelling in North America, had a wild idea that it might be her.

'In fact,' Pat told us later, 'he even saw you and me, Gwenda. Remember how we drove off sharpish when we saw those policemen in town this morning, thinking we were going to get a ticket? Well, Bud was one of them. He was about to ask us if we knew Patricia Beadle before we scarpered. Think of all the trouble that would have saved.'

The Canadian Rockies were even more magnificent than their American counterparts. We were all agreed on that. The craggy peaks sliced into a sky that looked as if it could never be a colour other than the deep blue it was at that moment. Snow was still lying in the hollows and on some of the gentler slopes, and thick green forests filled the valleys. We passed a field of ice that creaked and sighed like a door that needed oiling.

The night before Molly's birthday, we camped in Jasper National Park, by the shores of a pale green lake as glossy as an oil painting. Insects shimmered over the water as I got up to start breakfast. We hadn't mentioned the birthday for a few days, and guessed that Molly would think we had forgotten about it.

One by one the others woke, Molly the last of all. When she loped, rather sheepishly, out to join us, we burst into a chorus of 'Happy Birthday'. She was thrilled with her gifts – ski pyjamas and a Parker 21 pen – and the cake that we produced later when we stopped for coffee. It had been such a job trying to buy them when we were in Calgary as she kept popping up at everyone's shoulder whenever we thought we had got rid of her.

When had we agreed that we would drive to Alaska? I wasn't even sure. The idea seemed to have been suggested and accepted so readily. We had all exclaimed over the first sign for the Alaska–Canadian Highway (commonly known as the Alcan) that we had seen. I had used the opportunity to say – as casually as I could – something about 'popping up to Alaska' while we had the chance, and someone had laughed and said, 'I don't think it's a question of "popping". Have you seen how far away it is?' Then the three on the back seat had pored over Mrs Reid's book of maps for a while and announced that we might make it in a week, and that we had better get a move on as we had been told several times already that summer ended sooner up there.

So that was it. We were on our way.

The road was no longer a road, but a track. Clouds of dust were whipped up into the air when another vehicle passed by, encircling the car, so that I either had to stop driving until the dust had settled or slow down drastically, hoping that the track carried on in a straight line. Not that we were travelling quickly to begin with. It was impossible. Flatus staggered and lurched like a drunkard on the uneven surface, and at times bounced so high and landed with such a shudder that we feared the luggage would come off the roof, or that the car itself might fall to pieces. (We had been sending regular postcards to Bill and Tom at the garage, informing them of our progress but glossing over any car troubles.)

We closed the windows, but dust crept through the seals. It swirled around in little eddies at our feet, then settled in steadily growing piles on and amongst our bags and boxes. ('I can see the road moving beneath us!' exclaimed Molly. 'Since when did we have holes in the floor?')

It blew into our eyes and up our noses and sprinkled itself over our hair and skin, thinly at first, then totally transforming our appearances.

'I didn't know you were all so grey. How you've aged!' I said, after catching sight of my own face in the rear-view mirror and then the girls in the back.

We donned sunglasses and tied scarves around our heads, bringing the ends back up over our mouths and noses so that we looked like bandits. Every time we glanced at each other we collapsed into hysterical laughter.

It was a Sunday morning when we drove into Dawson Creek. It was a proper town, with houses and shops, and even a brand new Hudson Bay Company store right in the centre.

We dropped Celia off at church with a special mission, and went for a drive. She was waiting for us at the roadside an hour later and stuck a thumb in the air, beaming.

'He's only too happy to help.' She put on her fussiest Irish accent. '"Have you a little room somewhere, Father, to keep half a dozen suitcases and a pair of stag antlers? Yes, I did say antlers, Father. And two tents, and a great dirty old roof-rack, too. You'll hardly know they're there."'

We all laughed.

'Let's just say he was a bit taken aback, but pleased to be able to help.'

With the roof-rack fully loaded, the car stood eight feet tall. Taking only the essentials with us seemed like a good idea, and our best chance of reaching Alaska without mishap.

We had barely left Dawson Creek when we were hot and dusty again. We stopped to cool off by a river, and ended up spending the day there, swimming and dozing. We washed our clothes and draped them over the hot rocks to dry, then set off again in the late afternoon. Evenings were becoming cooler now, and the gentlest of breezes rustled at the windows. Travelling at this time also meant less traffic, and fewer dust storms. I went a little faster. Flatus without the roof-rack felt like a different car!

The pine forest rose steeply to the right, dropping away to the river on the other side of the road. It wasn't yet dark and a purple haze hung in the air. I was in my element.

At some point I became aware of a smell of burning, which I took to be a camp-fire in the trees. A few clouds of smoke appeared in the air from some invisible source, then vanished. Now the forest began to close in around us, and dusk turned swiftly into night. I drove on for another mile or two, when suddenly a tree crackled with flames beside me, as if somebody had flicked on a switch, and a low bush a few yards ahead sent a fountain of sparks into the road. Now I could hear the snapping and breathing of a large fire close by, though I could see no other signs of it. But I was scared. I did a panicky U-turn, and drove until the trees opened out and I was back in what remained of the daylight. I flagged down the next car and told them what I had seen.

The driver looked at me with amused impatience. 'That fire's been burning for weeks, ma'am. You just carry on straight through it.'

But I wasn't that brave – or foolhardy – and I retreated to a safer spot till daylight.

We could see the effects of the fire when we set off again at dawn. Charred trees, some still smouldering, covered the lower slopes and the valley floor. Pieces of ash fluttered in the air, and once, a small branch of pine, sparkling with embers, landed on the ground before us like a missile. We were surprised when we came across a gas station in a small clearing in the midst of this destruction.

Next to it was an attractive wooden cabin that looked like someone's home. A thin, efficient woman filled the tank, then cleaned
and polished our windows as if Flatus were a top-of-the-range
Cadillac rather than a seen-better-days Ford. Her husband sat on
a bench watching the procedure, smoking his pipe. I asked the
woman if she had been evacuated when the fire was at its peak,
and she shook her head vigorously and tutted.

'We would never leave our home. We pour sand and water on
the flames. My husband cuts the trees as they're burning to protect the house.'

She patted the car affectionately. 'You're done.'

The man began to cough violently, and spat on the ground.

'Can't say it doesn't get a little hairy at times,' she added.

The American west had seemed empty compared to the east, but
this was a whole new league of emptiness. Signs for towns merely
heralded a string of slightly sinister-looking caravans, usually sur-
rounded by car parts and bits of machinery, a scraggy dog and a
gas pump. Even in the quieter parts of the States there had at least
been smaller roads crossing the highway – reminders of lives being
lived in places just out of sight. Here there were none, just the one
road – if you could call it that – going on and on, as if it were
leading to a world where ordinary things had no place.

We were losing count of the days of the week, and of how
long we had been travelling the Alcan. Sometimes, remembering
a place we had passed or a person we had spoken to, we were
unable to agree on whether it had been that morning or the one
before, or if, indeed, it had been morning at all. Time, the be-all
and end-all in our lives as nurses, no longer mattered.

One night we drew up at a petrol station, but it was shut. We decided to wait there until it opened the next day – we weren't going to risk running out of fuel up here – and were just shaking out the bedding when we all stopped and stared. The Northern Lights were flickering and writhing above us. Nobody spoke for a few seconds after. We knew that we had witnessed something very special, yet it seemed hardly surprising that it had happened here.

When we woke the next morning the garage was still closed. We cooked breakfast, sipped our coffee slowly, looked hopefully up and down the road, then, after ascertaining that Whitehorse was not too far away, set off reluctantly. We made it to Whitehorse but, apart from filling the tank, drove straight on through.

The Yukon! The name itself seemed to belong to story books, and every view was as perfect as a picture postcard, every lake more blue and more beautiful than the one before, so that we kept stopping for photos, sure that we had discovered perfection each time. There was a new range of mountains in the distance now, shivering in a lilac haze.

It was the middle of August and even up here the days were still hot, but as we travelled northwards the leaves on the trees were beginning to glow, and occasionally a brilliant flash of red would catch our attention.

'You wouldn't want to be stuck up there for the winter, no sir!' said a man at a little outpost where we posted some letters one day.

'Goes once a week,' he had said, seeing our puzzled faces at the 'MAIL YOUR LETTERS HERE' sign. 'Long as the plane can land.'

After assuring us that he was expecting the plane that very afternoon, we had cautiously handed over our post.

'Sometimes the snow starts real early,' he continued. 'Can wake up snowed in, then it's all gone by lunchtime. But when it really starts, oh boy . . .'

My desire to reach Alaska was so strong, some days I barely slept. I told myself that I didn't need to sleep as much as other people did. Hadn't Pat and I proved it, with our back-to-back shifts in the last days of Cleveland, or when we were nursing our Yugoslavian friend Jadran? And again, with the few snatched hours that were sometimes all we managed at the Hotel Colorado? From time to time, Pat would take the wheel and I would doze off, my head drumming the window, almost soothing in its gentle rhythm. But then I would wake with a snap, and not feel comfortable until I was in the driver's seat again. Once, Pat said, when we had parked at the side of the road for a rest, I sat up with a start and grabbed the wheel frantically, a crazed look on my face. She had to wake me properly and assure me that we weren't moving.

In my head, I described what we were seeing to my parents. Sometimes I could even hear their voices, as if they were sitting beside me. My father saying, 'Aye, champion!' but barely looking up from filling his pipe. My mother more concerned with the way we were dressed – 'Those sleeveless blouses are really no better than underwear!' – and wondering when the next lavatory would be. Or Doug, winking as he told me about his latest girl-friend – the last one had been the captain's daughter, and I only hoped he knew what he was doing.

I must have drifted off to sleep, because now the car was glid-ing off the road and there was nothing I could do to stop it. It felt as if it were happening in slow motion. Flatus tipped on her side, everything shunted to the right, and settled with a dull thud. Then there was silence, apart from our quickened breathing and a whirring wheel that eventually stopped turning.

We were in a ditch about seven feet wide and four feet deep, tilted at a forty-five-degree angle.

'Is everyone OK?'

'I thought we were going to turn right over!'

'There's a precipice on the other side of the road, you know!'

'Does your door open? We can't get out of mine.'

'Yes, it seems to.'

'Let's get our cameras out!'

We were all taking photographs of the scene when two trucks drove up behind us, the first sign of life we'd seen for a few hours. Four men stepped out and asked if they could help. All were deeply tanned, with the thick, muscular bodies of those who do physical work for a living. The sort of men my mother warned me about. (Actually, my mother warned me about most types of men, though the appearance of these four – vest-style T-shirts showing strong arms, baseball caps, gum-chewing – would have given her palpitations just looking at them.)

The men took a few photos of their own, before attaching tow chains and pulling Flatus out of the ditch as if they did it every day. Their names were Jack, Clarence, Elton and Larry and they were farmers from Washington State, on their way to Alaska to go hunting before the winter months. There appeared to be no serious damage to the car, but they suggested that we follow them for the next few miles to be sure. When we all stopped at the next gas station to compare notes, the men invited us out to dinner later. We refused once – to be polite – but accepted quickly when they repeated the offer.

We had a shock when we discovered that we needed to put our watches back three hours. Now we knew why the gas station had been closed when we left it the previous morning.

There was no water for us to wash in at our meeting place.

'We can't possibly go in like this,' said Pat. 'I know we don't exactly need to dress up, but we're all stinking.'

We had to use some of our precious drinking water to make ourselves presentable.

'Why are we bothering?' asked Maureen, using the car window as a mirror to comb her hair, though it rarely looked messy. She sniffed her armpits. 'I don't suppose *they'll* be any better. Besides, they're probably all married men, old enough to be our fathers.'

'Isn't it nice just to have some male company, though,' I said, buttoning up a clean blouse. 'Anyone got any Pond's handy? My skin feels like sandpaper.'

'Well, they're obviously not fussy,' said Pat. 'I was looking—' She broke off giggling, and then began to laugh so much that she couldn't speak, setting the rest of us off as well.

Finally she wiped her eyes and composed herself. 'I was looking at us all back then and thinking what a sight we were. Like a bunch of wild women. They were obviously horrified, but too polite to say anything. Did you know, Molly, that you still had your scarf round your head, as if we were taking you back to your harem,' she began to laugh again, 'and when you realized that it was over your mouth, you just lifted the flap up and propped it on your nose to talk, as if it was perfectly normal. And you, Maureen, had these penetrating white eyes shining out of a filthy face – talk about *I Walked with a Zombie*!'

We were all weeping with laughter now, and though we pulled

ourselves together, we went inside to meet the men with such wide smiles, we could see that they looked a little worried.

The evening had been a great success – and the trout delicious – with no feelings of any sort of obligation, though Molly was sure that the men had combed their hair after removing their caps, and splashed their faces with cologne.

'I could smell it,' she insisted, 'and their hair had that slicked-down look that men's hair has when they don't wash it very much but still like to keep it neat.' She wrinkled her little nose.

We were still discussing the meal and our guests – who had said they'd be sure to see us in Tok, at customs – when there was a terrific clanking sound, as if Flatus had dropped anchor on to the gravel, and a sensation of being dragged forward unwillingly. We stopped with a jolt. We were in the middle of the road and it was dark. The four passengers got out and tried to push the car to the side, but it was locked in gear and wouldn't budge.

'If only the men weren't so far ahead . . .' someone said. It was what we were all thinking.

'If I can get a lift to Tok, I might catch them there,' I said, brightening. 'I can hear someone coming. Oh blow, it's coming the other way.'

To our surprise, the van now pulling up beside us was one that had overtaken us only a few minutes earlier. The driver, a sallow-skinned fellow with a long face and teeth that seemed too big for his mouth, said that he and his wife had heard the car making strange noises when they passed, and when they realized that we were no longer behind them, had come back to see what had happened.

We were all overwhelmed by their kindness.

'If you could run me along to Tok, that would be marvellous. Our friends will be waiting for us there.'

I was in their van before you could say 'Jack Robinson'.

As soon as we set off, I began to wish I hadn't been so hasty. I had seen doubt in the eyes of the others, but I was so impatient to catch up with the hunters – who would surely come back and tow us to the nearest garage – I hadn't given them the chance to speak. Now, I was like a prisoner in this van, and there was nothing I could do. It was no ordinary van, more of a home on wheels. A dirty, smelly home on wheels. What *was* that smell? It was strong and animal-like. Had they been hunting, too?

I had squeezed through a gap behind the driver's seat, gushing my thanks to the couple as I did so. The woman sat straight-backed, and merely looked at me briefly before turning away. Not quite the reaction I had expected following their solicitous enquiry. I sat behind them now on a bench of some sort, sur-rounded by bags and boxes and piles of items that I could not identify in the darkness. Something prodded my shoulder and I jumped and shot round, half expecting to find a creature or even another person there. But I had only brushed against a tool of some sort propped up behind me.

I tried to start up a conversation with my rescuers, but got only grunts in reply. A short while later, they drew a curtain between themselves and me. I wasn't sure whether to feel alarmed or relieved by this. But I wished, most fervently, that I hadn't come alone, and so willingly. Stupid girl, I told myself. Always in such a rush to do things, to please other people. The man's act of kind-ness ran through my head and began to take on more sinister connotations. In a landscape like this, how easy it must be to dispose of a body, to disappear and never be seen again! Hadn't we been warned about the sort of people attracted by Alaska – those running from something, those wanting a new start? Why had I been so trusting? How would my parents take the news when Pat rang and told them I was dead? (Poor Pat! I wouldn't like to be in her shoes.) Hadn't I always insisted to my mother that I would never go off alone with strangers? Yet here I was, a grown woman, almost twenty-five years old, doing exactly that. My anger at myself pricked and poked at my insides, and set my brain into such a flurry of activity that I felt like screaming.

We bounced awkwardly for a few miles, then came to a halt. The driver and his wife spoke in low voices, then the driver's door opened and he got out. This was it! My heart was beating inside my chest like a ticking bomb.

There was a squeaking sound, the van shuddered, and I realized that the bonnet was being raised. A mechanical problem! The woman shifted on her seat and got out of the vehicle too.

Should I squeeze out now and make a run for it? Of course not, it was a ludicrous idea, and it was freezing out there. It wasn't much warmer in here. There were some soft, rug-like items at my feet, but I decided I would rather risk hypothermia than wrap them round me. I wondered how long the hunters would wait for us in Tok. Had they actually agreed to meet us there? I wasn't sure now exactly what had been said.

Someone got back into the van – the woman, I thought – and turned on the engine, then got out again. A few minutes later they were both back inside and we set off once more. If they were going to murder me, surely they would have done it by now.

Later, we stopped again. I sat up with a start. To my surprise, I realized that I had been sleeping, albeit in an unsettled, sporadic way. I must stay alert, I said to myself. I heard the slamming of the van door, footsteps on gravel, then nothing. There was a small window beside me, but it was so dirty and spotted I could see nothing through it. The footsteps returned, someone wrestled with the curtain and a face bobbed before me.

'Customs is all closed up for the night,' said the man. 'Can't do nothing but wait. Plenty of blankets back there.'

I could have cried with relief and frustration. But instead I replied, 'Thank you,' in a dry, cracked voice. There was no alternative but to stay in the van till morning.

When I heard the sound of snoring from the front, I relaxed slightly, slipped off my sandals and curled my feet up beneath me to warm them. I even leaned my head against the smeary window. I thought that I was too cold and too anxious to sleep, but such strange scenarios played out in my head over the next few hours that I knew, in the morning, I had been dreaming.

Somebody was talking. I opened my eyes. A blanket was wrapped around me though I had no recollection of putting it there. The curtain had been drawn back and a stream of dusty light forced me to raise a hand to my brow. A voice said, 'We can go now. Might find your friends.'

Tok Junction, Alaska, didn't appear to be much of a place, but I had never felt so happy to be somewhere! For a few seconds, I felt something close to ecstasy – to be alive, to be out of the smelly van, to see the sun shining in a cold but flawless sky. A line of buildings straddled the highway: a couple of small hotels, a couple of stores, a chapel, another church-type building, a garage, a café, plus an assortment of houses. Further back from the road, other buildings could be glimpsed in the trees. It was bigger than it first appeared.

The café was a neat log cabin, its windows hung with cheerful curtains. Someone had planted some flowers and dwarf conifers in the strip of soil that ran around it. Only one car was parked outside, and there was no sign of the hunters' trucks. I guessed that they had passed through the previous night or, more annoyingly, been stranded at customs too, just ahead of us. Oh why hadn't I thought of getting out to look?

Well, it was too late now. I headed for the garage next door, hoping that the problem wasn't going to eat too deeply into kitty funds.

The garage was empty, and after waiting there for a while I went into the café. Two men in overalls, who I guessed were the mechanics, were eating breakfast. A man in an army uniform sat on his own a few tables away, talking to them across the room in a familiar manner. All three of them looked up as I entered. There was a woman at the counter. She had a kind, round face and frizzy curls tucked back over her ears in a girlish manner, though she was probably my mother's age. She put down the glass she was drying as I approached her.

She nodded sympathetically and pushed a cup of coffee towards me. The men would take me back to the car when they had finished eating. If I could just wait for half an hour, they'd be right with me. I sat down with my coffee. It smelt wonderful but my mouth felt strange, as if I had been eating cardboard, and I could barely swallow. I couldn't stop thinking now about the others. I knew they would be worried about me, but I was worried about them, too, stuck out in the middle of the road all night . . . I almost wept with gratitude when the army man stood up suddenly, introduced himself as Sergeant Miller, and offered to take me in his own car.

'We'll follow on with the wrecker,' said one of the mechanics, looking in no hurry to finish his food.

There were two other cars parked at the scene. Two men stood talking beside the raised bonnet, and the pair of legs of a third man stuck out from the back of the car. Pat, Maureen, Molly and Celia were sitting on a rug at the side of the road, as if they had nothing to do with the problem. Pat was even typing a letter! They all leapt up and came rushing over when they saw me, hugging me and casting curious, embarrassed glances towards Sergeant Miller at the same time.

'One of us should have gone with you. But you were off before we could stop you,' said Celia, hanging on to my arm as if I might try to leave again.

'Anything could have happened to you!' cried Molly.

'I'll tell you about it later. Have you been awake all night?'

They looked at me sheepishly. 'We slept in the car, right where she is. Don't ask us how. But now every passing man wants to have a go at fixing it.' Maureen jerked her head in the direction of the would-be mechanics. 'We can't keep them away. Verdict seems to be that it's the differential. And that we're well and truly scuppered.'

I could hardly bear to watch Flatus, her rear in the air, being towed backwards into Tok Junction as we followed in the car with Sergeant Miller. It was a sad moment, and one beneath the dignity of our trusty old friend. While the mechanics looked her over, we settled into the café, covering two tables with our writing paraphernalia. The coffee slipped down nicely this time.

We had just begun our second cup when people started arriving – men mostly, and many in army uniform. Some glanced at us shyly, and spoke to each other in loud voices, as if to mask their true intentions; others introduced themselves straight away. It was fairly obvious that they were all there to look us over.

'I don't think we've ever had five single ladies in Tok before,' said one of the soldiers.

'There is one, and we love her to death, but she's only thirteen,' said another, adding playfully, 'We're saving her for Ernie here. He's our baby, ain't you, Ern?'

Ernie, who was chatting to Maureen, pretended not to hear.

The morning customers gave way to the lunchtime crowd, including the Presbyterian minister, Mr Bartholomew, and his wife, who extended an invitation to the minister's ordination in a few days' time. The police commissioner, a small wiry woman who rolled her shoulders like a man when she walked, settled herself at a table in the corner and regarded us with bewildered amusement. By now, Mrs Post, who we had learned was the owner of the café and garage along with her husband, was barely able to cope as she attempted to wait on table, cook and wash up for what had been a never-ending stream of customers.

Seeing her struggle, Pat and I jumped up and started washing dishes, while the other three helped to clear the tables. She was overcome with gratitude, even trying to slip us the tips that had been left, which of course we refused.

An elderly man, his wife and two younger men who looked like brothers came in and sat silently at a table after the lunchtime rush was over.

Mrs Post nodded at them as she fried burgers on the grill. 'When'd you hear?'

'Oh, a coupla hours ago,' replied the old man. 'We came straight over.'

Mrs Post sidled up to me at the sink. 'They've driven over a hundred miles just to see you. Better mind out, they've been trying to marry those boys off for years.'

I looked over and saw that the 'boys' were at least forty years old. I caught one of them looking at me, and his eyes darted back to the tablecloth.

Some time that afternoon, Mr Post came into the café to find us.

'I'll be needing a third member,' he announced.

I immediately volunteered my services, but he laughed and said the third member was a part for the car. Normally, his spare parts were flown in from Oregon, but as he had promised to do the job as cheaply as he could, he had spent much of the morning ring- ing all the people he knew with old Fords within a hundred-mile radius. He had finally located the part he needed, and had just sent his mechanic on a hundred-and-eighty-mile round trip to collect it.

'Should have you on the road in a couple of days,' he said.

Mrs Post saw our disappointed faces. 'Don't you worry. I've got a cabin you can use out the back.'

The cabin had beds with soapy-smelling sheets, a bath and a washing machine. We decided that it might not be so bad to be stranded in Tok after all.

We spent the next morning helping in the café – which was still attracting more visitors than usual – and washing our clothes. Mrs West, an army wife who had brought her four younger children to meet us, offered the use of her tumble-dryer. We made several trips with wet washing between the cabin and her home at the camp, stopping to talk to people on the way.

Soldiers Dick and Mark took us water-skiing on the lake that afternoon. Only Molly managed to stay upright all the way round. I went flat on my face every time in the freezing water.

'I don't think Alaska is really the best place to learn to water-ski,' I said to Dick, my teeth chattering as I stood at the lake shore.

'You'll warm up later,' he said, winking. 'We're having a party for you at Rita's.'

'Oh ... actually we've been invited to dinner at the Bartholomews',' I said, surprised at how disappointed I felt.

Dick laughed. 'Don't worry. They'll be tucked up in bed by the time you get to Rita's.'

'Who's Rita anyway?'

'Rita's Trails Inn,' said Dick, fixing his eyes on me in a way that made my stomach flip.

'I think I might be tucked up, too,' said Pat. 'I'm absolutely jiggered.'

Dick wagged his finger at her. 'You can't deprive men of female company for just one night.'

We had been invited to Mrs West's for lunch the following day, but the car was ready earlier than expected, so we decided to carry on to Anchorage and Fairbanks and visit her on our return. We had to come back this way, anyway. The only road in Alaska formed a sort of triangle, with Tok, Anchorage and Fairbanks sitting on the three corners. We would follow the road round, and return to Tok in a couple of days.

We had spent a pleasant evening with the minister and his wife, eating a stew of rich, dark meat that none of us had been able to identify and nobody dared enquire about. At Rita's, all of the single army men were waiting for us — and some of the married ones too. Sergeant Miller said he was there to keep an eye on everyone and to check that the boys behaved themselves.

It all began in a highly organized manner, with each soldier waiting his turn to dance with a member of the opposite sex. There was a little tension at one point, when one of them — a lad of no more than twenty — was deemed to be taking more than his fair share of female partners. But as it got later, turns were forgotten and we had all paired off, while the less favoured soldiers began to drift homewards.

We had promised to meet the boys again the following evening, but had left word at the café that we had decided instead to move on while we could. There would be time for goodbyes later.

We had been driving for most of the day and seen very little traffic, when Molly gave a gasp.

'Do you see what I see?'

Ahead of us, parked at the edge of the forest, were two familiar-looking trucks, tarpaulin stretched over their frames. There was no sign of the hunters, but as night wasn't far off we felt sure that they would be returning soon to eat and sleep. I think we all felt excited at the thought of meeting them again, but tried to mask it by making ourselves busy, building a fire and preparing food. The sound of a bugle trembled in the night air. By the time the soup was bubbling, the men were appearing through the trees, smiling broadly.

We pooled our resources — soup, stew, fruit pie and tea — and sat around the fire, blankets over our shoulders. The air smelt of pine trees and a sharp, bitter smell that drifted from the lake on the other side of the road.

'Miss Molly, you heard the song about you?' asked Clarence, after we had finished eating.

'Oh, please, not that! Everyone plays it to me wherever we go.'

The men laughed and began to sing their own songs, taking it in turn to begin one, as if it were a well-rehearsed routine.

'This here's a cowboy song,' said Jack, when it was his turn. 'You probably heard it by now, "Git Along, Little Dogie".'

They all sang beautifully, though we hadn't a clue what it was about. We clapped our hands when they had finished, then Maureen piped up, 'But what is a dogie, if you don't mind me asking?'

'A dogie,' said Jack, pulling a sad face, 'is a little calf whose mammy has died and whose daddy has run off with another cow.'

I caught Maureen's eye and we both got the giggles.

'What's so funny?' asked Jack, looking at us and trying not to laugh himself.

'I'm sorry, but I've never heard anything so ridiculous,' I said, wiping my eyes.

The men looked at each other, shrugged, and pretended to be offended.

'Well, let's hear some of your songs from Great Britain,' said Clarence.

'"How Much is That Dogie in the Window?"' sang Celia, trying to keep a straight face.

When we had all pulled ourselves together, the men looking on indulgently, Pat and I had the bright idea of trying to teach the others some of our Geordie songs. We failed miserably with 'The Blaydon Races' – it was more complicated than we had thought, and nobody else understood a word. However, 'The Keel Row', with its simple chorus, was more successful, and soon nine voices thundered out into the night.

> *O weel may the keel row*
> *The keel row the keel row*
> *Weel may the keel row*
> *That my laddie's in.*

When we had finished, Elton scratched his head and said, 'Excuse me, and you thought our "Little Dogie" was funny?'

It was a cold and wet Sunday morning in Anchorage, and there was nothing to do except go to our respective churches, leaving Maureen to look after the car. After that, we drove down to the Cook Inlet, but low grey clouds hid the mountains and dampened our mood. We turned round and set off for Fairbanks.

The weather brightened. A small plane we had heard buzzing overhead came in to land beside us at a gas station. The huge head of a mountain sheep, its curling horns like an elaborate headdress, stared at us from the window. Molly went closer to take a look, then jumped back.

'Ooh, he's already butchered.'

We were supposed to have money to show at Canadian customs – seven hundred and fifty dollars for the carload – so we were quite prepared to be turned back. The army boys had threatened to tip off the officials, to ensure our return to Tok, but in the end we sailed straight through, relieved but perhaps partly missing the drama a return would have guaranteed.

We had reached Fairbanks, and driven from there as far north as the road would take us. We had also met our hunter friends once more. When we said goodbye to them that evening, after a trip to the cinema together, we knew that it must surely be for the last time, and the men had announced, solemnly, that it had been a pleasure to make our acquaintance and that they would never forget this trip as long as they lived. Back in Tok the next day, we had spent the evening visiting old friends, then been whisked off to Rita's, dancing until 5 a.m., when the owner finally turned off the jukebox and Mark brought the jeep round to drive six of us to a place he knew for breakfast. Celia and Pat had gone to bed by this point, but Molly, Maureen and I were quite keen on our partners, and happy to make the night last as long as possible. Dick was tall and blond, and I couldn't help wishing that I had met him at some other time, in some other place. He and most of the boys were stuck in Tok for another year, and there was little chance of our returning to Alaska. It had been a sad goodbye.

It was raining as we drove through the Yukon, and the track had turned to mud, though it was easier to drive in than the dust of the outward journey. We sat quietly, smiles flickering across our faces as we relived different memories.

Almost the whole of Tok had come out to wave goodbye to us – Mr and Mrs Post, the Bartholomews, Mrs West and her children, and others whose faces we knew but could not put a name to.

Mrs Post had given us a box of provisions, and Mrs West, too, had arrived with a large package she could barely carry. 'To be opened when you stop,' she said. 'It's just come out of the deep-freeze.' Inside it we found moose meat, home-made chocolate-chip cookies and raisin rolls.

The journey was uneventful until, after a stop to eat, we noticed that we were driving in a blanket of fumes, and making a noise more befitting a racing car than Flatus. A quick check revealed that the silencer had snagged on the rough ground and was hanging off. I fixed it with a length of wire lying at the roadside, but every few hours it worked its way loose again. When we smelt burning later that day I went straight to the silencer, but the problem was more serious – a hole in the radiator. We now had to make frequent stops to top up the water, and during one of those stops we discovered we were also leaking oil.

We found a mechanic who could mend the silencer, but radiators weren't his thing. They didn't seem to be anybody's thing. It wasn't until the next day, in the muddy streets of Whitehorse, that we found someone willing to fix it. When I asked the man what we could do in the town while we were waiting, he fixed his watery blue eyes on me and sighed. 'I've lived here twenty years now, and I ain't found nothing yet.'

The nights were cold and frosty. Now, when we awoke, the snow-line on the mountains had crept lower and the air took longer to warm.

Flatus was still leaking oil. At the next garage, the man thought that the problem was a clogged-up oil-cap and set to work, mending a flat tyre at the same time. A few miles further down the road we found a huge hole in another tyre, and had to change the wheel. And we were still leaking oil. We decided to forget about car troubles for a while, and cooked a meal out of all the goodies we had been given in Tok.

We had stopped at some hot springs on the journey up, and seeing the sign for them again was even more welcome. A raggedy old man followed us to the water as we set off with bathing suits, soap and towels, but he only wanted us to listen to the uranium in the ground with his Geiger counter. He told us he was a prospector, mining for fluorite, and gave us all a piece. We shared our soup with him, and he was disproportionately grateful.

'Next year they're mining this place,' he said sadly. 'Then where am I gonna go?'

The Summit. Mile 392. A garage, a café and a motel, at the highest point of the Alaska Highway. The garage had closed for the night, but it looked more promising than most of the others we had passed. We scrabbled together enough money to buy a burger each from a waitress whose mouth seemed to have forgotten how to smile, then spent the night folded into our seats inside the car. We woke up, stiff, cold and furry-mouthed, and were glad when the café opened and we could rush inside to its warmth.

We made our coffee last as long as possible, then went outside to make syrup sandwiches. We had agreed that until we were working again, we would cook our own meals and save the little money we had left.

The mechanic was a Scotsman of few words. He shuffled into the café later that morning, where we were sharing three bottles of Coke under the disapproving eye of the waitress. We needed a new block, he announced, and looked at us as if we were going to produce one from under the table.

It was a big blow. When he spoke again, it was to remind us that it was Sunday and the next day was Labor Day, and there was no chance of any parts arriving until midweek at the earliest. Each word was more crushing than the one before.

When he had gone, we looked at each other in despair. Where were we going to find the money?

'It'll cost more than the car did,' wailed Pat.

'A few hundred dollars, I should think,' I said.

Maureen spoke up. 'I've always got my savings. I can withdraw what we need, then you can all pay me back when we're earning again.'

'Oh, Maureen, would you mind awfully?'

'Oh, I'm so glad that someone was sensible in Cleveland, and didn't go off gallivanting all the time like Pat and I did.'

That evening we were eating scrambled eggs in the car park when Scotty appeared and told us gruffly that we could sleep in the garage if we wanted to.

'Did he almost smile then?' asked Molly.

Celia and I went for a walk the next morning, looking for something to lift our mood, though neither of us could have said what we were looking for. The road south stretched ahead, mile upon mile upon mile. We had bumped our way over every inch of it already. We knew that we were not going to find another Tok Junction round the next corner, however hard we looked.

A crow on a fence post thrust out his neck and cawed in a most menacing way as we passed him.

'Same to you,' said Celia. 'Oh, what an unfriendly place this is! I wish we were still in Tok.'

We got back feeling no better, but the others looked brighter.

'Guess what,' said Maureen, beaming, 'one of the owners has said we can move into a spare cabin and work for our keep. And she'll pay us one salary. Two of her staff are away. She says she doesn't really need five extra pairs of hands, but it'll make things easier for everyone for a few days.'

The days slipped into a routine as comfortable, as ordered, as being back on the wards. The garage-cum-motel was run by Della and her husband, Frank. Frank was the chef and Della the general manager. Then there was Scotty, the dour mechanic, and Doris, the scowling waitress. Actually, Doris was starting to thaw – Maureen said that she called her 'honey', and smiled when she showed her how to make up the powdered milk they sold as 'fresh cows' milk'. And Scotty, too, was becoming more communicative, ever since we offered to stick his personal laundry in the machine with the hotel stuff. We didn't think he looked after himself very well, and besides, it was hardly any extra work for us.

The motel had ten bedrooms, and as most people passed through quickly, the sheets needed changing every day. It was the job of two of us to sweep and dust the rooms each morning, strip the beds, and dust and wax the lobby floor. Two others took care of the laundry, hanging the sheets and towels out to dry in the breeze that was always blowing, before putting them through the electric press. There must be a knack to working this press, we thought, and we might almost have cracked it by the time it came to leave. The fifth girl helped Frank in the kitchen and café – serving, taking orders, washing up.

When we weren't working, we might be listening to music on the record-player Della had lent us, and anyone passing our cabin – two bedrooms and a living room, usually draped with washing – might have heard the sounds of Glenn Miller or the New World Symphony as well as the clack-clack of the typewriter.

Pat and I had adopted another job, too – working in the gas station, something I had long had a hankering to try. When a car pulled up, we put down whatever we were reading – I was already halfway through *War and Peace* – jumped off our stools and rushed out to serve petrol, check oil and water and clean windows.

'What a climate you have!' a woman said to me one day, from the comfort of her vehicle, just as the sky began to pelt me with hailstones the size of marbles. 'How do you put up with it?'

'Oh, the sun will be shining again in a few minutes,' I replied cheerfully, hosing down her tyres.

'Hey, don't you folks have neat accents!'

'Actually, we're English.'

'How neat – I heard there are lots of Indians round here.'

Passing hunters looked at our brown faces and asked about the game situation. 'Mountain goat, moose and caribou,' we recited, as if we had lived here all our lives.

One day a man asked Pat, 'Are there five of you? I've just come down from Tok, and everyone's talking about you. Say, you work-ing at every gas station on the highway?'

Everyone passing through had their own story. Families from the southern states, hit by the recession, were going to start a new life in Alaska, attracted by the higher salaries. Airmen were returning to their bases after time on leave. There were tourists, too, but fewer now that summer was ending.

One day an Irish nurse stopped on her way to Fairbanks.

'They're going to pay me twenty-seven dollars fifty a day,' she told us breathlessly, as we gathered round her in the café. 'I'll be able to bring my mammy and daddy out next year.'

We pulled horrified faces at each other over her head.

Frank said that 50 per cent of the Alaskan population had criminal records, and to be cautious with folk. And though it was true that there were some strange characters, people who didn't want to answer questions, who made little eye contact, even they were courteous.

At the end of the week, Della and Frank drove Maureen and Celia to Fort Nelson, ninety-two miles away, to see if the money had arrived in Maureen's account. When they had gone, Doris – now the sweetest person who had ever lived – baked a raisin pie and chocolate cake for us all, and used her key to open up the jukebox.

'Who'd ya like? Elvis? Phil and Don? Ah, Ricky Nelson, I just love that boy.' She gave a little wiggle.

Later that night I was in the cabin, reading my *Teach Yourself Spanish* book, when I heard a car draw up and doors slamming. A minute later, Maureen and Celia appeared. It was after nine o'clock.

'You've been gone all day! How did you get on?'

Maureen shrugged. 'We posted the mail, but no money. The Cleveland bank hadn't sent the message in code. We'll have to go back.'

'Oh no, poor you. And poor Frank and Della.'

'Oh, they didn't mind. They go every week anyway. It's just like popping down the road to them.' Maureen threw her jacket over a chair and went to boil the kettle. 'Cup of tea, love? Oh, how are you getting on with that?'

I smiled. 'How about "The fire hose is too short to reach the scene of the fire"? Do you think it will come in useful?'

Maureen shook her head. 'Well, you never know with us.'

There was only one dark spot in our new existence – pigs. Della kept a herd of them that ran loose in the grounds of the motel. Whenever we left the cabin they would appear from the bushes – running surprisingly quickly – and snap at our ankles. Even Celia, who had grown up on a farm, seemed nervous of them, though she tried not to show it.

'Just pretend they aren't there,' she said, raising her eyebrows in exasperation at the rest of us the second time it happened. 'Swing your arms like this to alarm them.'

But when the pigs showed no sign of being alarmed, and simply grunted with annoyance, the four of us ran ahead screaming, followed closely by Celia.

We tried different ways to leave – quietly, checking first that the pigs were nowhere in sight; with lots of noise and clapping of hands; singing nonchalantly. Nothing worked. And yet we watched Doris, Frank and Della put out the garbage and wander between the various buildings without being bothered.

Every week a film came to the maintenance camp nearby, and as there was so little else to do, every man, woman and child living in the vicinity – about a fifty-mile radius – would go to see it. All day Friday, the topic of conversation was whether the film had arrived or not. We had an idea it might be *Old Yeller*, which had been following us round the States like a faithful mutt ever since we watched it from outside a drive-in in Denver, too poor to pay for the sound. Not particularly wanting to cry through it again, we went for a walk.

It was a beautiful evening, the sky pale blue, apart from a strip of gold cloud that quivered in the west. We were chatting idly when a car came speeding up behind us and pulled up a few yards ahead. A man we hadn't seen before lowered the window and cried out, 'They won't start the film without you. And all the nurses are to get in free!'

It seemed rude not to show some enthusiasm.

I found Doris stoically holding the fort in the café and gas station, and insisted that she go instead of me, almost pushing her out of the door when she began to waver.

'Well, if you're sure. Gee, I don't often get the chance . . .'

When she had gone I wiped the counter – though it was already clean – then sat down on her three-legged stool, thoroughly enjoying the feeling of being in charge.

It wasn't a busy night. I served petrol to a man from Shrewsbury, who drove off chuckling when he heard of our plight. Two Mounties came in for coffee and a slice of pie. And I finished *War and Peace*.

'*The Story of Mankind*,' announced Molly, as they wandered into the café later.

'Pardon? Oh, the film. Who was in it?'

'Who *wasn't* in it? Vincent Price, Hedy Lamarr, Peter Lorre, Ronald Colman and the Marx Brothers, but not playing together.'

'Quite an oddity, but entertaining,' said Pat.

'What a blissful domestic scene!' said Maureen, finding me cutting Scotty's hair in the garage on our last night, as Celia sat darning his pants. ('I could hardly give them back without putting a stitch in here and there,' she said later.)

After ten days Scotty had admitted, reluctantly, that Flatus was ready, and I had driven up and down the road a few times, revelling in the clean sound of the engine.

'We're doing it again,' said Pat, as we began tidying up our rooms. 'Leaving somewhere just when we've settled in.'

Celia sighed. 'I think Doris is going to miss us. I think they all are.'

'Was it worth the long drive, girls? We might have had some money left if we hadn't come all this way.' And if I hadn't fallen asleep at the wheel, I might have added.

'Oh yes!' more than one voice chorused.

'I wouldn't have missed it for anything,' said Celia.

'I wonder if Alaska will change when it becomes a proper state next year.'

'I don't think it could ever change. Everywhere up here. It's just . . .' Maureen tailed off.

It was the Alaska Highway. That said it all.

Twenty-four hours later, a lorry flashed its lights at us several times on the road south. We pulled in nervously to see what was the matter.

'I've come from Tok,' said the driver. 'Mrs Post heard you were stuck somewhere and wonders if there's anything she can do.'

We were over a thousand miles from Tok. Sometimes it felt as if an invisible thread attached us to all the places we had ever been to.

8

The American Dream

Oregon to California, September–November 1958

'I wonder,' Pat said, 'if these are ripe limes, or unripe lemons.'

She, Celia and I were walking home from work in Woodland, California, down a lane fringed with fruit trees. Oranges and grapefruits, too, dangled tantalizingly close.

To get up in the morning and pick oranges from a tree in one's own garden . . . That was my idea of heaven. I ran my hand along a branch that drooped heavily over a fence.

'Hey, you there!'

A man was striding down his garden path towards us, and I felt, for a second or two, like a child caught in the act of misbehaving. I hadn't been intending to steal any of the oranges I was touching, though if one had come away in my hand, well, that might have been different.

I looked at Pat and Celia, wondering whether to suggest that we all make a run for it, but they were both looking at the man, smiling. Now I noticed that he didn't appear to be angry, and that he was struggling slightly with the awkward bulk of two large paper bags, one under each arm.

'I seen you this morning,' he said as he got closer, slightly out of breath, 'and yesterday, too. And I said to my wife, "That must be those English ladies living along the road who we read about in the paper. They sure seem to like our fruit trees." And she says, "Well give them a bag, they'd be doing us a favour. There's only so much juice you can drink after all." So here you are – oranges and grapefruits, and a few lemons. Hope you can use them.'

His wife then appeared behind him, and passed across a third, empty bag. 'Go on, take some more,' she urged. 'Make some of that English marmalade of yours.'

We walked back to Bob and Mary Ann's happily.

'Apples in Vancouver, filberts in Oregon, oranges in California,' I said, thrusting my face into the bag I was carrying. 'Oh, why don't oranges smell like this at home?'

'Don't talk to me about filberts,' said Pat. 'I'll never look at a nut again without thinking of sheer torture.'

We had picked up our belongings from the priest in Dawson Creek, then driven to Vancouver, where we camped in the garden of a family friend, Henry Maundrell, arousing curiosity – and disapproval – amongst the neighbours, as Henry's wife and son were away at the time. (Capable Henry had soon made position number four in our ideal husbands list.) Signs for filbert-pickers had accompanied us on our journey south, through Washington and Oregon, on our way to Eugene, to stay with Bill and Jo Ann Byrd, the climbing instructor and his wife we had met in the Tetons. They lived in a rented house on the banks of the McKenzie River, where it widened into a small lake. The shores were thickly wooded and the sun fluttered through the trees, making silver patterns on the water. We spent many hours on the

sundeck at the back of the house that overlooked this glorious
view, talking to our hosts, writing letters and helping to mind the
children. Teddy, aged three, had a trike he liked to cycle up and
down, while Terri, the baby, sat happily in her playpen.

As the chance of nursing jobs had looked slim at first, filbert-
picking, which had started as something of a joke – none of us
had any idea what a filbert was – had begun to look like our only
option, and we set off, hoping to make our fortune.

Celia was minding the children that day, so it was just four of
us who rose before dawn to get to the farm for seven o'clock. We
were given a basket and a sack each, and told which row to start
on. The filberts – which turned out to be hazelnuts – had already
dropped from the trees. The ground might be churned up and
muddy but scooping up the nuts was going to be easy, we
thought, and as some of the other pickers were elderly women,
we were quite complacent about the task ahead.

After twenty minutes in a crouching position, we had changed
our minds about this dream job. And about making our fortunes.
No wonder Jo Ann had laughed at us, and told us we had better
not bank on getting out of bed the next day. Our backs were
breaking, our legs had gone numb. We gave in and sank to our
knees in the cold, wet earth. A little while later, looking at what
we had gathered so far, we realized that if we were to make any
money at all we would need to use both hands.

We spent eight hours in the mud, pushing our baskets along in
front of us, picking as fast as we could. When we had filled a basket,
we emptied it into our sack. It was a hot day, and after a ten-minute
break for lunch we were still so thirsty that we sent Maureen off
to find a shop. She was gone for over an hour, and we practically
fell upon her when she reappeared with cans of warm Coca-Cola.

The afternoon wore on. The sun grew hotter. Finally, time was
up, and the sacks were weighed.

'Boy, you're quick workers,' said the farmer. 'Fancy coming back tomorrow?'

We had picked five hundred and thirteen pounds between us, earning the princely sum of fifteen dollars and thirty-six cents. We were so hungry, we spent it all on a meal on the way home.

Though we teased her about it, Molly wasn't the only one with romantic notions of California. Ever since we set out, I think all five of us had yearned to be here. Wasn't this the paradise state, where the sun shone, palm trees grew at the roadside, and film stars – as familiar to us as old friends – all lived?

Molly was impatient to get to California for other reasons, too; her aunt and uncle in Los Angeles kept writing and asking why they were having to wait so long to see her.

But first we had been invited to Woodland, not far from Sacramento, to stay with Bob and Mary Ann Jones, the fire rangers we had met in the Grand Tetons. We arrived to find that they had cleared out their garage for us.

'So that you can come and go as you please, and treat this as your home,' said Mary Ann, holding a wriggling Laura, who now wanted to crawl everywhere. 'You've got your own bathroom, too. No, honey, I'm not putting you down here.'

I spotted something black and shiny scuttle into a dark corner, and flashed a look at Pat and Maureen. They were both smiling, so clearly hadn't noticed it.

It was a spacious garage, with rafters where we could hang sleeping bags and wet towels, two large sinks and even a washing machine. The lawn, where the Joneses suggested we might prefer to sleep, was as springy as a feather bed, and Molly declared it perfect for exercising on, doing a cartwheel to demonstrate the fact.

'I shall eat what I'm offered,' she announced when Mary Ann was out of earshot, 'though I'm definitely on a diet the rest of the time. Don't let me forget.'

Mary Ann had already made some enquiries for us at the hospital. 'You're to go along and meet the director in a couple of days, and she'll see if she can help,' she explained at dinner that first night. 'Rice, everyone? This is one of my Mexican dishes. I hope it's not too hot for you.' She served each of us a large plateful. 'She sounded very interested in you, so I'm quite hopeful.'

'Perhaps she'll be another Mrs Reid,' said Celia.

'Could there be another?' wondered Maureen, gazing in disbelief at her helping. 'Oh, Mary Ann, this looks delicious!'

'And when you've a free day, I'll take you all to school,' said Bob, passing round the bowl of salad.

'To school?' Maureen frowned.

'To see the way it works here. And you could give a talk to my students. It's not every day we get British visitors. I just need to have a word with my principal.'

We all pulled worried faces at each other across the table.

'I don't think I'm ready to go back to school,' said Maureen. 'The nuns at my school put me off school – and religion – for evermore.' She smiled apologetically.

Bob and Mary Ann both looked interested.

'Really?' said Bob. He wagged a fork at us. 'Hey, you know that Mary Ann is the best cook in California? You won't eat like this anywhere else. Say, that sounds kind of sad, Maureen. Nuns, you say? But I think you'd be pleasantly surprised to see my high school. Not saying that some of the teachers don't have their own bad habits, though . . .'

'Bob, be serious,' scolded Mary Ann. But even Maureen was laughing.

With no prospect of work for a couple of days, we set off to visit Sacramento, the state capital, and got back to find Mary Ann peering anxiously down the road. The hospital wanted one of us on a private case and had agreed to hold it until six o'clock. I hurried in, and later that night, opening the door to my patient's bathroom, which adjoined the bathroom of the neighbouring room, came face-to-face with Celia. She had been called in straight after me, and the others were to start the next day. So we were all working as private nurses – at eighteen dollars a shift, which was beyond any of our expectations.

Pat was looking after an elderly lady who had suffered a minor stroke. She told me about her as we set off to play tennis one night at the local courts, with rackets borrowed from our hosts. We had left Molly behind, making a special dessert, and the other two were working.

'She looks just like Queen Mary, very regal, with that upswept hair, and she's extremely dignified. I can't believe she's eighty-two. I just sit and listen to her and fetch her whatever she needs, but she rarely asks for anything. Her family came out west in a wagon train before she was born, when her mother was expecting her oldest brother. Then her father had to go away for winter supplies, leaving her alone with a baby. Luckily the local Indians were friendly and they came to no harm. The family did well in the end, and the sons all followed different careers. It's more exciting than a book, listening to some of her stories.'

'It sounds like the story of America, doesn't it. It would make a good film. My patient is a jerky-maker. Apparently the only reason I've got him is because the local nurses didn't think they'd be paid. Fingers crossed. His family seem very decent.'

'What did you say he was?'

'A jerky-maker. It's that dehydrated meat they sell all over the place. At the end of the process you end up with something brown and shrivelled and full of protein.'

Pat looked at me and pulled a face.

'I tasted it, it's delicious. You start chewing on this stuff that looks like a piece of old leather, and then this amazing flavour starts to come out. They took it with them in frontier days. Your old lady probably grew up on it.'

We reached the tennis courts, and put a dime in the machine for the floodlights. It was a warm evening, with the slightest hint of a breeze. The night before, in the light of the street lamps, we had played croquet on Bob and Mary Ann's lawn until well after 10 p.m. And Bob was trying to teach us to play chess.

I reflected once more that if I were to settle in America, I would most certainly choose California.

When we got back, Molly was getting ready for bed. She proudly showed us her pudding – jelly with melted marshmallows – which we were to have the next day. Celia and Maureen got home and admired it as well. Then, when Celia and I were in the kitchen making coffee for everyone, we decided to play a trick on Molly, and pushed some more marshmallows into the not-quite-set jelly. The next day we would ask her how the marshmallows had become whole again.

We hadn't realized it was 31 October when Mary Ann burst into the garage one evening. 'Oh, I'm glad you're all here. We're having a party for you. You've got twenty minutes to dress up, the weirder the better. I'm sure you've got something amongst all your attire. I'm just getting Laura ready for bed. Come over when you're ready.'

She turned to go, then came back. 'In case you're wondering, Bob's taken the car to a neighbour's garage. You never know what they might have in store for you when you're a teacher. Last year one of his colleagues had his car pelted with tomatoes and his windows soaped.'

'The little devils!' said Celia. 'If I see anyone doing anything like that I'll give them a piece of my mind.'

Mary Ann left us and we sat down, temporarily stumped. Then Maureen stuck her cowboy hat on her head, and began putting together unlikely combinations of shorts and shirts. 'How's that? Oh, and my black tights. Is that crazy enough?'

The rest of us hunted through our bags and cases. I wore my old jeans and a shirt, blacked my face, pulled a cut-off stocking over it, and put my joke-shop teeth in, topping the look with my big straw sunhat. Weird was the word. I even found an old pair of crutches in a corner of the garage, and hobbled off on them. Pat managed to turn herself into a forty-niner, and Molly was a woman of the Twenties, who we all thought looked rather elegant. Celia was almost as odd-looking as I was, with a stocking on her head, sunglasses, and jewellery made out of whatever was lying around, including film reels.

Inside, the party had started. The house was decorated with balloons. We bobbed for apples, passed matchboxes between our noses, and ate lots of good food. We met Mary Ann's younger brother, John, who had completed a year of college but was now planning to drive across the States.

'You won't believe this,' he told us. 'I've been in Portland with some friends and there was a story on the radio about you all.'

'A story about us? In Portland?'

'Sure. About these five crazy girls who'd driven down the Alaska Highway in an old car. I told everyone you were staying with my sister and that I was going to meet you soon, but nobody would believe me.'

As the party was winding down, John told me that the hospital had just rung, wanting me to go in. I thought he was joking until Mary Ann – wearing what looked like an upside-down bedpan on her head – said that unfortunately it was true.

What a job I had scrubbing the black off my face! I couldn't get it off entirely, and was left with an odd greenish tinge to my complexion. I apologized to my patient's family. His three-year-old grandson, dressed in a duck costume, was rolling around on the floor of the private room, high on candy and in danger of tripping up one of the elderly visitors. I decided that my appearance was the least of everyone's worries.

With all of us on private duty, the kitty was beginning to build up again and we were able to pay Maureen back for the new engine. Cases finished, new ones started. One day none of us might be needed, the next, we were all employed. Pat found a regular job at the children's clinic, shepherding her patients to and from their appointments with the doctor. She confessed that she spent most of the shift chatting to the other nurse there.

We began thinking about our next trip. We fancied Hawaii – we had seen flights advertised at ninety-nine dollars one way – but it was still a bit of a dream at this stage. Slightly nervously, we wrote and told our parents that they wouldn't be seeing us at Christmas after all, that the new year seemed more likely, but best to say Easter to be on the safe side. 'We might never be here again' was our constant justification for delaying our return. Mexico was another place that kept coming up in conversation. If we *were* to drive all that way, well, the truth was, we had no real idea when we would be home, other than some time in 1959.

When we all had a few days free, we hurried off to San Francisco before the phone could start ringing.

'I don't think I ever get sick of seeing anywhere new, do you?' Pat said, sighing with pleasure as we approached the Golden Gate Bridge, and we all agreed.

I was overwhelmed by the city. The pretty white houses with their wrought-iron gates and shutters, and cheerful plants hanging outside. The streets that appeared to be almost perpendicular, lined with parked cars that seemed about to topple over (we scraped the bottom of Flatus trying to get up one of them). The friendly people, who all wanted to stop and help us when we were lost. The view of blue water from every hill.

'They say that girls in San Francisco have the best legs in the world from walking up and down these streets,' said Molly, striding energetically ahead. 'Perhaps we should move here for a while.'

'Perhaps we should just stop eating magical marshmallow puddings,' said Celia, fending off a playful slap from Molly, who had been taken in by our trick.

I had sent my camera a few weeks earlier to the Kodak factory for a repair, and after we had picked it up we sat looking out on to a rocky island in the bay, wondering what it could be. When we discovered that it was 'the Rock', or Alcatraz, we could hardly believe that such a forbidding place could look so appealing.

We decided to take a cable car to Chinatown. As we were about to board, it swung away from us – we hadn't realized it was on a turntable – and we chased it, trying to reach the door. In fits of laughter, we gave up and ran the other way. By the time the door met us, everyone else had jumped on and there were no seats left. We couldn't speak for laughing, and wished one of us had taken a film of it all.

We visited Fisherman's Wharf at night, and decided to treat ourselves in the most famous of all the restaurants, the Fishermen's Grotto. We ordered Lobster Newburg, and tried not to notice how finely dressed the other customers were. Still, nobody bothered us, and we had a table by the window, where we sat watching the brightly coloured lights of the harbour buildings, and the fishing boats bobbing in the water.

We were too full for pudding, and as there were people waiting for a table we moved on. An hour later, walking past a café, we changed our minds. I had a banana split, Molly a Hawaiian Sundae, Pat a Mr Bunny, Maureen a Peter Pan Glory and Celia a couple of bars of chocolate.

We got back to Bob and Mary Ann's to a pile of letters. Mrs Cashmore from Helena had written, thanking us for the English socks we had bought the doctor in Vancouver, and inviting us to their home for Christmas. We didn't intend going back that way, but we were touched by the invitation.

Our dear friend Margaret had recently gone back to Cleveland after a holiday in the San Fernando Valley. We were sad to have missed seeing her, due to our later-than-planned arrival in California, especially as she seemed unsure about her future. There was talk of her going to work for one of the sons of her old employer, who was married and whose wife was expecting a baby. We wrote back, hoping that everything would work out well for her.

There was a letter for me with unfamiliar handwriting. I turned it over, and found it was from Cleo. I took a deep breath and began to read. Actually, it was a lovely letter, though it made me feel a little sad. I read parts of it out to the others. He told me that winter had arrived in Glenwood Springs, the summer guests giving way to skiers, who came back to warm up in front of fires burning in the lounges.

'It sounds very romantic,' said Maureen. I fluttered my eye-lashes at her.

'Our friends there all say hello, and they miss us. That's nice. And the owners of the old people's home in Denver came out to see us again, after we'd gone. What a shame.'

'Anything else?'

I put down the letter. 'He says he's sure we'll meet again, and that he'll wait for me. Oh, I feel so mean. After that terrible tragedy, too.'

'And such a super chap,' said Pat. The others nodded.

Laura had learned to walk in our short absence. She wobbled past us, her arms rigid, followed by a watchful Mary Ann, who raised her eyebrows at me but didn't ask any questions.

There was a letter to us all from another Colorado friend, Robert Loewe, the pianist and adventurer, who had set off on his own travels. He had already been to stay with Molly's and Pat's parents and was on his way south, en route for Europe. He had enjoyed his 'teas' with both families, he said, and he also men-tioned an evening walk down to the Tyne, returning home to a lovely fire at Mr and Mrs Beadle's.

'Funny, all this talk about fires. And here we are still in T-shirts,' said Celia.

'I wonder if we'll ever see him again,' mused Maureen.

'Oh, he was quite a character,' Celia began telling Mary Ann. 'Did we ever tell you about our dinghy ride on the Colorado? You wouldn't believe—'

'Honestly!' Pat, who was reading a letter from her parents, made all of us look over at her. 'My mother still hasn't worn the housecoat I bought her months ago. She says she's saving it for best. It's only a housecoat! Sorry, I didn't mean to interrupt, but aren't parents maddening sometimes. Now she wants to know what I want for Christmas and where to send it. Do you think I'll ever wear a twinset out here?'

One evening we were all relaxing after dinner when the phone rang. Bob answered it, and came back to say it was for one of us. Thinking it was the hospital, none of us wanted to take it – we'd all been working and nobody felt like going back that night. In the end Molly relented, and we heard shrieks of delight coming from the other room. It was Joan, asking what was keeping us, and saying that she was going to England for a holiday, and we were not to leave California until she got back. We all queued up to speak to her.

'Could you come to us for Christmas?' she asked.

'Oh, Joan, we'd love to, but we just might be in Hawaii,' I confessed.

'Oh, no contest then. Don't forget your surfboards.'

At the Hospital for Tropical Diseases in London, the consultants were always looking up people's backsides and it was our job to clean the instruments afterwards. One day I stuck a cloth into the tube of a sigmoidoscope and it didn't come out the other end. No matter what I did, it was completely stuck. I had the bright idea of burning it out with a little alcohol and a match, and succeeded in not only blowing the cloth out but in blowing a hole in the tube as well.

Sister almost took to her bed. 'That is Sir Neil's special instrument,' she exploded, her face even redder than mine. 'Oh, what is he going to say?' She stood there, wringing her hands, as we both looked at the damaged piece of equipment, willing it to mend itself.

'Well, there's only one thing for it. You can do his next clinic and tell him what happened when he refuses to perform the examination. Now tidy this mess up. Oh dear, oh dear, I just don't know what will happen.'

I spent a sleepless night before the clinic, worrying about it. I had worked with Sir Neil Hamilton-Fairley before, and he had appeared to be a quiet, dignified gentleman, not pumped up with his own importance as so many consultants were. But consultants were used to being obeyed. In fact, the way some of the sisters fawned around them, it was surprising they didn't ask us to kiss their feet – or even their backsides. So perhaps I wouldn't have such an easy ride after all.

The day dawned – I had rather hoped it wouldn't – and I stood at the instrument tray, my apology prepared. The patient lay on his left side, his knees drawn up to his chest, breathing heavily. Sir Neil asked for the sigmoidoscope. Hoping that my trembling fingers didn't give the game away, I handed over its replacement, determined not to meet Sister's eye.

Sir Neil took it. He didn't give it a second glance. He began to insert it.

'Just breathe slowly, love,' said Sister. 'It might feel slightly uncomfortable but it shouldn't hurt.'

'Have you ever had a tube shoved up *your* arse?' growled the patient. 'Cor blimey, gov! What's the view like then?'

Sir Neil hadn't noticed the absence of his 'special' instrument, and how could anyone in their right mind really believe that he might have done? It was just a blooming tube, after all. I had to force myself not to flash Sister a victorious grin.

This all came back to me as I spent a worried night on Bob and Mary Ann's lawn. I couldn't remember feeling so nervous since that long night, two years earlier. The next day, Molly and I were going to Bob's high school to talk to the students. We had all refused at first, thinking what a sophisticated, confident bunch American youngsters were. The very thought of sitting in front of them terrified the life out of us.

'Aw, come on,' coaxed Bob, when we voiced our fears. 'This is your chance to do your bit for Anglo-American relations. They don't know a thing about your country or your government. You could tell them anything and they'd believe you.'

In the end, Pat, Maureen and Celia had informed me and Molly that they had held a meeting and reached a unanimous decision that we would be ideal for the job.

'Flatten yourself against the wall when the bell goes,' said Bob, and as it did, doors were flung open and dozens of students streamed down the corridor.

'It's like trying to paddle the wrong way up the Colorado,' I whispered to Molly. She smiled, but it was a wary smile. I knew that she felt as nervous as I did.

Most of the pupils were already in Bob's classroom as we got there, sitting at their desks, or even sitting on them. Everyone was talking loudly. The noise level went down slightly when we entered, and heads turned to see who the new arrivals were, but then the hubbub resumed almost as quickly.

Bob sat us in the front row. 'Don't look so scared,' he laughed.

He cleared his throat and the class began to pay attention.

'All right, folks.'

Everyone took their seats, chairs scraped on the floor. He was just beginning to introduce us when the door burst open and a boy walked in, spoke to a couple of other students as he passed their desks, and thrust a piece of paper at Bob before sitting down noisily, making a comment to his neighbour as he did so. He shut up quickly after a stare from Bob.

When everyone was quiet, Bob began again. He talked about his own trip to Europe, and told a few of the funny stories we had heard before. It was obvious that his pupils liked him. Then he asked if anyone knew anything about Great Britain, as he always called it.

Somebody knew we had a queen. Somebody else knew that the British people lent the Americans a hand in the war. We smiled sweetly.

Bob produced a map of the world and, with Molly holding the other end, asked who could show him where Great Britain was. The class went quiet for a while, then a girl spoke up. 'I guess it's, like, somewhere in the Atlantic Ocean?'

'Come and show us,' said Bob.

She wandered nonchalantly to the map, stood back for a couple of seconds, then pointed to Greenland.

When I was asked to point out where it actually was, there was some laughter about its size.

Bob decided that I ought to speak now. I stood up, hoped that my voice wasn't shaking too much, and told them about the Queen and the Royal Family and our main political parties, aware that it didn't sound terribly interesting – to me or these young-sters. Nobody had heard of Macmillan.

Then it was Molly's turn, and she told them – at Bob's insis-tence – about the National Health Service, and that at least produced some 'Oh's and the murmur of what sounded like sur-prise, or even approval.

I looked at the class as she was talking. Though it seemed ter-ribly warm to us, they all wore their outdoor jackets and coats – the boys' emblazoned with 'Woodland Wolves', which I guessed must be a sports team. Most of the girls had long, wavy hair, and looked unsettlingly glamorous, especially as they wore their own clothes. I watched in amazement as one girl rummaged through her handbag, took out a comb and began to style her hair, regarding Molly with great interest as she did so.

When Molly had finished, Bob asked if anyone had any questions. This produced a buzz of conversation amongst the students, and a few shouted remarks. Bob insisted they raise their hands and speak one at a time.

'How old are you when you start dating?' asked one girl.

I noticed that the cuff of her bobby socks matched the material of her checked dress. Ah yes, dates! We might have known they would come up. Even the newspaper reporters who had interviewed us were keen to know about our love lives.

'Well, me and Robbie McLeod said we loved each other when we were five, but I don't really call that dating,' said Molly.

'Do you go to drive-ins for your dates?' asked another girl.

'Oh, we don't have drive-ins,' I said. 'Though we have cinemas, of course.'

'Where do you go on dates if you don't have drive-ins?' somebody else asked, in an appalled voice, and a few others voiced their disbelief at this sad state of affairs.

'We have dances, like you do, and cafés. Or we might go for a walk.'

The questioner looked distinctly unimpressed.

'How many dates do you have a week?' asked the hair-combing girl.

I could hear Molly sigh beside me.

'Do you have a steady back home?'

'Have you had any dates in Woodland?'

This was followed by some giggling, and the names of a couple of boys were called out, producing loud protests.

'Steady on, guys.' Bob clapped his hands. 'You must have questions about something other than dates. Come on, we've got visitors from Great Britain. This doesn't happen every day. Think of their country, think of their history. What would you like to know? Yes, you, Maggie.'

'How old are you when you learn to drive?' Maggie examined her nails as she spoke.

'Ah, now there's a more interesting question!' Bob was almost shouting with relief.

'Seventeen,' Molly and I answered together.

'You like American cars?'

'Boy, you should see *their* car!' said Bob. 'How many miles have you done so far?'

'The milometer broke a long time ago, but the last time we worked it out it was about thirty-six thousand,' I replied.

Some of the boys whistled. Even the girls opened their painted lips.

'Neato!' someone cried.

'What make is she?'

'A Ford V8. She's super.'

'Super,' mimicked a voice from the back row.

There followed a series of questions about cars. How fast were we allowed to drive? How much was an Austin Healey? And an MG? More my type of question.

'Does your date pick you up in his car?'

'Actually,' Molly began, 'not many youngsters have their own cars. They can't really afford them. We're more likely to walk or take the bus.'

More gasps.

'Any more questions?' asked Bob. 'Yes, Billie-Jo.'

Billie-Jo smiled at the boy sitting beside her, before asking, with a hint of a sneer, 'Do you have television in your country?'

Molly breathed out noisily beside me. I looked at her and

nodded, indicating that this one was hers. I hoped that she wouldn't be too sharp in her reply.

'Television,' began Molly, with an icy smile, 'was invented by a Scotsman.'

Voices simmered, then came to a rapid boil.

'Uh-uh.'

'No way!'

'But my mom says—'

Bob laughed heartily. 'Good question, and even better answer. One up to the Brits!'

He rubbed his hands together. We might not have been enjoying this much, but he certainly was.

Bob admitted at the dinner table later that the average American teenager's knowledge about the rest of the world might be sadly lacking.

'But let's be fair,' said Celia, after we had told the others about our experience in the classroom, 'how much did we know about America before we came here? I for one didn't know that much.'

'No, I suppose apart from film stars and a few famous landmarks I didn't either,' I admitted.

'And certainly nothing about government, except the name of the president,' added Maureen.

'Ah well,' said Bob, 'at least you knew enough to drive that old car of yours on the right side of the road here. Did Mary Ann and I tell you about our arrival in the UK?'

We all shook our heads.

'Well, we had sailed from Calais to Dover, and it was late when we arrived. The ferry docked, and we cycled down the gangplank to begin our journey round your jewel of an island.'

We sat back, smiling at each other across the table.

Bob continued. 'At least, now, we shared the same language as our hosts after our weeks in Europe. No more having to remember if we needed to say "*buenas noches*" or "*bonne nuit*". Then suddenly, out of the darkness, we heard our first English voice. Was it welcoming us to this merry old land? Nope. "Wrong side, Yank," was what it said. And that was our introduction to the United Kingdom of Great Britain and Northern Ireland.'

'They were being kind, of course,' added Mary Ann, putting the salad on the table. 'We could have been killed if we'd gone any further like that.'

'"Wrong side, Yank!"' repeated Bob, thumping the table. 'It sure woke us up. But they were friendly folks in Dover. You heard about no room at the inn? Well, that's what happened to us. We were looking for somewhere to stay for the night and having no luck. One lady told us she was full, but to come back later if we couldn't find anywhere else, and we were so desperate we had to do just that. She kicked her son out of bed and gave us his room. Poor kid had to sleep on the sofa.'

'Did she really?' said Celia.

'Hey, Celia, don't sound so surprised,' I said. 'The English are nice people.'

'I'm surprised, too,' said Pat. 'We find Americans like that wherever we go, but we always wonder, "Would the British do this?" I mean, how many of the people we know back home would do what Bob and Mary Ann are doing now – putting up five people they met for a couple of days in a national park? They're not as outgoing, and I think a lot of them are suspicious of strangers.'

But Bob and Mary Ann wouldn't hear of it.

'Did I ever tell you about the good folk we met at the cricket match?' asked Bob.

9

A Perfect Cloud

Honolulu, Hawaii, December 1958

Our apartment was a couple of minutes' walk from the beach, tucked between some of the big hotels and a block up from the Moana, where we had stayed on our first night in Hawaii. It was a tiny, one-bedroom place, with a kitchenette and small living room, only meant for two and barely big enough for our luggage, never mind the five of us. Cases were pushed under beds, balanced on cupboards, or tucked into any corner they would fit. We had piled two of them on top of each other, turning them into an extra table, and covering them with a couple of island-print tea towels we found in a drawer. With our assorted camera bags strewn around and Pat's typewriter sitting importantly on the dining table, it looked rather like the office of a crew of photo-journalists, except that they would not have been coming and going dressed in bathing suits and with towels slung over their shoulders, like we did.

It was December, and we had made it to Hawaii. We could hardly believe our luck. Even the warm rain that was falling when we landed in Honolulu could not dampen our enthusiasm. We had been greeted at the bottom of the steps of the plane by a smiling islander, who presented us with *leis* of purple and white flowers. The staff inside the airport smiled as we retrieved our luggage, the porters smiled, the drivers smiled beside their steaming cabs and gestured to the rain apologetically. The long and bumpy flight – Molly had been sick, and I might have been too if I hadn't taken a tablet – was soon forgotten.

Our rooms at the Moana Hotel overlooked Waikiki Beach. A band was playing in the courtyard below as we went to bed. The strumming of the guitars and ukuleles and the plaintive singing lulled me to sleep after the long day. The waves, crashing rhythmically in the background, were like another instrument. When I woke up, the heady scent of jasmine filled the room.

We spent the weekend on the beach and vowed that we would look for work on Monday. A girl from New Zealand got talking to us. Nell had been travelling round the world on her own, and was sailing home on the SS *Oronsay* that had docked from San Francisco earlier that day. Her blue eyes were striking in her deeply tanned face.

'The hardest part was when I ran out of water in the desert. I thought I was a goner then.' She sucked on the slice of pineapple we had given her, and looked thoughtfully out to sea. Surfers, like predatory seabirds, formed a line where the dark water in the bay changed to a paler shade.

'Have you tried that?' She pointed at the surfers. 'It's terrific, but – strewth! – you can get a battering if you're not careful.'

The five of us looked at her, and then each other, admiringly.

'Our own trip sounds very modest compared to yours,' said Maureen.

Nell shrugged. 'Once Christmas and summer hols are out the way, it'll all be over. I'll be behind a desk again.'

'I suppose this will end for all of us one day, too,' Maureen said sadly. 'You're going to college, then?'

'Nope, I'm a teacher. Got a job lined up in Auckland. Let's hope the little buggers behave.'

She continued to gaze out at the ocean, as if it was luring her back. As if the next trip was already taking shape in her mind.

We took her back to the apartment for a meal, leaving the door open to catch the breeze. A walkway leading to the other apartments passed in front of it, and at one end a communal flight of steps led straight down to the street. Other residents hovered at their doors, chatting at the railing and making the most of the late-afternoon sun. Cooking smells drifted through open windows.

An American girl we had said hello to earlier waved as she passed by again, then retraced her steps and stuck her head inside. She was wearing cropped white trousers and an embroidered Chinese-style shirt, her hair in a girlish ponytail.

'Sorry, I won't disturb your meal. But, gee, it's great to see so many people! I live round the corner and normally it's just dead round here.'

We invited her to join us, and her eyes lit up as she came into the room.

'Don't get up. No, nothing for me, thanks. I'm Marcia. My husband's in the navy – aren't they all? You don't really all live here, do you?'

We explained who we were, and Nell introduced herself.

'Oh, why is my life so dull?' she wailed, slipping off her pretty sandals and placing them neatly by the door.

'You live in Hawaii!' scolded Molly. 'How can that be dull?'

'Now, where do I start . . .' She put a finger to her lips, and considered her answer. I offered her my seat as I got up to prepare pudding.

'The beach. And shopping. The beach. And more shopping. That's it. I don't even like the water much. It gets kind of boring day in and day out. I've got a little job in real estate, but it's . . .' She shrugged.

'But there must be lots of you in the same boat,' I said from the kitchen, 'what with all the services that are based here. I thought you'd all have a grand time together.'

'Oh, I've got a few girlfriends, but most of them have kids. And so many of them are kind of small-town in their outlook. Now, if they were here, they'd want to know how many children you wanted, and what you thought of the latest chocolate pecan cake mix.'

We all laughed.

'Pineapple?' I asked her, as I cut up two of them. 'We've got some passion fruit or banana ice cream to go with it. Now, *there's* a reason for living in Hawaii!'

'No pineapple, thanks. I'm sick of the things. Ice cream sounds delicious, though. Say, would you all like to come round tonight and watch television with me?'

'Oh, Marcia, that's so kind,' Pat said quickly, 'but we've promised to take Nell back to her ship, and she's going to give us a guided tour.'

'Oh, I'll run you all down there in the car. Bob's away. Might be a bit of a squeeze, but you're all skinny lizzies. We can watch TV another time if you like.'

Marcia's boredom was our gain. She was a friendly girl, and she couldn't do enough to help us. She lent us books about the islands, made a list of useful telephone numbers, and spent ages making her own enquiries about nursing jobs. She asked us what we liked to eat and did our shopping at the Commissary for servicemen, saving us a small fortune.

In the International Market Place, she told us what was genuine Hawaiian and what was actually Polynesian or Japanese.

'If you want something to take home, you want it to be authentic,' she said, expertly rifling through rails of brightly coloured clothes. We thought that everything looked beautiful, but she seemed to know what was good quality and what was tourist tat.

'Did you know that sarongs are not Hawaiian? The traditional costume is the *muu-muu* – that's what you see the hotel staff wearing – but they can look a bit frowsy in the wrong material.' She held one up to prove it, and we nodded wisely.

'Jeez Louise! Have you seen this one?'

The garment she was holding now was in midnight blue, and the neck and hemline were trimmed in mink.

I thought about the mink stole I had promised my mother, and smiled to myself. Somehow I couldn't picture her in a mink-trimmed *muu-muu*.

We would not be able to work as nurses. Marcia had found out that we needed to register, and that the process would take several weeks.

'I suppose you can't blame them,' said Pat. 'They don't want everyone flocking here and taking jobs from the locals.'

'They don't know what they're missing,' said Marcia, indignant on our behalf.

We spent a couple of days trailing round shops and hotels to see if they needed any Christmas staff, but nobody was hiring. The chance of living like islanders for a few weeks was diminishing fast, but still, nothing could take away our pleasure in being here. The sun was hot, the trade winds delightfully cooling; even the rain felt welcome, leaving misty rainbows over our new-found paradise.

In between our job-hunting we went to the beach, and back to the apartment for siestas. We ate so many pineapples that our mouths bled. Marcia said we should sprinkle the fruit with salt first.

We spent our evenings in the Banyan Court of the Moana Hotel, where the staff greeted us as if we were still staying there. Marcia let us borrow some of her pretty oriental shirts and blouses.

'I buy so many clothes. I could get by without shopping again for the rest of the year. Well, a month or two, at least. Isn't it great that we're all the same size!'

It was true – apart from Celia being a few inches taller, and Molly a little shorter, we fitted into each other's clothes perfectly.

In the Moana's Commonwealth Room, we found comments in the visitors' book from a group of Geordie servicemen whose ship had recently docked in Honolulu.

'Howay United!' one of them had written. 'It's alreet,' stated another. A feeling of nostalgia washed over me. I could hear the men's accents as I read, and it was a strangely comforting sound.

One night, watching the Dixie Cats play as we sat under the banyan tree, we got talking to some Australian boys, who told us that we must hire a car and explore the rest of the island.

'It's nothing like Waikiki,' they said. 'It's so commercialized here.'

We went on with them to the Royal Hawaiian Hotel, and walked past Dorothy Lamour in the lobby.

'Wait till we tell Marcia,' said Pat and Molly together.

Marcia found us cleaning jobs for a couple of days in some new bungalows on the edge of town. We also put an advert in the *Honolulu Star-Bulletin*: 'Five versatile British nurses touring the world desire work of any kind'.

In the meantime, Pat practised her typing and went off for an interview to be a Kelly Girl. She was away for ages, and I was convinced she had not only passed the test but started work. She returned eventually.

'I'm not fast enough. Now you know why I wasn't a secretary for long. But I might have another go later in the week.'

We woke one morning to the sound of the phone ringing. Molly, who was lying right beside it, answered sleepily. It was a naval officer's wife in Pearl Harbor who had just had a baby and wanted some help for a few days. This was a perfect job for Molly and Maureen, who had worked on the maternity ward in Cleveland.

We were having breakfast when it rang again. Someone needed a gardener. Then a recently widowed man wanted help with cleaning.

We decided to take it in turns to go to the beach that morning, so that somebody was always around to answer the phone. Celia picked it up on our way out, as I was throwing juice and pineapples into a cooler bag.

'Did you say you wanted us to sell fire hose?' She grinned at us all, then had to turn away. 'I'm sorry, I still can't catch it. Ah, fine hose? Yes, er, I'm sure we could have a go . . . And how many of us will you be wanting? Yes, we'll find you. See you tomorrow. Thank you.'

She collapsed into the chair, putting her hands over her face. 'What have I done? We're going to be door-to-door salesmen.'

'Oh, Celia, as if it would be fire hoses!'

She laughed. 'That's what it sounded like. I really couldn't understand him very well. At least stockings won't be so awkward to carry. Can you imagine us with great hoses round our necks? "How many feet would you like, sir? Fifty? Kindly wait while I uncoil myself."'

We were all laughing when the phone rang again. Maureen picked it up, turned rather pink, and flung it back down.

'I'm not going to give him the satisfaction of thinking he's shocked me,' she said. 'Whose idea was it to say we'd do work of *any* kind?' She looked straight at me, then chuckled to herself. 'Honestly, there are a lot of weird people in this world.'

It rang again. 'No, leave it, it's sure to be him.'

We all stared at the phone, willing it to stop.

In the end, it rang for so long that Molly picked it up, holding the receiver a few inches from her ear, as if the distance would protect her from any unsavoury intentions. It turned out to be a reporter from the *Star-Bulletin*, thinking that we would make a good story. Molly was on the phone for ages, answering questions about our travels in the polished manner of one who has told the same tales many times before.

Finally, she was finished. 'The photographer is coming round at four o'clock. We must make sure we're all here then. Now, who's for the beach?'

Molly and Maureen went first thing the next morning to look after the newly delivered mother, so that left Pat, Celia and me to see the man about the fine hose. We took the bus into town and found his office down a narrow road, squashed between a laundry and some sort of drinking den.

He was on the telephone when we entered the room, a cigarette burning itself out in an ashtray. His voice, which had been raised, changed to a gentler tone when he saw us.

'Hey, buddy, we'll talk about it later. I'll be seeing you.' He put down the phone and stood up to shake our hands. He wore a short-sleeved shirt with a tropical-fish design, and had a pen tucked behind one ear. He looked us up and down.

'English? Irish? That's just swell.' He rubbed his hands together. 'They're honest accents. Did you know that? You can sell anything with voices like that. Folks trust you. That's what this game's all about. If someone trusts you, you can sell them their own grandmother.'

We looked at him suspiciously and he gave a nervous laugh.

'Anyway, these are the Bibles.' He picked up a huge tome from his desk.

Pat and I looked at Celia. 'Oops,' she whispered.

'I'm terribly sorry,' she said to our prospective employer. 'I misheard you on the telephone. I couldn't possibly sell Bibles, and nor could my friends.'

The man nodded his head vigorously, as if he couldn't agree more. Then he began talking very quickly about the importance of Christianity on the islands, and how a large family Bible was an asset to any household. He removed the pen from his ear and went to the desk where he scribbled something on a pad. He held it up to show us what he had written. 'Five dollars commission' was underlined three times, as if we might not have believed it otherwise.

'That's five for every Bible,' he said.

'Five dollars!' I exclaimed, and Pat nudged me in the ribs.

'That's all yours, with every sale, and it's all you need to take from your customers. I collect the rest later. But they get the Bible straight away. See – you get the easy part!'

A few minutes later, we were lugging three heavy boxes on to the bus.

'I'm not sure that God will really like me doing this,' said Celia, sweating slightly. 'Bibles aren't supposed to be forced on people.'

'As if we could force anything on anyone,' I said. 'If they like them, they like them. If they don't, they don't. And five dollars apiece!'

'Did you see his office?' Celia continued. 'He had all sorts of things in there. I reckon all that crack about being a good Christian was just a load of old flannel. He'd probably sell the Muslim holy book if it fell off the back of a lorry. As well as his grandmother, the poor soul.'

'What would she be doing on the back of a lorry?' said Pat.

Celia took one of her Bibles out of its leather casing. 'These are very fine, though.'

'So they should be for forty dollars,' said Pat. 'Do you think they can afford them in our apartment block? I'd have thought we'd have more luck in the posh part of town.'

'Remember what he said,' I reminded her. 'People don't think about money when they're buying a Bible. They're buying something that's more than a material good.'

'Hmm. Sounds like you've been well and truly suckered.' Pat made a fan out of the piece of paper bearing the office address and began to waft it in front of her pink face. 'I think we got the short straw today.'

Back at the apartments, I knocked on the door of one of our neighbours. The man always nodded to us when we passed each other on the steps. His wife, who looked Japanese, went out early every morning in a tight-fitting suit, her hair pulled harshly into a bun, her lips a strange shade of orange. Back home in the evening, we would see her setting off for the shops in a flowery *muu-muu*, her hair hanging freely, looking like the younger, prettier sister of the woman we had seen earlier. He was scruffy, usually unshaven, and pottered in and out all day, a cigarette clamped constantly between his lips.

He nodded when he saw me standing there, and even went inside to turn down the volume on the television. I felt embarrassed, and very insincere, as I began my sales pitch, aware that I was apologizing for what I was doing in a way that was surely not in the door-to-door salesman's handbook. He took the Bible from me, didn't open it, but turned it over in his hands a couple of times. Celia and Pat were hiding round the corner, in fits, having nominated me to go first. The occasional sound of their muffled laughter was close to setting me off too. Our neighbour handed the book back to me, and I was all ready to thank him for his time and to take my leave when he went back inside.

I turned to the others apologetically. Pat mouthed, 'Well?'

I shrugged in reply, and was about to put the book back in the box when he returned, thrusting a five-dollar bill into my hand. I was so surprised, I forgot to give him the Bible at first.

'Are you . . . I mean, thank you very much. I hope you enjoy it.'

I rejoined the others, unable to wipe the smile off my face.

'See, it's easy.'

'"I hope you enjoy it!"' mimicked Celia. 'It's not the latest Agatha Christie, you know!'

'We'll probably have his wife round later demanding a refund,' said Pat.

'Don't say that. I feel guilty enough as it is. Come on, let's try our luck at a few more. Look at this.' I waved the five dollars at them. 'We're going to be rich, girls.'

Nobody else was buying that morning. One woman shut the door in my face as soon as she saw the box at my feet. An older woman peered out from behind her curtains and shooed us away with her hand, a worried expression on her face. We took the bus to Pearl Harbor to try our luck on a navy housing estate. Looking out at the calm water, it was hard to think of what it must have been like on that fateful morning seventeen years earlier.

The Bibles were getting heavier. We were wearing skirts and blouses and court shoes, which had seemed like the right thing to do, but I could feel wet patches under my arms and my petticoat sticking to my legs.

'I'm always going to be nice to travelling salesmen from now on,' Pat said, after our umpteenth 'No thank you' or hurriedly closed door.

'What do you take us for – a bunch of heathens?' said one angry service wife. 'You think we don't have Bibles of our own?' A small girl peeped out behind her. 'Go and play, Susan,' she shooed.

'We don't think that at all,' said Celia soothingly. 'Oh, what a pretty child!'

'Yes, well . . .' The woman wavered. 'Just seems a strange thing to be selling. And who has that sort of money to spend on a book?' She folded her arms across her flat chest.

'Yes, it is rather a lot,' said Celia, in her melodic Irish voice, a voice that softened most people. 'I'm quite tempted to give them away – I'm sure that's what He would want us to do – but I think we'd get into trouble for that. I suppose it would be stealing, in the eyes of the law at least, if not in the eyes of the Lord. Oh, what a dilemma it is to be a good Christian!'

The woman seemed captivated by Celia. She smiled and nodded. Pat and I stood back, impressed.

'Mind, they must have been expensive to produce with all these colour pictures, and the leather binding. Smell it, it really is leather.'

The woman tilted her head up as Celia brought the book to her nose, and gave a girlish laugh.

Soon she was telling Celia the names and ages of her three children, and how her parents were coming to visit from Michigan for Christmas, and nobody made pumpkin pie like her mother.

'Celia, you sounded like a real salesman there,' I said, as we trudged away at last. The woman hadn't bought a Bible, but we had been invited to coffee the next day.

'Yes, and it's the last time you talk me into anything. If we hurry back now, we could have lunch on the beach.'

Joan Nakamura had been living in Cleveland for a year, and recently returned home to Hawaii. She was a friend of Enrique's, and he had written to us insisting that we phone her. When we did, she invited us to accompany her to a party that night.

'Enrique is a honey,' she agreed, as we walked along a road of low white bungalows with overhanging eaves and shadowy porches. She was a strikingly pretty girl, with long shiny black hair and almond eyes. 'And you must know Barbara, too.'

'Barbara, um . . .' I tried to remember the surname of our American nursing friend – the one who had made us laugh with the tale about the tea cosy.

'Barbara Cook,' she said. 'You didn't know her?'

I was about to ask why we ought to know this Barbara, when Joan stopped.

'This is it.'

A path, overgrown with large, red-leaved plants, led to a small porch. Shoes – perhaps about twenty pairs – were lined up neatly on the steps.

'You can always tell where the party is by the shoes,' Joan laughed.

There was a wide mix of guests of many races, and everyone was just as friendly as Joan.

One of them turned out to be the chief photographer for the *Star-Bulletin*, who said he had been developing our photos that day.

'I never dreamt I would meet you myself!' he gushed.

As the night wore on, a boy in a shirt the colour of the ocean picked up a steel guitar and began to strum it gently, accompanied by his friend on the ukulele. Two girls in island dress performed a dance called Lovely Hula Hands, which they tried to teach us. We felt big and clumsy beside them, but they were both patient, and complimentary about our efforts. Apparently Molly and Maureen were both naturals, which they seemed to find as funny as we did.

Inevitably, somebody asked us to entertain them with a traditional song or dance of our own. We should have been seasoned performers by now, but as usual, we spent more time racking our brains than singing. Then Molly suddenly remembered 'My Bonnie Lies Over the Ocean', and we wondered why we had never thought of it before. Our new friends joined in with the chorus, clasping their hands together pleadingly, and finding depths in the song that I had been unaware of before.

'I'm so glad that Bonnie came back,' said one of the Hula

Hands girls, with a tear in her eye, after we had sung it for the third time.

We couldn't believe it when somebody told us it was 3 a.m.

Marcia's husband, Bob, took us in the car to return the Bibles. The salesman was standing smoking on the step. We had already spoken to him on the telephone to tell him we were coming.

'See, I knew you could do it. Don't give up so easy. You're naturals.'

We told him that carrying the boxes around in the heat was no joke.

'Yeah, I get it, ladies. Tell you what, I've got the ideal thing for you. Magazines. But all you do is carry one with you to show your customer – they get theirs in the post when they sign up, see. Nothing to carry at all, except the forms to fill in. You don't even need to take any money from them. But gotta make sure they sign.'

We declined his offer and were about to leave when he nudged Pat, who was standing closest to him. 'See them vacuum cleaners. I take them to the north shore and I plug 'em into the cigarette lighter on the car and the folks go crazy for them. 'Course they're not going to do anything 'cept make a nice coat-stand when I'm gone. They've got no electricity, see!' He began to wheeze with laughter. 'I've sold a few. Good money, too. Would you believe how stupid some folk are?'

'That is thoroughly dishonest!' said Celia. 'You should be ashamed of yourself taking advantage of people like that.'

'No, you don't get it. It's a status symbol for them folk. Makes them feel important. And like I said, if folks—'

'There's no excuse for it at all. Come on, girls, let's not waste any more time here.'

Molly, Maureen and Celia went out with some RAF boys we had met in the Banyan Court, while Pat and I volunteered for a baby-sitting job. The unpleasant smell hit us as soon as we entered the apartment. I tried not to notice how dirty the place was.

The child's father was uninterested in the references we tried to show him.

'I'm a qualified nursery nurse,' I told him, 'and we're both registered nurses, with wide-ranging experience of—'

'Yep,' he muttered, grabbing his car keys.

I asked him about the child's bedtime, but he shook his head as he made for the door.

'He'll fall asleep when he's good and ready. His mother will be in around midnight. Sometimes one.'

He ruffled the boy's hair and was gone.

Pat went into each room, sniffing, trying to locate the offending item, then gave up and began to tackle the kitchen. Every surface was thick with grease, and the floor covered in sticky yellow patches.

Charlie was a two-year-old with large, watchful eyes and a hesitant smile. Though he regarded me cautiously, he didn't seem upset about being left with strangers.

I bathed him – after scrubbing out the bath and disinfecting the sink and toilet – and put him into his pyjamas. The smell of the bleach, mixed with another, unidentifiable smell, turned my stomach.

Charlie's father had been right. The child had no intention of sleeping just yet. I played various games with him and, after about an hour, succeeded in settling him on my lap for a story. To my surprise, he had a well-stocked bookcase in his room, though most of the books did not appear to have been opened. In the middle of the second story, his head lolled heavily against my arm. It was twenty past ten. If I'd closed my own eyes, I would have fallen asleep, too. I forced myself out of the chair and carried him to his cot. Pat and I both did some ironing, then flopped down, exhausted, and waited for his mother to come home.

She arrived a few minutes after midnight, and asked if we could return at seven-thirty the next morning. She had two jobs, she said, a daytime job and a night-time job. Pat asked what her husband did, and she raised her eyes and said, 'Messes around in cars most of the time, but you better ask him.'

I dragged myself out of bed just as it was getting light. Both of Charlie's parents were up, and more smartly dressed than they had been when I last saw them. They left with barely a word. Charlie was still sleeping. The kitchen looked better in the light of day and after its good clean by Pat, though the smell of disinfectant every-where still made me feel queasy. I found a clean cup, rinsed it several times under the hot tap, and helped myself to coffee. I was drinking it at the kitchen table when Charlie tottered in, his expression cross and sleepy, his hair sticking up in a way that made me want to run my fingers through it.

'Mama?' he asked me. 'Mama?' he called to the rest of the house.

I sat him on my knee and told him that Mama had gone to work, and that we would go to the beach later. He seemed satis-fied with that.

Pat arrived as I was getting him washed and dressed, and we hunted around for something to give him for breakfast. I opened the door of the fridge for juice and milk and what I saw made me slam it shut again immediately. A large brown cockroach was

sitting on a plate of some congealed leftovers, waving its anten-
nae at me.

I would have screamed if Charlie hadn't been there. I could
cope with most insects, but not cockroaches.

'That does it,' I said to Pat. 'No, don't look. You'll have a fit.
We're taking him home. How would you like to come and have
a special breakfast with us, Charlie?'

I grabbed some spare clothes for him and we left.

Maureen had gone to a gardening job, but Molly and Celia were
having breakfast when we got back. They squealed over Charlie.

'What a little angel!' said Celia.

'Och, look at that wee kiss-curl!' said Molly.

Charlie gazed back at them both with his big eyes, then, rather
endearingly, turned and pushed his face against my legs.

'He's never been shy before,' I said, as if I'd known him all his
life.

'How about a nice biscuit, Charlie?' said Molly. 'A cookie, I mean.'

He slowly turned his head. Molly patted the chair beside her
and I lifted him into the air as Pat whipped a cushion from
another chair and put it under him. He sat at the head of the table
like a little lord.

At the beach later, we were surprised to find that he could
almost swim, albeit in a splashy dog-paddle that made it look as
if he was drowning. He loved the water, and as soon as he was out
he wanted to go back in again. We took it in turns to entertain
him, and he basked in the attention. Maureen got back to the
apartment for lunch at the same time as we did, admired our little
charge, then waved a newspaper in our faces.

'Have you seen this yet? I'm surprised no one's been throwing money at you on the beach. Listen to this: "*Five fun-loving British nurses on a lark have hit a financial snag and are now looking for any job a-toll, reh-ally to buy return tickets to Cleveland, Ohio. The girls – three brownettes, one brunette and a blonde –*'"

'Am I a brownette or a brunette?' I asked her.

'Why are you reading it in that funny voice?' asked Molly.

'Because, love, that's how they've written it. Not only are we practically beggars but we talk funny, too. Well, you do, you're the one they spoke to.'

'Ooh, you wee—'

'Well, what else does it say?' I flopped back on one of the armchairs, pulling Charlie on to my lap. He snuggled back for a few seconds, then wriggled down on to the floor, where something had caught his attention.

Maureen summed up the rest of the article for us. 'We slept in national parks to save money – big deal, isn't that what they're there for? – we're down to our last dollar, and we're hungry. In fact,' here she put on her most pitiful voice, 'we've never been this poor before. Oh, boo-hoo.'

'That's journalists for you,' said Pat, preparing lunch. 'It was almost as bad in Colorado, if you remember. It'll all be forgotten tomorrow. Fish and chip wrappings, or whatever they do with old newspapers in Honolulu. Right, five coffees coming up. Is it safe with the little one?'

Just then Marcia knocked and came flying through the door, brandishing the paper. 'Have you all seen this? You didn't tell me they'd taken your photograph. Trust you all to be pictured with a pineapple! Don't you all look cute! You look so pretty in profile, Maureen. Let me look at you – tilt your head a bit.' She almost stumbled over Charlie. 'Oh, who's this little one?'

The little boy was sitting happily on the floor, making a puddle out of our wet costumes.

Later, after we had eaten and Charlie was taking a nap on one of the beds, there was a sharp rap on the door.

'The Bible man?' said Pat, biting her lip.

But it was the landlord, looking furious, and telling us that he was sure he had told us most clearly that children were not allowed in the apartment.

'But we're only looking after him for a few hours,' said Celia, putting on her nicest smile. 'His own home is rather, um . . .'

'That's not my problem. Kids make a mess. Either he goes or you go.'

We were already quite attached to Charlie, and had promised to look after him again. But minding him in his own home was out of the question. We had little choice but to leave. Marcia was helping us pack as Grace Murata popped by with her baby daughter. Grace's husband, David, had gone to college with Bob Jones, and these friends of friends were offering us the use of their car for a few days as they were going to another island for Christmas. Baby Ruth, with her shock of black hair, white dress and matching lace-up shoes, was as cute as a doll. She slept for the whole visit, and we were all desperate for her to wake.

'You're leaving already?' Grace looked at the open cases.

'A spot of landlord trouble. We're just moving house. We're quite used to it.'

Our new home was an empty room in a guest-house down the road. The manager asked how we would all fit in, and Maureen said it was bigger than our tent, so we'd be fine.

We were glad, however, having dropped the Muratas off at the airport the next day, to leave the hustle of Honolulu, with its hotels and offices and endless apartment blocks, and head inland. We passed isolated farm buildings, pineapple plantations and fields of sugar cane. Birds were singing from deep inside the thick trees. Trumpet-like flowers waved their gaudy heads from the roadside.

We had lunch on a hill overlooking a rocky headland. A finger of white sand was being pounded endlessly by great rolling waves.

'Who said the Americans had spoilt Hawaii?' Pat shook her head slowly.

We all agreed that we would love to bring our parents here.

'As if they'd ever come . . .' someone added.

We walked down to the beach. Thick, glossy blades of grass struck our bare legs. The surf crashed and fizzed like boiling water.

When we got back that evening, the manager had pushed a note under our door. It was from Joan Nakamura, who had spent ages trying to find out where we were. Enrique needed to get hold of us, she said, and we were to call him urgently. It was getting late, too late to ring Cleveland, and we spent an anxious night wondering what had happened. It was hard to think of a reason that didn't concern the illness – or worse – of one of our parents.

The others watched me as I dialled the number of Enrique's office the following morning on the manager's phone. In other circumstances, I would have been looking forward to hearing his voice again.

'Hi!' He sounded as bright as ever. 'How are you all? We've been worried sick about you.'

'You've been worried about *us*?'

'There was a story in the *Plain Dealer*. I think they picked it up from the Honolulu paper. I've got it right here. Says you're all stone broke and need to get back to Cleveland. Tony's been organizing a fund-raising campaign among the ISG crowd. He's collected quite a bit already. I don't think we've got enough to fly you home, but tell me, Gwenda, honestly, would you like me to lend you some money? I know I'd get it back. It's not a problem.'

I felt a stinging sensation behind my eyes. Our families were fine. Our friends were fine. What's more, they still cared about us, all these months after our departure. I tried to speak, but my voice wobbled. Pat, Maureen, Celia and Molly looked as if they were about to burst into tears. I had to mouth at them all that everything was fine, and force a grin.

'Tony even went begging to your hospital director,' Enrique chuckled. 'You know Tony, he's very insistent. Think he got a guarantee that he'd have you all back.'

I thought about what we had been doing on the island – lazing around on our lilos, sipping drinks under the banyan tree, the odd job here and there – and felt incredibly guilty. I swallowed hard.

'You're very quiet, Gwenda. Are you still there?'

'Oh, Enrique,' I burst out. 'We're so lucky to have friends like all of you. Please say thank you so much to Tony and to every single one of the others. But we're fine. We're absolutely fine. The paper here went over the top with a story about us. That reporter has a lot to answer for.'

Enrique laughed. 'Well, I did think if you were going to be broke and hungry, Honolulu was the place to be. Now, shall I keep sending your post to Hawaii? It's all building up again, and Christmas parcels, too.'

I looked at the others. We'd been discussing our options in the car the day before.

'I think you'd better send it to Joan's in LA. We probably won't be here much longer.'

Pat and I went to meet a man a few blocks away about model-ling work. He asked us if we would consider 'life modelling'.

'We'll do anything,' I said. 'Can we start now?'

'What exactly do you mean by life modelling?' asked Pat.

When he had told us, and before I had chance to consider, she had grabbed my arm. 'Certainly not. Let's go, Gwenda.'

More welcome was the invitation to the USS *Finch*, in dry dock in Pearl Harbor. The men had read about us in the paper, and said that while they couldn't offer us work they would be happy to treat us to a night out. We dressed up in our glad rags, and two cars came to collect us. The married officers had gone home to their quarters, and we had the ship more or less to our-selves with the bachelors. There was as much steak as we could eat, then we had coffee and talked and talked. They wanted to show us round, and we almost broke our necks in our high heels on the ladders. As there was no alcohol on the ship, we went for a drink afterwards to the officers' club at Hickam Air Base, more sumptuous than any hotel we had seen.

They dropped us back at the guest-house just after midnight.

'Didn't they all look super in their uniforms,' I said.

The others nodded, dreamily.

It was hard to believe that it was Christmas. Coloured lights winked in the shops, and little Christmas trees adorned the lamp-posts. One night we were visited by barefoot carol singers.

We went to Midnight Mass at Honolulu Cathedral, and Marcia and Celia went to a Catholic service. The choir sang beautifully, and for the first time it did feel Christmassy, and I thought about everyone at home who would now be getting up on Christmas Day.

In the morning we went straight to Marcia's with gifts for her and Bob, and to help with the dinner. She had bought us each a pinny with a map of the islands on it and a little towel attached to the side to dry our hands on while we were working – it was the handiest thing – and a pair of ivory earrings.

'Marcia, you are so generous. There are five of us and only one of you,' Pat said, but she just shrugged.

'Aw, it's been so peachy having you here. I wish I could take you all with me everywhere we go.'

We all lent a hand preparing the twenty-four-pound turkey, then set off for the beach, where bobbing heads shouted 'Happy Christmas' to each other across the waves.

'We were supposed to be home,' I said to Pat as I dried myself. 'That's three Christmases in a row we've been away.'

'I know, but haven't they all been special, in their own way? Remember how happy everyone was in Cleveland last year. You'd think we'd given them all a thousand pounds.'

'Yes, I wonder where they all are now . . .'

Back at Marcia's, we dressed up in her Hawaiian clothes, put flowers in our hair, and went for cocktails in the top-floor lounge of the Princess Kaiulani Hotel.

'Princess Kaiulani was an amazing woman,' said Marcia, pointing out a picture of her. 'The heir to the Hawaiian throne.'

'Oh yes, I've been reading about her,' said Celia. 'Didn't she travel to England at some point?'

'She was educated there. Her father was a Scot, and the family knew Robert Louis Stevenson, who came to live here. He was very fond of the princess, and knew it would be hard for her to leave the islands. The monarchy was abolished while she was away, and it broke her heart. She came home again, but died very young.'

'Is that her with the peacocks?'

Marcia nodded. 'They say that at the moment of her death, the peacocks in the grounds of her estate began to screech and nothing would make them stop. Her father had to have them shot.'

White clouds fuzzed up over Diamond Head, but the sky behind us was flat and blue. Cars droned by on the road below, quieter than usual.

Back at Marcia's, we opened a bottle of champagne and toasted our hosts and everyone at home. Bob was making his speciality – a pear and cream cheese salad – which we ate with the turkey. That night we sat and watched television, and for once didn't moan about it. The film showing was *A Christmas Carol*, and we sat and sobbed our way through it.

On Boxing Day I went to pick up the Muratas from the airport, and to thank them for the loan of their car.

'Don't you want to stay and see more now?' teased David, tall and lean, with thick dark eyebrows and twinkling eyes. 'There are more islands, you know.'

'It's going to break our hearts leaving here,' I replied.

In the Banyan Court that night, we met three British boys from the RAF. They were stationed on Christmas Island, and overjoyed to be in 'Lulu' on leave.

'You're five plucky ladies,' said Johnny.

They told us about weapon-testing near the island, and how they all had to turn away.

'They made us cover our eyes but we could still see the flash,' said Philip. 'It seemed to go right through you. Then we were allowed to look, and there was this great big cloud, so perfect, but sinister at the same time.'

'Told us we were a part of history. Say, anyone fancy a dance?' asked Bert.

Marcia drove us to the airport, and insisted on waiting with us even though the flight was two hours late. Joan Nakamura turned up with her sister, and put *leis* of mauve orchids round our necks.

'I think you'll all be back one day,' she said, smiling. Grace Murata had said the same thing that morning when she popped round to wish us well.

Marcia hugged us all as we left her, and presented us with another *lei* each. A child walked past wearing one made with sweets and chewing gum.

'If you are leaving here by ship, they say that if you throw your *lei* into the water and it floats back to the shore, then you'll return to Hawaii.'

'Perhaps you could come and see us in Los Angeles first,' suggested Molly.

Marcia smiled and shrugged. 'We'll see.'

As I looked out of the plane window and saw miles of ocean trembling before us, Hawaii already seemed like a dream.

We all agreed that we were going to miss Marcia.

10

Fit for a Star

Los Angeles, California, December 1958–June 1959

Just off Sunset Boulevard, on our way to the library in Beverly Hills, we came across a camera crew at work and pulled over. A couple of men in suits and trilbies were standing together, talking and smoking. It was hard to tell if they were actors or on the production team. Another man, in shirtsleeves, leafed through pages on a clipboard and shouted out to someone else, who may have been the director. A woman appeared to be dusting a flight of steps. Two huge lights cast a strange, other-worldly glow on the street.

Three policemen were standing on the corner. One of them came to the car window and told us we could get out and watch if we were quiet. I thanked him, and moved forward a few yards to park. As I did so, Flatus made the most peculiar roar, like a lovesick dragon, and everybody looked in our direction with horrified expressions. Red-faced, and trying not to laugh, we got out as quietly as we could and went to stand by the policemen. One of them raised his eyebrows and made a tutting sound, though he smiled as well.

Suddenly, everyone went quiet. Someone called, 'Action!' and we noticed a blue Cadillac that had been parked at the far end of the street beginning to move closer. It stopped in front of an apartment, an actor got out, walked up the polished steps and opened the front door.

'Is he famous?' whispered Maureen, between takes.

An electrician looked us up and down as if we might not be human, before saying, '*That's* Henry Fonda.'

We nodded wisely, as if we'd known all along.

'I'm sorry about the car – she doesn't usually behave like that,' I offered by way of appeasement.

'Don't worry, we'll send you the bill,' he replied.

After we had watched this scene several times, then watched Fonda leave the apartment and retrace his steps to the car even more times, we decided that acting wasn't all it was cracked up to be, and slipped quietly away.

The stout woman who stamped our books was unimpressed by what we had seen.

'They were always filming on my road when I was growing up,' she said, looking at us over the top of her stern spectacles. 'Drove my folks crazy. But we kids got roped in as extras. Got paid for it, too. I sometimes think I've been in more movies than Charlie Chaplin.'

We looked at her with new respect.

We were regular visitors to the library. Working at night, on private duty, I often had little to do except sit by my patients as they slept. Reading kept me awake, and stopped me from dying of boredom. Some of the other private nurses curled up in a blanket and went to sleep, but I couldn't have done that while I was on duty. I reflected that they were probably married, with children, and were far more in need of sleep than I was.

We lived where Hollywood rubbed shoulders with Beverly Hills, in an apartment with a shared pool just off Sunset Boulevard, at the top of La Cienega. Those neighbouring blocks of Sunset, with their restaurants, bars and clubs and constant, preening procession of cars, made up what was known as the Strip. Our windows looked out on to the back of Dino's, Dean Martin's restaurant, and we often saw the chefs eating and smoking on the balcony when they weren't busy. If we looked the other way, the city of Los Angeles was spread out below us, disappearing into the haze. In the right light, the smog sometimes gave the place an ethereal sort of beauty.

There seemed to be studios on every corner.

'Not actresses, are you?' asked the man at the gas station. 'We've enough of them already. And most of them are waiting tables.' He pointed at the young lad working alongside him. 'There's another. Thinks he'll be the next Jimmy Dean.' He snorted. 'Course, they say the future's TV these days. Give me the movies any day.'

We had to agree.

Celia saw Yul Brynner in the street, and Molly came home all excited one day because Mr Magoo – or at least a man who had something to do with the hopelessly near-sighted cartoon character – was on her ward at La Brea.

'Better be careful he doesn't mistake you for his wife,' said Celia, picking up a box of Cornflakes and squinting at it.

One day he was allowed out to sign a contract and never came back.

Pat nursed a film producer at the vast Queen of Angels Hospital where she had become a regular, and said that he was the most nervy man she had ever come across.

'Hopeless as a person,' she said despairingly, 'like top people often are.'

Once again we had persuaded our landlord to allow five of us to stay in a one-bedroomed apartment, explaining that as we all worked different shifts, we would rarely be there at the same time. It was expensive but we needed to be somewhere central, and we liked to be able to say we lived in Hollywood.

The A1 Nurses Registry had signed us up straight away. We had to pay them 10 per cent of our earnings, but we were still making more than we had ever made in our lives.

I suppose money was the main reason for staying put in the City of Angels. Other cities were nicer – San Francisco, for example, and Denver. Other hospitals were more welcoming – the staff in Helena had been like family to us. Not that they were unfriendly here – we were treated kindly almost everywhere we went – but it was harder to forge lasting relationships on private duty, and I, for one, was moving around constantly between different workplaces.

Our prime motivation now was to make enough money to get us to New Orleans for Mardi Gras. Driving more than halfway across America for a few days then driving all the way back to start earning again for our final trip was a crazy idea, really. Perhaps LA was inching its way into our hearts, after all.

Olov had come to meet us off the plane from Hawaii, while Molly's Aunt Meg was waiting to whisk her away. Jean and Joyce, her teenage cousins, skipped impatiently from one foot to the other as we said our goodbyes. We all felt rather emotional at the thought of being parted for a few days.

Olov let me drive his car, a 1958 Ford Skyliner, which had a roof which opened and closed at the push of a button. I had never seen so much traffic. Every major carriageway was at least four lanes wide in each direction. Los Angeles was alive with cars, as if *they* were the life force of the city, and the buildings and people just accessories to them.

It was wonderful to see Joan again. At first sight she appeared slightly less girlish, her hair more carefully styled, as if she had grown into whatever a married woman was supposed to grow into, but once we got talking we were soon giggling like old times. She was clearly happy, and she enjoyed her job at a nearby hospital. She had stacked our Christmas cards and presents from home into neat piles, and we all admired each other's scarves and stockings and initialled handkerchiefs, as well as Pat's twinset. We had some surprises, too – a card from the post office workers in Denver being the least expected, and a very welcome cheque for ten dollars from Mrs Reid in Helena.

We were up early on New Year's Day to go to Pasadena for the Tournament of Roses Parade. Anyone with a bit of wall space was selling a seat for four dollars and some people had been there all night, but we managed to find a good place to stand. The day was warm and sunny, the palm trees fluttered gracefully in the breeze and the crowd was happy.

I remembered a parade in Cleveland for Flag Day, where we had witnessed the participants walking out of step, chatting and chewing gum, in a way that had made me nostalgic for the sedateness of a London ceremony. But this parade was sheer theatre, and like nothing we had seen before. Every inch of every float was covered in fresh flowers – even the wheels managed to look beautiful – and their violent perfume made the air throb.

Immaculately dressed film and television stars waved at us as they passed. We recognized Roy Rogers and Hopalong Cassidy, but a lot of the faces were unfamiliar. When great cries erupted from the crowd for an ordinary-looking man with a pot belly, making little bows first to one side of the road, then the other, we enquired who he might be.

A young girl of about eight or nine screwed up her face in disbelief. 'You don't know him from the TV?' she asked.

'We don't have a TV,' said Celia, and the girl gaped at us, then nudged her mother, to pass on the alarming news.

'I don't think people at home realize how big television is here,' said Pat, as we made slow progress through the crowds to find Olov's car later, 'though it might be going the same way, heaven forbid. Did I tell you that Dad's choir is disbanding, because everyone wants to stay in and watch some programme on a Tuesday night? I'm absolutely flabbergasted.'

We had stayed with Joan and Olov for a few days, before flying to San Francisco to bring back Flatus from where we had left her with friends of friends. On our last night with them, we sat in the darkened room and watched the movie film Joan had taken during her trip home. Her parents popped up in front of us, shooing the camera away with bashful waves of their hands, before coyly pointing out domestic objects as if they were the Crown Jewels. We moved to London, where Joan had caught up with a friend from Mount Sinai. It was a London of smart policemen and double-decker buses. Did London really look like that? I had a strange feeling that I was watching some picture-book England, an England that didn't really exist. The people, in their dark coats and hats, seemed to blend into the buildings behind them.

The screen twinkled with light, and a piece of twirling tape announced the end of the show.

'I feel a bit homesick after that,' admitted Pat.

But Joan said briskly, 'Just remember that most of the time I couldn't take any film because the weather was so awful. I think the sun shone the day I arrived and the day I left. Why doesn't Olie find you some nice American boys so that you can all stay here? What fun we'll have!' She turned to Olov, who was packing up the projector to take back to the hire shop. 'You must know some, darling. Can't you invite them over?'

Olov, wisely, stayed out of the conversation.

Joan had made us a cheesecake for pudding. It was the first time any of us had tried one, and I wondered if anything in the world could be as delicious.

We had everything that we needed in our Hollywood apartment, except for a phone. I rang the telephone exchange to see if we could have one installed, and the woman who answered had an English accent. We started chatting, and before I knew it she had invited all five of us to her apartment for dinner. She also let us have the phone without paying the twenty-five-dollar deposit.

Margery Barzey was blonde and plumpish, a few years our senior. She had come out to the States several years earlier to work for a family in the east – 'sheer drudgery', she sighed. But she had stuck it out for the duration of the contract, before arriving in California, flat broke, and wondering what to do next. An agency found her a job in Beverly Hills, and she ended up as governess to the children of one of the big studio chiefs.

'I had to teach them manners, but they were away at school most of the time, so I was really more of a companion for their mother. I was treated like one of the family, and I met all the stars. It was a wonderful life.'

We asked her why she had left, and she disappeared into her bedroom and came out a few seconds later with a fur coat and two luxurious evening gowns.

'Because it wasn't *my* life,' she said, stroking the coat as she laid it over a chair for us to admire. 'The family bought me these. And many other gifts. When I was with them, everyone treated me like royalty because of who they were. But I knew that if I'd been on my own, no one would have given me a second glance. Now I'm living my own life, and I love it.'

Ella lived 'above the smog line' (we soon realized that nobody lived below it, or confessed to it anyway). She was a snob, opinionated, almost brutal in some of her remarks, yet we got on like a house on fire and I grew fond of her during the few days she was my patient.

Her shrunken torso barely made a rise in the bedclothes. With her little walnut head, topped with smooth white hair, perched on a pillow, she gave the alarming impression of having no body – something dreamed up by the studios, perhaps. But she could talk. Boy, she could talk. It had taken a while to get used to her New York accent, still strong after thirty-odd years on the west coast. She fell asleep talking, woke up talking, and sometimes spoke when I thought she was sleeping, coming out with, 'Did I tell you 'bout when I was in the Bowery in twenny-two, dem folk, I tell you . . .' or, 'You hear about Buddy Holly and Ritchie Valens? Oh, dem poor boys . . .' before dropping off again.

She had a directness that could be disarming. When I asked if I could get her some juice one morning, she barked, 'Juice?

Gemme some cawfee.' I should have been used to it by now, but I still flinched inwardly if somebody didn't say 'please' or 'thank you', those words had been so ingrained into my upbringing.

But she listened, too, and seemed genuinely interested in my family and my travels in America. The fact that I had visited the city of her birth had been a great ice-breaker, and she often spoke to me about New York as if I, too, was a native.

One of her daughters came barging through the door one night.

'Hey, Mom! Sorry I couldn't get here earlier.' She clutched an expensive little fur jacket around her thin shoulders, as if the warm room was freezing, pulled a chair up to the bed and lit a cigarette. 'You must be the agency nurse.'

'She's Gwenda, and she's English. Gwenda, this is Peggy. And don't believe a word she tells you.'

Peggy ignored this remark.

'English. Wow! And where did that name come from? That's a new one on me. Hey, sit down and talk to us.'

Peggy talked almost as much as her mother. She worked as a dancer in a show I hadn't heard of. But her job 'sucked'. Everything sucked.

'You married?' she asked out of the blue.

I laughed and shook my head.

'Oh, aren't you the lucky one. I was happier when I was single. Most of us are, eh, Mom? That's what they don't tell you.'

Her mother had closed her eyes now, deliberately, I suspected.

'Well, gotta go. Someone's waiting.' She winked at me. It was one-thirty in the morning. Her heels clattered down the corridor, then I heard them returning. She put her head round the door and beckoned to me.

'I was supposed to tell Mom, my sister's coming tomorrow. I'll let you give her the news. They don't get on.' She gave a slightly sinister laugh, and disappeared with a wave of her elegant hand.

Weren't Americans funny, I thought, after she had gone. Nobody at home would believe half the things they came out with.

The next night, I found both daughters present. Peggy was standing at the window, smoking.

'Mom's dying.' She paused, her voice trembling slightly. 'Would you believe it? And you were the first nurse she got on with.'

Her sister, Gloria, sat by the bed, her back very straight – perhaps she was a dancer, too – her expression hard to read. Other family members came in over the next few hours to say goodbye. One youngster solemnly handed round chocolates from a box on the bedside table.

'You know I don't eat candy,' snapped Gloria.

Ella died at around three-thirty. I was used to patient deaths, but I was sad to see her go. I combed her hair and put her teeth in. The funeral parlour took care of everything else, and with Jewish patients, we didn't even touch the body. It was all a far cry from last offices back home, where we washed our patients, stuffed all orifices with cotton wool, and wrapped the bodies in a shroud before a porter took them to the morgue.

Slowly, the relatives began to drift away, apart from Peggy, who remained in the position at the window from which she had barely moved all night. I stood beside her, and watched the headlights of a car swooping into the canyon like a great bird, then surfacing again a few seconds later.

'She was a remarkable woman,' I said.

Peggy stubbed out her cigarette into an overflowing ashtray.

'She wasn't much of a mother, you know. Oh, she was quite a character, but she was a selfish woman. We only came out west because she was chasing some fella. That didn't last five minutes. Gloria never forgave her for taking her away from New York. And Mom never forgave us for being more successful than she ever was.'

I tutted in sympathy.

'But she got nicer as she got older. Guess we all do. Hey,' she tapped the pocket of her trousers, then delved into her handbag. 'You said you liked a good show. Got you tickets for mine. There's a couple, if I can only find them.' She frowned. 'Dang! Guess I've left them behind. Maybe next time, huh? Well, it's been good to know you, Gwenda.' And she stuck out her hand rather formally.

I drove to Queen of Angels and sat reading in the car, waiting for Pat to come off duty.

'I've found out why that nun is so bad-tempered,' said Pat as she climbed into Flatus. We had all been shocked when she came back from work, telling us tales of the battleaxe in charge – all of us apart from Maureen, who said she wasn't in the least surprised. 'Apparently she hasn't had a night off for twenty-seven years. Can you imagine it?'

Neither of us could.

I told her about Ella and Peggy, and Pat said, 'It makes me quite grateful for my stable upbringing.'

The luggage rack fell off somewhere close to the Arizona border. Luckily, nobody was behind, and we managed to tie it back on. Arizona was miles and miles of straight desert road, with only cacti to look at. Texas was worse, with nothing but gravel and sand. I thought it would go on for ever. But the people were friendly. We sat and listened to one gas station attendant's life story, before he treated us all to a cup of coffee and a piece of pie.

The girls crocheted as I drove. Sometimes Pat and Molly took over. We stopped to cook our meals – usually ham and eggs bought from shacks at the roadside. Otherwise, we kept on driving.

In Louisiana, the countryside turned to swamp. Trees, dripping with Spanish moss, dotted muddy fields. People were fishing in small boats. The houses didn't look fit to live in. By the time we got to New Orleans, every hotel and motel was full. We were resigned to a night in the car when we tried a guest-house on Canal Street, and they found us a room. We all collapsed into bed.

We were up early to drive to the docks the next day, and saw a banana boat unloading in the fog. After that, we walked around Le Vieux Carré and found it charming but dirty, with litter blowing everywhere. We headed to the famous Antoine's for dinner, but there was a huge queue. There was a queue outside most of the French restaurants, but we finally found one that wasn't too busy and had a tasty Creole dish before watching our first parade. We all agreed that it was disappointing after the Tournament of Roses, though the atmosphere on the streets almost made up for it. Torch-bearers walked beside every float, and the people on them threw necklaces and little favours to the crowd, which we all leapt to catch.

On Shrove Tuesday, we got up at sunrise and put on our fancy-dress costumes. Molly wore ski pyjamas, Celia had pinned little flags to her clothes, Maureen was Dick Whittington, and Pat and I were in pyjama suits and straw hats. The streets were quiet, and we didn't see anybody else dressed up. Feeling rather foolish, we headed for the Café du Monde, thinking that things might liven up after breakfast. We were about to go inside when Pat announced that she wanted to go back to the guest-house.

'Look at us. We're a laughing stock,' she muttered, when I asked her why.

Molly agreed, and said perhaps we should all go back to get changed first, and I was beginning to waver, too, when Maureen put her foot down.

'We've come all this way,' she said. 'Who cares what anyone thinks? We haven't exactly worried about it up until now.'

Her argument seemed to do the trick, and we all followed her inside. Unfortunately, the service was pretty bad and the croissants weren't very French, which didn't help anyone's mood, but at least by the time we left, small crowds were starting to assemble on the streets.

Pat still insisted on going back to change.

'But look, there's Pocahontas! And that one looks like a flapper girl. Oh, why didn't we think of that?' I said, trying to lift her spirits.

She remained unimpressed.

Someone pointed to Maureen and said, 'Oh my, it's Robin Hood!'

Pat rolled her eyes.

'Well, I don't suppose they've heard of Dick Whittington,' said Maureen, shrugging.

Our attempts to cheer up Pat were going down like a lead balloon, and we all trailed back to the guest-house with her. When she said that she'd like to stay behind on her own, I decided that she must be unwell, though she brushed off our concerns. We had just agreed on a time to come back for her, and were going out the door, when she changed her mind and said she was coming after all, so off we trooped, just missing the Zulu Parade.

As the afternoon wore on, the costumes of the crowd became more colourful and outrageous, and the big parade put smiles on all our faces. Later, we had a siesta, then met a group of South

African boys doing a tour like us, and spent the evening with them. It poured with rain for the last parade, but Pat was happy and laughing again, and nobody cared about the weather.

In a bend on the Mississippi, as it makes its lazy way down to the Gulf of Mexico, stands a former sugar plantation, home to a leprosy hospital called Carville. As part of our tropical diseases training, Pat and I had spent three-week stints at Jordan, the hospital for leprosy in Redhill, Surrey. Leprosy was now known as Hansen's disease but old habits were hard to break and most of our patients still called it by its former name, including Mac, who we used to take on outings, and still kept in touch with. While we were at Jordan we had come across the *Star*, a paper published by Carville patients and sent all over the globe, and it had been a dream that we might visit the hospital one day.

We were warmly welcomed at Carville by Pete, the patient-guide, a young man probably in his late twenties. He wanted to show us everything, and we were amazed at what there was to see. Carville was more like a small town than a hospital, with its own chapels and churches, shops, school and library, and even a golf course and softball park.

Pete led us down long covered corridors that linked different hospital buildings, providing shelter from the sun or the rain. He chatted as he walked, and told us about their Mardi Gras celebrations the day before. An old woman coming the other way, propelling herself in a wheelchair, thrust her ruined hand at us as if she were offering it for our inspection. She only wanted us to shake it, and when we did, and greeted her warmly, she nodded happily and carried on. The sun came out from behind a cloud and filled the air with golden light, casting shadows of the arched windows at our feet. But then the ringing of a bicycle bell on the corner ahead shook me, reminding me of the bells the lepers carried in biblical times, and for a second I shivered and felt the presence of all who had walked these corridors before.

We spoke to one old man who told us about the first patients at the hospital. 'They brought them at dead of night, up the Mississippi, on a coal barge, 'cause no one else would take them. No one wanted anything to do with them. It wasn't just the poor either.' He shook his head grimly. 'There's one lady here, came from high society, she did. Her family had all these plans for her, she was at every party, she even had a rich husband lined up. Then she got the leprosy. They never told her friends where she went.'

Another patient happily told us that the drugs they had been using had worked so well for her that she was preparing to leave.

'Sometimes we go out dancing,' said Pete, his eyes twinkling. 'Though we don't usually tell folks where we're from.'

In the peaceful graveyard, matching white headstones were neatly lined up under massive oak trees. The information on many of them was sparse, a reminder that though times were happier now, some patients had gone to their graves under false names, abandoned by the people they loved.

'It's home,' said Pete, shrugging. 'We had a new doctor came here, said that those of us whose conditions were arrested should leave, but a lot of folk didn't want to go. What did they have to go back to? This was all they knew. Now, those who want to can stay.'

We met the crusading Stanley Stein, founder and editor of the *Star*, who was blind as a result of the disease, and had our photos taken for the next issue. And before we left we had highballs with Dr Meyer, the medical director, a fine man who had spoken out against the compulsory isolation of Hansen's disease patients.

As we left, the heavens opened and the white plantation house was lit up by an electrical storm. Maureen shuddered. 'I'm just thinking what it must have been like for those first patients sixty years ago. The house looks quite creepy now.'

'It's a disease of ignorance more than anything,' said Pat as we drove away, the road before us already swimming with water. 'Hansen's disease is almost impossible to catch.'

'I'm so glad that we went,' said Celia. 'I've learned such a lot. Thank you both for taking us.'

'Did you see how pleased that old lady was when we shook her hand?' said Maureen. 'I really felt that it was worth going just to see her face.'

I remembered something that had happened at Jordan, and couldn't help smiling as I told the others. 'One of the patients was Indian, and he was making chapatis. They encourage them to live independently, you see, very like Carville. Well, have you ever seen the way they make them – tossing them from one palm to another? The trouble was, he'd also just murdered some poor chicken, and his hands were dripping with blood. When he offered me a chapati, what could I do? If I refused, it would seem as if I was snubbing him for having leprosy. If I ate it, well . . .'

'You took one, of course,' said Celia. 'You couldn't offend him.'

'Dead right. I ate some of it, then I disposed of the rest while he wasn't looking. I just didn't fancy the blood that went with it.'

The rain continued all night. We had planned a scenic route back to California, but in Oklahoma the rain turned to snow and there was nothing to see. New Mexico and Arizona were freezing, the Painted Desert and Petrified Forest obscured by blizzards. Plans to carry on to the Grand Canyon, Las Vegas and Death Valley were abandoned when a lady warned us that the roads were almost impassable. We turned back for LA and crawled home.

It was a relief to get back to the apartment, to switch on the heaters and run a hot bath. I was first for a soak, and when I lay back and closed my eyes I felt as if I were driving still, and could see the road like a conveyor belt rushing towards me. I snapped out of my trance when someone shrieked, a babble of voices all started up at once, and Molly burst into the bathroom. This wasn't too unusual, as the bath was blocked in with a coloured-glass screen and door, which was handy when two of us needed to use the bathroom at the same time.

'You won't believe it! Enrique's getting married!'

'I think I must have had soap in my ears then. I thought you said that Enrique was getting married.'

Molly flung open the screen door and waved a piece of paper in my face.

'He certainly is, and he's full of it. She's called Barbara. And she's English! I always thought he had a soft spot for an English accent. She's from London, though, so more like Maureen, I suppose. Now, what else does he say . . .' She paused for a few seconds. 'Here we are . . . she didn't arrive until after we left, and . . .'

I wasn't often speechless, but I think my mouth was probably hanging open then. Was there a tiny bit of resentment, too, to think that our loyal friend might have other priorities in his life now? Perhaps, but I pushed such uncharitable feelings aside. We didn't own Enrique, even if we sometimes thought we did.

Celia called across from the living room, 'I thought you and Pat said he was a diehard bachelor? It sounds as if he's been quite a fast worker.'

'Oh, I do hope she's good enough for him,' I heard Pat say.

Molly had sat down on the closed lid of the lavatory. She carried on reading, loud enough so that we could all hear, though Maureen was now standing at the bathroom door.

'He says she's a very nice girl, and that we'll all like her very much. Well, I'm sure that's right. We've always liked his friends before.'

'When did the public meeting start in here?' I asked. 'It wasn't cold two minutes ago, then there was this almighty breeze . . .'

'You've been in there for ages,' said Molly.

'Didn't Joan Nakamura in Hawaii ask us if we knew a Barbara?' said Maureen. 'Perhaps she knew all about it and assumed we did too. He's been a bit of a dark horse, hasn't he?'

'Well, I think it's lovely news,' called Pat. 'And now we need to decide what to buy him as a wedding present.'

'If you come out now, you can be the first to read Robert Loewe's letter,' said Molly, standing up. 'Here, I've got your towel. My turn.'

Piano-playing Robert was 'living like a bum' in Spain, he wrote, and had no plans to leave just yet. I wondered if he'd met someone, too. And there was another wedding: Bunty told us that she and Alex had set a date, and would be moving to California soon. She also passed on the sad news that Miss Harrison, our director of nursing from Mount Sinai, was very ill.

I thought longingly of the old days in Cleveland, and wondered who of the old gang would still be there when we eventually returned.

I had started to think again about the mink stole I had promised my mother. If I was to buy one anywhere, Los Angeles was the place to buy it. I decided not to take another night off, and to see how much money I could make. Our policy was six shifts a week for the kitty, and anything else was our own to keep.

We were living quietly. We didn't go sightseeing, as someone was always working and we didn't want to do anything without them. Any spare time was spent reading, crocheting, or trying out new recipes. I had picked up a shop-soiled copy of *The Joy of Cooking* for two dollars fifty, almost half price, and in it discovered many of the recipes that friends had cooked for us over the past couple of years. The Farmers' Market, a few blocks away, sold all the ingredients we needed.

The odd excitement broke the calm. One evening we looked out of the window to see Dr and Mrs Cashmore, our friends from Helena, Montana, on the pavement below. We were delighted that they should take the trouble to pay us a visit. They brought a letter from Mrs Reid, asking if we could go back to St Peter's Hospital for the summer. We told the doctor and his wife that we would think about it, though I'm sure they could tell by looking at us that a return was unlikely.

On another evening we invited Margery Barzey for dinner, and she arrived positively buzzing about a series of ghost stories she and some friends had written for television.

'If I get the green light, fingers crossed – and better cross your toes as well – I'll treat you all to a night on the town. Where shall we go?'

Pat and I went to a store on Wilshire Boulevard and bought Enrique's wedding present. It was a pair of candelabra in sterling silver that could also be screwed together to make one big piece. They cost ninety dollars, and we could hardly believe we had spent so much of our precious money on a gift. Molly and Maureen thought they were lovely, though Celia confirmed our doubts and asked us if living in LA had made us go a bit doolally.

I took Pat with me for moral support when I went to look at furs.

'Are you sure they'll let us in here?' Pat looked at me, then down at her own shorts and T-shirt. The shop window was lined with mannequins wearing very expensive coats.

We should have dressed up a bit, I could see that now, but we were here. I took a deep breath. 'This is America, remember. Anything goes.'

The lady who showed us to the salon was charming, in a severe sort of way. I tried to tell her that I only wanted to look through a rack of mink stoles to find one that I liked – and could afford – but she wasn't really listening. She told us to make ourselves comfortable and let them do all the hard work, and disappeared to fetch us both an iced tea. I shivered in the fierce air-conditioning – a hot drink would have been more welcome – and looked deliberately around me, everywhere but at Pat.

'What are we doing here?' Pat barely opened her lips. 'You won't be able to afford anything in this place. Let's scarper.'

But already two very tall and very attractive girls were sashaying towards us. One of them wore a full-length fur, the other a neat jacket which I knew my mother would love.

'How much is this one?' I managed to croak, as the one in the jacket stood right in front of me, a hand on one hip. The manager had now returned with our drinks, and it was she who told me the price. I heard Pat splutter.

It didn't get any better. I began to feel despondent. All those extra shifts and my goal still seemed unreachable. I thought of all the money we had spent on travelling, on having fun, on Flatus, and I couldn't help feeling guilty. Surely I could have put a little bit away from time to time?

Then, finally, one of the girls appeared in a mink stole, and I knew it was the one. It was expensive, but if I carried on working seven days a week . . . Well, I had set my heart on it anyway. I asked the manager if she could keep it for me for a couple of weeks, and to my surprise she agreed. I made Pat swear she wouldn't tell Celia about it.

When I got home, I rang the A1 Registry and asked them to find me double shifts from now on.

Driving along the Strip the day before Easter Sunday, a car sat on my bumper all the way home. Whenever we stopped at lights I could see the driver craning forward, his face almost touching his windscreen. I eventually realized that he was trying to read the stickers on the back of Flatus, of which there was quite a collection after our many months on the road. I couldn't help thinking that he looked remarkably like Gary Cooper.

The next day we walked to Beverly Boulevard for the Beverly Hills Easter Parade, where film and television stars drove by in white Cadillacs, accompanied by crippled children from the Shriners Hospital.

'There he is! It *was* Gary Cooper!' I cried to the others, as I saw him leading the parade. 'Oh, doesn't he look like a nice ordinary chap.'

Los Angeles was beautiful in the spring. Pink and white geraniums grew like weeds at the roadside, and the grass was such a shiny green, it hardly looked real.

It was the hottest 1 April on record, according to the radio, and after having our apartment swimming pool to ourselves in the winter months we were now often joined by other residents. We felt quite resentful having to share it.

Bunty and her new husband, Alex, came to stay for a couple of nights. Bunty surveyed our living room from the front door. 'Well, darlings, this all looks rather familiar.'

It had begun to take on the appearance of a warehouse, ever since we had discovered Lynn's discount house and started going mad on the three-dollar dresses there, as well as presents to take home.

We tried out a new recipe for our visitors, baked ham in a spiced sauce, and invited Joan and Olov to join us. A few days later, Bunty wrote from their new home in San Francisco, thanking us for our hospitality. She also said that she was five months pregnant, but hadn't liked to tell us in case we were disgusted. We wrote straight back to say how thrilled we were.

Our last weeks in LA were busy ones, but we managed to squeeze in a visit to Disneyland. We had wondered if it could be quite as 'fabulous' as Americans told us it was, but we weren't disappointed. From the moment we entered, we felt as if we were in another world. Everything we gazed at was perfect, right down to the smooth pavements we walked on and the neat shrubs in the flowerbeds. We were thrilled to fly over London town with Peter Pan, and to narrowly avoid being eaten by a crocodile in Adventureland.

Molly got a pass from a set director who came into the doctor's office where she was working, and we spent a morning in Paramount Studios. We saw one set all ready for filming, and the star, Shirley MacLaine, waved to us and said, 'Hi, girls!' She wore thick make-up and her hair was a strange mixture of red and darker shades.

We couldn't get over how real everything looked. Carpenters were working on a replica hacienda for a Marlon Brando film; even the scratches and bloom on the doors had been painted on, to give the effect of age.

After the tour, we stood for a while looking at a line of cars parked outside the offices, wondering who they might belong to. The guard told us that the really famous Hollywood stars, like Fred Astaire and Gary Cooper, drove old 1949 Studebakers so that nobody bothered to look twice.

'Now that old ramshackle thing on the end . . .' He pointed to Flatus. 'That'll belong to one of our top people. A real character, I'm telling you.'

We all looked at each other, trying to keep a straight face.

'Perhaps it's Shirley MacLaine's?' I suggested.

'Oh, not a lady. That's no lady's car! Nope, I'd say that belongs to a man who don't have to prove nothing to no one. Bob Hope, I guess, or Jerry Lewis. Nobody else'd get away with driving an old wreck like that.'

I sometimes worked from three in the afternoon until seven the next morning, sleeping in the cool of the porch for just a few hours – five or six was a luxury – before getting up to go shopping or back on duty. One day I bought a cheesecake to share, but it was so delicious I kept going back for another slice. Molly found the empty box in the bin later and wouldn't let me live it down.

I had enough to buy the mink stole sooner than I had expected, and broke the news to the others. I was so excited at keeping my promise to my mother, I decided that I didn't care what anyone else said, though I couldn't really blame them for thinking that spending a few hundred dollars on such an unnecessary item was madness after all our careful budgeting. I needn't have worried. Maureen, Molly and Celia all agreed that the stole was lovely, and said my mother would be delighted.

'While we're all together for once, I've got something to tell you, too.' Molly's eyes had filled with tears. My pleasure evaporated and a feeling of dread wound itself into a tight knot inside me.

'Don't all look like that! I'm not dying or anything! It's about the rest of the trip.'

We had decided to travel back to Cleveland via Mexico, visiting first some of the places we had still not been to – Yosemite, Las Vegas and the Grand Canyon. A pile of library books about Mexico sat on the coffee table.

Molly took a deep breath, and said in a teary gabble, 'I've decided not to go back with you all. I'm going to stay behind and work and stay with Aunt Meg for a little longer. They really want to see more of me and—' She broke off and gulped back a small sob.

'Oh, Molly!'

She pulled herself together. 'I'll still get to Cleveland about the same time as you do. That's the plan, anyway. Now, don't try to change my mind because I've been thinking about it for ages. I could do with the money. And don't,' she frowned at us all, 'start me off.'

It was hard to imagine carrying on without her.

'It'll feel like a body part is missing,' said Maureen, to nods from the rest of us.

'Especially in the back seat, with only two of us,' added Celia.

'I'd have thought you'd be happy about that,' said Molly. 'Think of all that extra space.'

The rent was paid until 11 June, so it was countdown until that date. One evening towards the end of May, Ann Carroll, an old friend from the General who had been working in Toronto, arrived at the apartment with three friends. They were in a super new '59 Chevy, which they had hired in Salt Lake City after dropping off a brand new Ford Thunderbird.

'It's just a shame we've got to give it back,' said Ann, as we stood admiring it.

We were all getting ready for work when they arrived, and left them to make themselves at home. The next day we took them to Lynn's, and what a time they had! Two of the girls were from Australia, and on their way to San Francisco to catch a ship home. They insisted they were only going for a couple of Lynn's seventy-cent blouses, but they both went wild and spent nearly all the money they had left. And Molly came back with seven dresses. Ann said she was going to be the best-dressed woman in Scotland.

Ann and her friend May were about to start work at Cedars of Lebanon Hospital and would be moving into the nurses' home, but for a few days the four new arrivals shared our cramped quarters. As the five of us were all on night duty, it worked out well, and our friends thought that being able to wake up and jump straight into a swimming pool was simply the last word.

Parking Flatus one morning, I saw the manager of the apartment block coming towards me. After exchanging pleasantries, he asked how many people were living in number eleven, because he thought he had seen four new faces down at the pool.

I put on my most incredulous expression. 'Do you really think that nine people could fit into an apartment for two?'

He agreed that it was impossible.

We began to pack up. Every time we looked at each other, some-body would start crying and set the rest of us off. 'I wish I was coming with you all!' sobbed Molly, making it even worse. We were sending most of our luggage ahead. A patient's wife in Beverly Hills had given me an unwanted trunk, which I was grateful for. I had done a lot of shopping.

Then one day the trunks had gone, we had cleaned the apart-ment ready for its next occupants and Flatus was packed. Molly's Aunt Meg came to pick her up. Molly said she didn't know why we were all blubbing as she would see us in Cleveland in six weeks' time, then burst into tears herself.

When we had all pulled ourselves together, we gave her a silver charm for her bracelet, a car that looked remarkably like Flatus, and that started her off again. She solemnly presented us with a toy dog – rather like a shorn poodle – that a patient she had been fond of had given her.

'You're to put Sammy in the front of the car with the other mascots,' she commanded. 'You can give him back to me in Cleveland. So, you see, we *will* meet again.'

We shut the front door for the last time, and our Hollywood lives came to an end.

11

Winners and Losers

California to Mexico to Missouri, June–August 1959

Before leaving Los Angeles, we had needed photographs for our Mexican visas. When we heard about the clever contraptions that took passport-size photos while you waited, we just had to try one out. We sat, one at a time, in a little kiosk, put a quarter in the slot and composed ourselves for four flashes. That, at least, was the idea. In reality – having never seen anything like this before – we found it impossible to keep a straight face. Pat was first, and though she started off looking serious, by the time the second flash exploded she was grinning wildly. It was my turn next, and the sound of the others in fits of laughter outside the booth – now whirring and shaking as it prepared to spit out Pat's photos – set me off too. Maureen gave up entirely, and sat back roaring with laughter. Needless to say, the Mexican official wasn't satisfied with any of the pictures and insisted on us having them taken again, at the price of two dollars per person.

Pat sent the rejected photos home, along with some other recent snaps, and her mother wrote back, commenting that Pat looked 'typically American'.

What was typically American? We no longer knew. So many things that would have drawn comment from us when we arrived in the States two years earlier felt normal now.

Men doing the grocery shopping.

People talking about themselves in a way that we would have considered to be 'showing off'.

Hospitals advertising themselves like packets of cereal.

People of all shapes, sizes and ages wearing skimpy clothes on hot days.

'She probably thinks that I look a bit loud,' said Pat. 'Isn't that what we used to say when we first saw men in flowery shirts? But do you know what, I'm going to miss that sight when I get home. Men dress so conservatively there.'

It felt strange without Molly, and we were all subdued at first. It had been the same before whenever one of us was missing, regardless of which one it was – that one absence made a far bigger hole than seemed possible. With five, there was always one person willing to provide what was needed: to put the kettle on, offer to cook tea, lift the mood on the odd occasion when it needed lifting, be sensible when the others were getting carried away with some hare-brained idea. We were like a jigsaw made up of five pieces that fitted together in different patterns at different times, but always fitted perfectly.

Pat and I were going to spend a few days with her Aunt Anne and Uncle Bill in Detroit before returning to Ohio. Of course, they wanted to see Pat again before she left for home. We had sent our trunks to Detroit from Los Angeles, feeling that we had already burdened Enrique with quite enough. The plan was to put Maureen and Celia on the bus to

Cleveland from there. But first, we had a few thousand miles to travel.

In Yosemite National Park we spent our days hiking, swimming and floating down the river on our lilos. One night we saw the famous Firefall, where the burning embers of bark from the red fir pine were tipped over the top of Glacier Point, a ritual started the previous century by a hotel owner and now one of the most popular attractions in the park. As the embers fell three thousand feet into the valley below, it was like watching a molten waterfall.

We had our first glimpse of Las Vegas in the light of the morning, a wobbly outline of towers in the distance that looked as if it might disappear if we blinked. It was too early to go gambling, so we parked in a campsite at Lake Mead, where children were crying because their feet were burning and several people looked as if they were suffering from heatstroke. A hot wind blew across the hostile landscape, like the blast of heat from a furnace. Even the lake was warm.

'Oh, I could just die,' moaned Pat.

'Just think of Ireland – green fields and all that lovely rain,' said Celia.

'I promise I will never complain about waiting for a bus in the cold ever again,' said Pat.

In the evening, we showered, dressed in all our finery, and set off down the smooth wide highway for the great gambling city. Oh, the lights of Las Vegas! I was quite prepared to hate the place, but in truth I had never seen anything like it. I was captivated. We were all captivated. Red and gold, blue and green, pink and yellow . . . lights of all colours flashed on and off, spilled on to the pavements and flickered across our awestruck faces. A neon cowboy waved a hand at us, and smoked a cigarette with the other. A steam train came chuffing out of the side of a building. Hotels and bingo halls and parking lots all shouted out their presence as brashly as any casino.

We parked outside the Golden Nugget and went inside. It was like walking into a fridge. For a few seconds we just stood there, letting the icy air wash over us.

I couldn't get over the intent expressions on the faces of some of the gamblers. They didn't look as if they were enjoying themselves. Some of them were working two machines at the same time with a grim, mechanical rhythm.

Ella, my patient in LA, had given me a 'lucky' dollar before she died, and I had decided to save it for this visit. I used two quarters on a slot machine, lost them both, and changed the rest into nickels, which I tried on another machine. I won a few, carried on playing, and eventually lost them all. Celia and I stood and watched a man feed a one-armed bandit from a bucket full of nickels, one after the other, until the bucket was empty, then wander off, seemingly unperturbed by the small fortune he had just thrown away.

'That machine will explode if it doesn't spill out its jackpot soon,' I said like an expert.

Celia agreed, and after just a couple of tries, one of her nickels did the trick and a cascade of coins tumbled into the tray. She gave us all a dollar each. That made up for the one I had lost, and I decided that was enough gambling for me. I watched Celia for a little longer, then went to see what the others were doing.

Maureen and Pat had gone to the roulette table, where they sat very seriously with their five-cent chips, looking like a pair of seasoned gamblers. The man beside them, who was playing five-dollar chips, grabbed my hand when they got up to leave.

'I've been winning ever since you've stood there,' he said. 'You're my lucky charm. Don't go yet.'

I'd never been one for superstition, but it was quite flattering. After winning again, the man thrust two of the chips into my hand, saying, 'Have a go, and keep what they win!' I told him I'd rather have the ten dollars, but he ignored that remark. I lost, but he won again. I decided to slip away before his fortune began to change.

Pat, Maureen and I wandered off to some of the other casinos, collecting souvenir books of matches and anything else that was free. When we got back to the Golden Nugget, Celia was still attached to a slot machine and in a world of her own.

'A true Irish woman,' said Pat. 'Mind, aren't the Irish supposed to be lucky?'

She was – again – and came away, with some persuasion, three dollars in profit.

We went for a meal before leaving Las Vegas, and the waitress presented us with ashtrays and key rings.

'Come again soon, winners!' she called as we got up to go. 'Everyone's a winner in Lucky Number Grill!'

We walked back to the car, feeling strangely satisfied.

'That place gives you ten dollars to spend as soon as you step in the door,' said Maureen, pointing at a sign across the road.

'Can't we walk in, collect the money, then walk straight out again?' I asked.

'Las Vegas wouldn't make much if everyone was like us,' Pat said. 'Not including you, Celia.'

Not even the sight of the Grand Canyon could fight off our tiredness when we arrived there at five in the afternoon. We shook out our tarpaulin, spread out our sleeping bags and lay down on top of them for a nap. I woke up some time in the night, my arms feeling shivery, and crept inside my bag, noticing that the others had already done the same. After that I didn't stir till morning, when I got up, feeling refreshed, at around seven. There was even a gentle breeze blowing. Eggs and pancakes started the day off nicely, especially when we remembered that we hadn't had our evening meal the day before.

We spent some time in the visitor centre, and decided to take a mule ride down into the canyon the next morning. Walking was not recommended, except for the very fit and those used to arduous climbs, and we supposed, reluctantly, that we didn't quite fit the bill, though I would have liked to try.

Later that day a green MG parked beside us, and the driver turned out to be an Englishman. Peter came from Kent and had been working in New York. He was now on his way to LA, where he hoped to find another job.

'But first I'm going to hike the canyon,' he declared.

When we voiced our concerns, he laughed. 'That's just to stop overweight Yanks thinking they can do it and having to be rescued. A friend of mine walked it, and he's no athlete. I'm sure if I can do it, you all can.'

That was all I needed to change my mind. Celia said she was coming with me, while Pat and Maureen decided to stick with the mules. I couldn't help feeling that if a mule could do the walk, then I could too. I also thought I would feel a lot safer on my own feet.

Peter woke us with a cup of coffee the next morning. He had already lit the fire. We had a good breakfast, then he, Celia and I set off at six, down the Bright Angel Trail, with two sandwiches and two plastic water flasks each. We reached the halfway point, Indian Gardens, at eight, and cooled off in the fountain. It grew hotter as we descended – we had been told that there could be a thirty-degree difference in temperature between the rim of the canyon and the base. It didn't take long to reach the bottom. The Colorado, green and fast, swung its way through steep-sided red and black cliffs.

'Just think,' said Celia, as we cooled our feet in the rushing water, 'we were sailing on this river a year ago. In fact, I'm surprised we're not still on it now.'

We told Peter about Glenwood Springs, and our adventure with Robert in the dinghy.

'You've had some good times here. Aren't you ever tempted to stay?' he asked us.

I looked at Celia, who was smiling into the water. In her face, I saw all the things we had done together over the past fifteen months. In some ways, I thought, it would be easier to stay than to go.

'I love it here, but it's time I went home,' I said finally.

'I'd like to go back and work in LA.' Celia held my gaze for a few seconds. 'I like it there.'

'Might bump into you then,' said Peter. 'Hey, did you see the size of that lizard?'

Whatever Peter had seen had disappeared behind a rock, but I watched a smaller one on the ground beside us dart forward all of a sudden. Something hung from its mouth, like a black bead. It swallowed. Then it was perfectly still.

'It's probably a good job Pat and Maureen aren't here,' said Celia, biting into her sandwich.

A man wearing shorts, a T-shirt and a pair of sneakers walked briskly towards us as we ate our lunch. He stopped to talk for a while, and asked us what we were taking with our water. We told him they were salt tablets, to help replace the salts we were losing in our sweat.

He laughed. 'Sounds like a load of old baloney to me. You know what your best medicine is? The mind.' He tapped his head. 'Did you know that? Not many folks do. There's no such thing as hunger, no such thing as thirst, no such thing as pain, not if you tell that to your brain before it gets to hankering after things it can't have.'

'Actually, we're nurses, and I'm not sure I really agree with that,' I began, but he was already getting to his feet.

'Best to keep moving. Told the wife I'd be back for dinner. It's neat down here, but I must say I prefer the view at the top. Enjoy your day!'

We watched him disappear back along the trail.

'Let's give him a good head start before we set off,' said Peter. 'I don't fancy being stuck with him on the walk back.'

Later that morning we caught up with him. He was sitting on the ground, in the full sun, panting heavily and looking very red.

'My leg's all seized up,' he said as he saw us. He grimaced. 'Like a cramp? And I feel kind of sick.'

He looked quite pathetic. Somehow, we managed not to gloat.

'You're dehydrated,' said Celia. 'Now, drink this, just a few sips to start with. I can't believe you haven't any water with you, and that you're not wearing a hat.'

'You need to get out of this sun first,' said Peter, taking one of his arms. Between us, we managed to yank him up, and found a large rock nearby that offered shade, for the time being at least. He began to feel better, and when we were satisfied that he wasn't in any danger we left him with one of our precious water bottles and carried on to the nearest emergency phone. The cost of the mule rescue service had to be paid by someone on the surface before help would be dispatched.

'My wife's going to kill me for this,' muttered our patient

before we left him. 'She told me I was crazy before I started. If I'd known you were both nurses, well . . .'

Celia rolled her eyes at me over the top of his glowing head.

While we were phoning, we met the people who had taken the mule rides, but there was no sign of Maureen and Pat. Then we heard someone say, 'Gee, I felt really sorry for those two English girls.'

We asked what had happened, and were told that the man in charge had sent them back to hire long-sleeved shirts, then had gone without them.

'Well, what a cheek!' I said, as we continued our ascent. 'Though I suppose they can always go tomorrow.'

It felt hotter than ever, and as we climbed, wearily, back along the trail, I hoped that we hadn't overestimated our capabilities.

'If you ask me, I'd say they saved their money,' said Peter. 'Did you see how saddle-sore those riders were? Must be torture being stuck on the back of one of those things for hours on end.'

The last two miles were particularly hard work, but at last we reached the top. The riders got back at the same time, and they did look fed up and uncomfortable.

We met Pat and Maureen in the grocery store.

'Thank goodness,' they said, rushing over. 'We went to the lookout building to see if we could see you, and saw a mule rider setting off with a spare mule. We hoped it wouldn't be for one of you. Oh, this is Eddie.' Maureen took the arm of the boyish-faced fellow behind them. 'He's just started work at the hotel here.'

Our camp-fire was enlivened by our new friends. Eddie, who came from Chelsea, had been at sea for ten years and wanted to spend some time on dry land. With his sailors' songs and Peter's Cockney repertoire, we had an even more raucous sing-song than usual, aided by the bottle of port that Peter produced. It was after one in the morning when Eddie looked at his watch and groaned, saying he started work at five.

I could get used to this, I thought, as I awoke once again to coffee at my side, and the sight of Peter crouched over the fire. Later, he drove Pat and Maureen to the airfield in the MG, as they had decided to take a flight over the canyon rather than brave the mules. They came back enthusing over the sweeping view and the colours of the rocks, though it had been rather rough.

We decided to leave that night, and spent the rest of the day packing, and lazing around with our new friends. Peter had a portable gramophone, and we played his new Harry Belafonte record over and over again.

Peter decided that he would head off at the same time as us, and we gave him Molly's and Ann's addresses in LA. Eddie, who had fitted in with the crowd right from the start, said he didn't know what he would do without us.

We gave Peter a push start and travelled together until he took a road headed west, while we carried on in the direction of Phoenix and the Mexican border.

We stopped in Phoenix at the home of Florence and Lloyd Langer, a couple we had met briefly in the Grand Tetons, and who, it seemed, had been awaiting our arrival ever since. There we stayed in air-conditioned luxury, dashing between house and car, and one day braving the savage heat to witness cacti blooming on the edge of town after an unexpected shower. Their dog, JinJa, was treated like a child, and sat with us at the table for meals, his bowl and plate set out before him.

A few days later, we were driving through the Mexican desert state of Sonora. If we had thought we might be used to the heat by now, we were wrong. At one point, the temperature was one hundred and thirty degrees. Grass shacks and simple shelters made of sticks, topped with thatched roofs, were the main dwellings in some places. People were washing in what appeared to be pools of dirty rainwater, yet they all looked clean. Some of them smiled and waved to us. For a long time, the only things we saw growing were cacti, and low trees and bushes that dotted the scrub. Then, to our surprise, the land would be cultivated, with cotton and other crops.

Often our way was obstructed by bony cattle, and mules piled high with firewood or pots and pans. Their owners always seemed most cheery when we passed them, or perhaps it was just the sight of Flatus that put a smile on everyone's face. Our rusty old car both looked and sounded as if she might fall apart at any moment, though even more eye-catching was the roof, with our trusty antlers still pointing forward and the luggage piled precariously on top.

We had never felt so thirsty. We stopped at one place advertising Coca-Cola and drank two king-size Cokes, then, when that didn't quench our thirst, followed it with five glasses of water.

With the heat came insects, bigger than we had ever seen and more numerous. At one stop for petrol and cold drinks, I was practising my Spanish with the attendant when I heard Pat knocking frantically on the car window. She opened it a chink, and said through gritted teeth, 'Behind you!'

She was pointing at the biggest, ghastliest bug I had ever seen – about three inches in length and three-quarters of an inch wide – crawling along the ground towards me. Celia had stood on something a fraction of the size once, in Bob and Mary Ann's garage, and it had made the most awful crunching noise. I could no sooner have done anything to this creature than murder a small animal.

Suddenly, it produced a pair of enormous wings, and its lumbering body took to the air. I could hardly believe that anything this size could fly. I screamed and ducked, feeling it brush against my hair. It landed with a crunch on the car windscreen. Pat and Maureen's faces were like something from a horror film, their mouths open in silent screams, pinned to their seats as if being sucked backwards by some powerful force. They wouldn't come out of the car, even though they were being boiled alive inside.

We crossed the Tropic of Cancer during the night, and when daylight came the scenery had changed to banana plantations. Papayas and pineapples also grew at the roadside. The thick, damp air wrapped itself around us and sapped our energy.

Later, we began to climb. Up we went, into countryside that reminded me and Pat of the Lake District. The hillsides were bright green, interlaced with little stone walls, and when it began to rain we felt quite at home. The air was now delightfully cool. Towns became more frequent and more Spanish in character.

We arrived in Guadalajara at midday, found a hotel and slept for sixteen hours.

We spent a few days in the city and visited the surrounding villages. We bargained in the markets, ate tree-ripened bananas and exotic fruit, and wherever we went, children gathered round us. We visited sumptuous churches – even the smallest village had one – and sat beside fountains in the squares, watching the old men greet each other as they watched the world go by.

'Don't those little girls look beautiful,' said Maureen. 'I wonder if English children are as appealing to Mexican eyes as their children are to us.' One of them, who allowed us to take her picture, was no older than seven or eight and carried her brother or sister on her back, wrapped in her *serape*. A shock of dark hair was all that was visible of the baby.

'I do worry about those little ones suffocating,' said Celia. 'But isn't it marvellous, keeping the hands free like that.'

We practised our Spanish on the children and found that we could converse a little with them, though their giggling and shyness kept the conversations short.

All the people seemed so contented with their lot. In one village, a man who spoke good English told us that as long as he had what he needed, he wouldn't cross the road for a million dollars. I thought his words had the beauty of a piece of poetry, and stored them away in my memory.

The night before we left Guadalajara, there was a terrific noise at the window, as if someone was throwing pebbles to attract our attention. It turned out to be hailstones, the diameter of sixpences, clattering down from the sky. We watched from the window as the water on the street rose to cover both pavements, then rushed away in a brown torrent. In a few minutes, our room was flooded. We moved all our belongings on to the beds, and mopped the floor with sheets and towels. We all stripped down to our underwear, except for Maureen, who had visions of us being rescued from the rooftop and kept her skirt on so that she wouldn't be seen in her knickers. The lights went out and we were quite scared, but the manager came along and gave us a candle and told us that it wasn't unusual. The rain finally stopped and we were able to go to bed, minus any bedding.

We left Guadalajara on a smooth, surfaced road, then discovered that it was the wrong one. Looking at the map, we could see that it eventually joined the road we wanted, so we decided to stay on it. All went well for a few miles until we reached a tiny village, where it turned into a deeply rutted track. Up and down we went. We worried that Flatus wasn't up to such rough terrain, and that the luggage might fall off the roof. It was a relief to make it out the other end, and to see a decent road beneath us again, but each successive village was worse than the one before.

At the approach to one tiny place, we started to cross a narrow bridge, only to find a donkey, half a dozen hens and a bus coming towards us. There was nothing to do but reverse, and when the bus drew level, the grinning driver pointed to something behind me. It was a traffic light. I hadn't seen one for so long, I had just driven through a red light.

We came to Guanajuato, an old colonial town, famous for its well-preserved mummies. Having read about this attraction, we expected to see a signpost for it, but there didn't seem to be any. The town's streets were narrow, cobbled and twisting, with high walls on either side, so that it became easy to lose all sense of direction. After driving round in circles for a while, we asked a group of boys in a square if they could point the way. They babbled something back at us and waved their arms.

'Did anyone get that?' I asked.

'I think they want to come with us and show us. They'll want paying, no doubt.'

'We've never been defeated yet. Let's have another go. I think one of them said something about *derecho*, or was it *derecha* . . .'

We set off and, after a few twists and turns, ended up back in the same square, where the same boys found our return highly amusing. With their big dark eyes and flashing grins, it was hard not to laugh with them.

We saw a car that looked as if it was full of tourists, and all got lost together in another part of the town. One of the passengers got out of this car to ask for directions. He was wearing a police uniform. Whether it was out of fear or respect, he was given what appeared to be very precise instructions, and he indicated that we should follow him. We left the town and climbed up a hill to a cemetery, picking up another lost party on the way.

Hanging around the cemetery were the usual groups of youngsters, offering to keep an eye on the car in exchange for a few coins. One young lad, probably about ten years old and the leader of his group, walked round Flatus, appraising her.

'*Muy pobre*,' he said finally, shaking his head in disappointment.

I folded my arms in mock anger. 'She might be *muy pobre*,' I replied, 'but *muy largo*.' I stretched out my arms as wide as they would go. 'The journey. Er, *el viaje. Largo*.' I pointed to the north, or where I thought north might be. 'Alaska,' I said. I pointed to the middle distance. 'California. *Aquí*.' I pointed to the ground.

My mixture of stilted Spanish and sign language seemed to do the trick. The boy smiled and nodded eagerly, '*Ay, muy largo! Sí, claro*.' He spoke to his cronies, and I caught the words '*Estados Unidos*'. They all looked at Flatus with a little more respect.

Pat didn't want to go down into the vault, but the three of us went to see what was quite a gory sight. The mummies were all standing up, pleading at us with their gaping jaws and cavernous eye sockets. Some of them were fully clothed; others were naked, with jutting shoulders and hips and shrunken torsos. A child clutched a doll, and another was dressed up like some macabre angel. In a corner of the rather smelly tomb was a pile of skulls and bones which hadn't survived the mummification. We were glad to get back into the daylight.

We put our sleeping bags down at the roadside that night because it was too hot to stay in the car, and awoke the next morning to find ourselves in the middle of a market. Around us were stalls selling baskets, clothes and piles of crockery. A small boy stood close by, solemnly wafting a palm wand over a display of cut fruit to keep the flies away.

Seeing us stirring, heads turned and there was much chatter and activity. The boy was pushed forward and shyly offered us a plate of his fruit, which we felt obliged to eat in spite of the flies. Then, when we were ready to go, they quickly – and with little fuss – made a space for us to drive away.

We were all touched by these small kindnesses. Earlier in our Mexican journey, two men in a passing truck had stopped to help us change a tyre at the roadside, refusing to accept any payment. And a garage owner had gone to great lengths to find a couple of cheap retreads for us. Yet Ella in Los Angeles had more or less begged me not to go to Mexico. We would be knifed, she said, or robbed at gunpoint, or at the very least the car would be broken into. Would she have believed me if I had told her that Flatus no longer locked, that the passenger door did not even close properly – we had to fasten it shut with a piece of rope – and yet we had not lost so much as a sticker from one of the windows?

In the late afternoon we reached Mexico City. We found a hotel that we liked the look of, and the kind man on the desk lowered the price to one hundred and twenty pesos for each double room, but it was still a bit much for our budget.

'*No mucho dinero*,' I said, shrugging, as we made our way to the door.

'*Ah, estudiantes?*'

'Actually, no, *enfermas*,' I said.

He looked at us with concern. 'You are sick?' he asked in perfect English.

'Sick? No. Oh, I see, not *enfermas*,' I laughed. '*Enfermeras*? We are nurses.'

'Ah, nurses. Of course.'

He gave us the rooms for sixty-five pesos instead.

'I'm not sure I like to admit to being a nurse these days,' said Pat, taking a look at herself in the mirror when he had left us. We had two rooms next to each other, which shared a bath, shower and lavatory. 'Whatever will people think? We look more like a bunch of charladies. Except that I'm sure they look more presentable than we do.'

Celia wanted to rest for a while, which wasn't like her, but the rest of us set off to explore the neighbourhood. We discovered that we were very near the office of Señor Ruiz, a friend of Enrique who was receiving our post for us, but when we got there the office was closed. By now, the smell of food was making us hungry. We went back to see how Celia was feeling, found her revived and took her with us to eat. She and Pat had steaks, and Maureen and I had a spicy Mexican meal with chicken, beans and tortillas.

That night, both Celia and Maureen were violently ill. The next morning, Pat joined them. I could hardly believe that I still felt well, and moved around very cautiously at first, half expecting to have to make a rush for the bathroom. When I realized I was fine, and I had done what I could for the others, I left them to recover, and set off to find Señor Ruiz and do some sightseeing.

Señor Ruiz was a tall, dignified man in a dark suit, who wouldn't have looked out of place with a copy of *The Times* and an umbrella on the Tube. He was most concerned to hear about the others, and told me what medicine I should buy for them. He insisted that we call him if we needed anything, and if he was not there, he said, his staff had been instructed to help.

I quite enjoyed the strange feeling of wandering around on my own, though I didn't like to go too far, and checked on the others at regular intervals. Celia was sitting in a chair, writing, by the late afternoon, and felt well enough to come out to eat, and the other two were much improved and able to read their letters.

Pat's mother said that it had been lovely weather for Race Week – where she had won a nice bag – and that they had been basking in eighty-degree heat. We all groaned in envy at the thought of such pleasant temperatures. And we had a card from Peter, who had arrived safely in Los Angeles and had already been in touch with Molly.

What a beautiful city Mexico City was, with its parks and fountains, old and new buildings bumping into each other, and streets lined with flowers and grassy verges! We took the bus downtown. The traffic raced madly, and the buses didn't even stop properly, with people leaping on and off wherever they fancied. Luckily, the driver noticed we were novices and stopped for us so that we could all get on and off together.

We spent ages looking at the beautiful paintings in the Palace of Fine Arts, then walked past the House of Tiles to the main square, the Zócalo, which housed several historic buildings. We almost got into trouble at the National Palace when Maureen took a picture of the courtyard and inadvertently included some of the military. She thought they would confiscate her film, but they only asked her, politely, not to take any more. We were sight-seeing for eight hours, and got back to our hotel exhausted.

We were getting ready to go out to eat when Pat asked me if I thought Celia looked a bit peaky. 'In fact, I hate to say it, but I really think she looks a bit yellow.'

'Are you sure she isn't just dirty?' I examined my own reflection. I'd never been such a dark brown before. But I realized that I knew what she meant. 'Are you thinking what I'm thinking?'

'Hepatitis. She hasn't been quite herself lately, though you wouldn't know it most of the time. She probably hasn't even noticed herself.'

'Perhaps we should bring it up later.'

I can't remember whose idea it was to go to a bullfight. We had been to markets, museums and galleries, climbed the pyramids at Teotihuacán, seen the Shrine of Our Lady of Guadalupe. I suppose a bullfight felt like another once-in-a-lifetime experience, a rare opportunity not to be turned down.

Summer was the season for novice bullfighters, but there was still a huge crowd in Mexico City's Plaza de Toros. The band played, the atmosphere was electric. We paid a few pesos for cheap seats in the sun and sat back. I felt a bit jittery, not knowing quite what to expect.

The matador and some minor toreros came on first, teasing the bull with their capes, before leaving the ring for the grand entrance of the picadors. They sat on padded horses and drove lances into the bull's neck, making the blood gush down his back. The bull, angered now, tried to gore one of the horses.

'I wish he would go for the man instead,' whispered Pat. 'What's the poor horse done wrong?'

A man beside us, who looked rather like Señor Ruiz, explained in English what was happening.

'He is making the bull lower his head. It is safer for the matador that way. He will be watching now, very carefully, to see how the bull behaves.'

Suddenly Maureen burst into tears. 'I don't care about the matador. What about the poor animal?' she sobbed. 'I don't want to see any more.'

Pat took her outside and returned ten minutes later, saying that Maureen was going to wait for us in the street until it was over.

'I can't say I'm enjoying it that much myself,' she added. 'It might be different if the bull at least had a chance. But do look at Celia.'

Celia was clapping her hands and shouting with the crowd, who cried, 'Olé!' with every successful manoeuvre.

After the picadors came more toreros, who thrust barbed sticks into the creature's shoulders. The first bull we saw had grown very weary by this stage, and looked ready to lie down and give up, but then on came the matador in his fine costume, attempting to woo the crowd with some fancy cape-work and tormenting him further, before finishing off the listless beast with a sword.

We stayed for another fight, then, when we could stand it no longer, dragged Celia away with us.

'I'm not ill,' said Celia that night over dinner. 'Certainly not ill enough to see a doctor.'

'You've got some of the symptoms . . . you've said yourself you've been under the weather.' Pat spoke gently. 'If it *is* hepatitis . . .' She trailed off. 'Well, it's best to know.'

'We did eat at some pretty dodgy places on the way down,' I volunteered, wondering what the chances were of all four of us coming down with it. I caught Celia's eye, then looked away. I couldn't bear it. I so wanted to be wrong but I had seen plenty of hepatitis cases, and it was clear to me now that Celia was suffering from the disease.

'We don't have to go to Acapulco,' I added. 'If you don't feel well enough, we could drive straight back to Cleveland. We'll drop you off there before Pat and I go to see her aunt and uncle in Detroit. If we go non-stop, we'll be there before we know it.'

But Celia insisted that we carry on with our plans. So we went to Acapulco. Celia slept a lot, and she certainly wasn't the Celia we all knew and loved, but she still accompanied us on all our outings. I knew she would enjoy La Quebrada, where a man climbed a steep cliff, prayed at a little shrine at the top, then executed a perfect dive into the water below, narrowly missing the overhanging face. It was so brave, and so foolhardy, it gave us all a thrill.

But even Celia knew by now that she needed medical attention, and as she clearly had no intention of being admitted to a Mexican hospital we began to head northwards.

What a time the customs men had at Laredo! The luggage rack was three tiers high and packed solidly, but they insisted that everything come off. We had all bought tequila in Mexico, including some miniature bottles, but were told that miniatures were illegal in Texas and that they would have to be confiscated.

One of the men let me have a swig of mine first, and laughed at my horrified face as I felt it burning inside me.

Maureen had moved into the front with me and Pat, so that Celia could stretch out and sleep on the back seat. When she wasn't sleeping, she sat and gazed out of the window at the scrubby vegetation with blank eyes, though occasionally she joined in our conversations and we almost forgot that she was ill.

After much discussion, she had agreed to go back to Molly in Los Angeles from the next airport. She had wanted to go by Greyhound at first, but we wouldn't hear of it, and we had managed to cobble together the airfare from kitty money and some emergency funds.

We put Celia on a plane in San Antonio. Buying the ticket felt wrong. Everything felt wrong. If we had become accustomed to being four instead of five, it hadn't happened easily, and to see our number diminishing further was heartbreaking. Yet we knew there was no alternative.

Just before she left us, she said, in a voice in which her old enthusiasm was still discernible, 'Remember, we met at the tea-party. All those months ago. When you get back, have a cup of tea for me there!'

We watched her walk away from us and tried our best to be brave. Then, when she had disappeared from view, we all had a good old cry together. This wasn't how our adventure was supposed to end.

'But nothing can spoil our memories,' said Maureen, wiping her eyes. 'I'll always picture five of us when I think about this past year and a half. And Flatus, of course.' And that made us cry even more.

We spent the rest of the day sleeping in the airport TV lounge, before setting off again at night. When we stepped outside, the still, heavy air briefly felt welcome after the chill of the air-conditioned building.

We phoned Molly from a gas station, and were relieved to hear that Celia had arrived safely, was comfortable and would see a doctor the next day.

'She started to feel better as soon as she got here. Says the heat was terrible.' Molly's chirpy voice made me wish we were all together again. 'Don't worry, she'll be fine. Give my love to the girls – and Flatus. Oh, and thanks for sending Pete to us, he's such—' The line hissed and crackled, then went dead.

In the middle of the night, we stopped for petrol. The forecourt of the gas station was black and shiny. It looked as if a thick layer of oil had been spilled and allowed to congeal. But when the attendant came out from the hut to serve us, his bare feet made a crunching sound and something dark and sticky oozed up between his toes. Then the black carpet came to life, ripples crossed its surface and it disintegrated. Now I saw that what had appeared to be a solid mass was, in fact, hundreds – perhaps thousands – of flying cockroaches, now swarming in the air. I had got out of the car to stretch my legs, and one of them flew straight at me, disappeared down the front of my blouse and came out through my sleeve. Pat and Maureen's screams would have woken the whole town if we had been in one. They refused to leave the sanctuary of Flatus, even though they were both desperate to spend a penny.

The man filled the tank, whistling. 'They won't hurt you,' he said, to no one in particular, shaking his head. Then he tapped on the car window with his free hand – making the girls jump and scream again – and repeated it more loudly, wagging his finger at them as if they were naughty children.

I was doing my best to be brave. 'They're enormous!' I said, managing a laugh. 'I've never seen anything like them.'

He gave a leery grin. 'Don't y'all know, everything's bigger in Texas.'

We began to judder violently if I drove faster than thirty miles an hour. We crawled along, not even managing to whip up a breeze. For a while, we seriously considered abandoning Flatus and hiring a car for the rest of the journey. Getting a puncture seemed like the last straw, and we had no option other than to change the wheel for one of the retreads. To our relief, that solved the problem.

Sometimes I slept for only a couple of hours before setting off again, reluctant to stop for long when we were going well. The sooner we got to Detroit, I told myself, the greater the chance that Flatus would make it. I think I drove in a trance for much of the time. Texas became Oklahoma, and then we were crossing the border of Missouri. We saw a sign for St Louis, and all burst into song with 'Meet Me in St Louis'. It seemed to cheer us up. Losing Celia had brought home to us all the fact that our adventure was coming to an end, that real life was about to claim us once more. And while I was excited about my eventual homecoming, something stabbed my insides when I realized that I would probably never be as free again as I was now.

'What's the first thing you're going to do when we get back?' I asked the others, as we drove past flattened cornfields the size of small towns.

'Buy a bottle of Pretty Feet,' said Maureen, quick as a flash. 'I think I could start a new career as a firewalker after going barefoot for so long.'

I caught sight of my face in the rear-view mirror, the whites of my eyes a stark contrast to my brown skin, dust engrained in my hairline.

'We've turned into wild women,' I said. 'Nobody in Cleveland will know us. At least we've got a few days to get human again at Aunt Anne's.'

Pat bared her teeth at us both, before saying, 'Well, if he's not too scared of us, I'm going to give Enrique the biggest hug he's ever had – whatever his new wife thinks. She'll just have to lump it.'

We discussed again, for about the hundredth time, what sort of woman our friend might have married, and whether she could possibly be good enough for him.

'What about you, Gwenda?' asked Pat. 'What will you do first?'

That was easy. 'I'm going to drive into Tom and Bill's garage, tooting the horn and shouting, "Look at us! We made it!" I can hardly wait to see the look on their faces.'

12

Changed But Still the Same

Detroit to Cleveland, August–September 1959

We drove into Chicago at night, the lights of the city strung out like necklaces around the lake shore. It reminded us all of our arrival in New York, late one May evening, two years before. Both were sights that lifted my heart, that made me feel that somewhere in the twinkling darkness there was room for everyone.

We parked at a turnpike plaza to sleep, so that we could get washed and make ourselves presentable the next day, before setting off for Detroit and the home of Aunt Anne and Uncle Bill.

Detroit had changed since our last visit. There were new buildings, and roads where none had been before. We made a couple of wrong turns before finding the street that we knew so well. Even the house, as we drew up to it, looked different. The grey and white bungalow was freshly painted, the flowerbeds newly dug, and some small trees had been planted in the front lawn.

'Uncle Bill's been busy. I wonder if he's finished the back porch,' mused Pat.

'Hmm.' I was more interested in the shiny red car that stood in their driveway.

Uncle Bill had just got in from work, and in no time at all he had given us jobs to do, as if we had seen him only yesterday, while he busied himself cooking steak. After a leisurely lunch, we all went to pick up Aunt Anne from her office, and some of the people remembered us from earlier visits and wanted to know how we'd got on. It felt like a proper homecoming.

In the car on the way home, Aunt Anne kept turning round and beaming at us, and saying that she couldn't believe we were back again, and how well we all looked, and how they had loved hearing from us.

That evening we set to work on our neglected bodies. We tackled our feet, and removed all the hard skin. We steamed our faces and applied whipped-up egg whites. We finished off with a layer of Beauty Ice. 'Thrill to instantaneous results,' said the label. When I looked in the mirror, my skin just looked pink after so much attention.

After the weekend, Maureen took the bus back to Cleveland, where she was going to stay with her old room-mate, Tommy. We knew that we would see her again very soon, but how odd it felt to watch the bus slip away from us, and to see her face, slightly anxious, at the window.

'Just the two of us now,' said Pat after we had waved her off. 'It must mean something.'

'Like what?'

She shrugged. 'Like it's time to go home. We don't want everything to start feeling like an anticlimax.'

Pat's aunt and uncle were desperate for her to stay longer, so we set about trying to find work in Detroit. We were going through our money fast. Developing some films had set us back twenty dollars each. There were more to develop, but they would have to wait. Pat wanted to buy some extra suitcases, and we both needed new white stockings for nursing again.

After leaving the bus depot we began our trawl of the hospitals, but the story was the same wherever we went – we needed Michigan registration. We carried on regardless, visiting the smaller ones as well as the bigger institutions, thinking that if any of them were desperate they might waive the rules. But we had no luck.

We both felt our spirits lift when we saw there was a letter from Celia waiting for us back at Aunt Anne's. She had written it from Cedars of Lebanon Hospital, where Ann and May were working, and where she was undergoing tests for infective hepatitis. She said that she was finally starting to feel better.

'I have to be careful not to tell the nurses what to do,' she wrote. 'But I do try to be on my best behaviour, knowing how annoying those patients are who always know best. I suppose it's been a humbling experience. I'm just thankful I carried on paying my insurance. I'd be facing the workhouse otherwise.'

'That's true. It's a good job it wasn't you or me,' I said to Pat.

'I think we'll have to get ourselves a shot of gamma globulin, just to be on the safe side,' said Pat. 'We'll have to do it as soon as we're back in England. It would cost a packet here.'

It was a lovely summer's evening as we drove into Cleveland a few days later. Our search for work in Detroit had proved fruitless, but we would see Aunt Anne again when she and Uncle Bill brought our trunks over. Uncle Bill was going to hire a trailer especially for the job. We were relieved to see that our old home still looked familiar. There was Terminal Tower, and the sober, handsome buildings of Public Square. The Old Stone Church looked slightly out of place, just as it always had done. There might have been a new building here or there, but nothing had changed too much.

The rush-hour traffic had died down, leaving a lazy drone in the air, and I had that pleasant feeling of wondering where other people were going, and hoping they were all as happy and excited as we were.

We were on our way to Enrique and Barbara's, as they had invited us to stay with them. It had always been the plan, before Barbara came on the scene, that we would land on Enrique for our first couple of days back, but we had wondered if the offer still stood. However, he had assured us that we were very welcome, and that Barbara had insisted on it. Still, I felt a little anxious at the thought, and I knew that Pat did too.

'As we're so close, shall we pop along to Bill and Tom's first, to see if they're still working?' I suggested.

Pat smiled, and I knew she had been thinking the same thing. 'They'll get the surprise of their lives. When did we last send them a postcard?'

Neither of us was sure. Our list of correspondents had grown steadily longer with each new stay, so nobody heard from us as regularly as they might once have done.

I pictured the way their faces might look when we appeared. If Tom were there, he would take off his hat, scratch his head, and say, 'Well, I'll be darned,' before giving us both a hug. Bill would probably have his head under a car. He would wriggle out at the sound of an arrival, jump to his feet, then offer that shy dawning smile of his that didn't give away quite how pleased he was.

As we turned the corner that would give us our first view of the garage, I could feel my heart thumping wildly.

But where was the garage? There was no sign of it. Yet there was no doubt that this was the right spot. The ground where it had stood was flat. The place where our kind-hearted friends had spent so many hours lovingly tending Flatus had become a parking lot.

When I felt that I could speak, I said in a small voice, 'Now we'll never be able to say thank you.'

'That's America for you,' said Enrique, as we sat down with highballs after a warm welcome. Barbara sat beside him, smiling but saying little. I wondered if she minded her husband being such a good friend to so many people. It struck me that Enrique was the sort of man you would have to share. Not romantically, of course. You could tell that he adored his wife. I sneaked a look at her. She was very pretty, with reddish-brown hair, large eyes and pale freckled skin, about our age, I thought. But he was the sort of man who was always going to belong to the rest of the world, and who knew how many people he would collect over the years. I caught Barbara's eye, held it for a moment, then she beamed at me and pointed to my drink.

'I'll top you up,' she mouthed, then said quietly, as she took my glass, 'Thank you for coming. He's so thrilled that you're with us.'

And in that instant, all my reservations blew away.

Enrique looked at her, distracted for a second, then carried on. 'You hear about it all the time. Some guy goes back to see his birthplace and finds there's a turnpike running through it.' He chuckled. 'Gee whiz, it's a funny old country.'

It was impossible to thank Enrique enough for what he'd done for us, but he had more up his sleeve. He suggested that Pat's aunt and uncle bring our luggage there, and that we use his garage to do our packing, especially as we had already stored some of our belongings with him. Then, when we had news of a ship, he would send our trunks on ahead. We had always intended to sail home. Our flights out had been paid for by the hospital, then deducted from our salaries over several months so that we had hardly noticed the expense, but there was no question of flying now. Doug had given me the address of a cargo company that might have a ship leaving Montreal in about a month's time, and I decided to write the very next day to enquire.

Barbara insisted that we ring Maureen and let her know we were back. We'd been apart for just a few days but we couldn't wait to speak to her. She was already working, and had told Miss Harrison to expect us. 'And I've bought my ticket home,' she added sheepishly.

There were letters to open, too, but we saved those until we had gone to bed. Molly wrote and told us she had left Los Angeles and was now in Ames, Iowa, waiting to be godmother to her friend Betty's new baby.

'I can remember being at Betty's as if it were yesterday,' said Pat. 'But can you believe that when we were there we hadn't met Bob and Mary Ann, or Robert Loewe.'

'Or Bill and Jo Ann. Or Dr and Mrs Cashmore.'

'Or Marcia. Or Mr and Mrs Post in Alaska. And that soldier you fancied.'

'Ah, the Alaska Highway! Doesn't it seem a lifetime ago! Longer ago than Ames, for some reason. I wonder why that is.'

The next morning we went straight to Mount Sinai and asked if we could make an appointment to see Miss Harrison.

'Gwenda Brady and Pat Beadle,' said a voice behind us. 'I was wondering when you two were going to show up. Come on in.'

Miss Harrison showed us into her office. She looked thin, but cheerful. Her skull had a slightly fragile appearance; her hand, when I shook it, felt like a dry bundle of twigs. We chatted for a while – she was keen to know how some of the hospitals we had worked at compared to Mount Sinai – then we told her that we hated to be presumptuous, but if there was the chance of work we would take any job and any shift available.

'We'd like to go home a little better than paupers,' I said. 'I think our families and friends are expecting us to be rolling in it. They're in for a shock.'

'Our money is all tied up in our memories,' added Pat.

'And what memories!' said Miss Harrison. She sat down suddenly, as if the thought of everything we had done was too much for her. 'You'll have to excuse me. I get very tired these days. Such a drag.'

We gave her a little toy bear we had bought in Montana, and she touched it with fingers that trembled slightly.

'Thank you for keeping in touch,' she said when we left. Then, as we said goodbye to her secretary, she came out of her office. 'I appreciate that you took the time to write to me.'

We started work the next day. Pat was back on her old ward and I was on the private wing, both of us on day duty. I had been shown round this wing on a tour of the hospital when we first arrived and remembered feeling quite detached from it, as if it were more an industrial unit than a ward. Ah well, beggars can't be choosers, I thought.

One of my patients was on the phone to his doctor when I arrived.

'Yes, Doc, I know, but I just don't fancy getting up today. The nurse says I need to start putting some weight on that leg, but hell, no. It's my leg and I think it wants to rest.'

I said a silent prayer for patience, and waited for my phone to ring. Sure enough, a few minutes later, I had a call from the man's doctor, asking me to humour my patient in his desire to stay in bed.

It was a funny way to work, I thought, but I enjoyed my shift and the time passed quickly.

We were surprised at how many people in the hospital remembered us. Doctors would stop us in the corridor and ask how the trip had gone, and whether the old car had seen us out, and we would bump into British nurses we had known, many of them still working on the same old wards, and some still having travelled no further than the neighbouring state.

Even Mr Lewine, the hospital director, said, 'Welcome home! Glad to see you made it,' and clasped my hand when I passed him in the car park. I remembered how Tony had shaken his tin at him when he had been collecting money for us, following the story about our desperate plight in Hawaii, and felt quite embarrassed.

Sheila Mack was good fun, and we were only sorry that our spells in Cleveland had not overlapped sooner. She had been a year ahead of us at the General, but all the January starters did days and nights at the same time, so I had worked with her and got to know her then. Now living in our old apartment with a girl called Isabel, she invited us to stay there while we got some money together and waited to hear about a ship. Though Enrique and Barbara insisted that we stay for as long as we pleased, it didn't seem right to impose on them for any longer.

We pulled up at East 100th Street and sat for a while, the car windows open, thinking back to when we were last there. We had left our old home that April morning in a terrific downpour. Now, the heavy, drowsy heat felt thick enough to stir. I had forgotten how uncomfortable Cleveland could be in the summer months, how you could break into a sweat between the shower and the bedroom. How I longed, at times like this, for our LA apartment and its swimming pool.

Sheila and Isabel were both at work, but they had given us a key. The apartment looked almost the same, apart from some personal knick-knacks lying around. The green-check curtains that Margaret had given us still hung in the kitchen. The fridge that we had posed proudly beside two years earlier stood humming in the same corner, but how small it looked now!

'I feel as if we're welcoming you to *our* home,' I admitted to Sheila on her return. 'We've even got your tea ready.'

She put her hands on her hips and said most indignantly, 'Everyone has only just stopped calling this "Pat and Gwenda's place". No doubt it'll start all over again. But my, what a healthy colour you both are!'

Maureen and some other British girls came by later that evening.

'Maureen, we've missed you!' I exclaimed as she came in. 'And you've had your hair cut! What's wrong with Brady's salon, then? It's always been good enough for you before.'

'You look lovely,' said Pat. 'I think we're all fed up with our identical styles, even if they *were* cheaper.'

'The cheek of it!'

Maureen laughed. 'You two haven't changed. And I'm pleased to see that you've still got Flatus. What's going to happen to her, though?'

'I don't know. Someone will want her.'

The present company all looked doubtful about this.

One of the girls, Evelyn, was getting excited about taking her

American husband back to England to meet her parents. She had just found out she was pregnant, and we were all over the moon on her behalf.

'Where do Brad's family live?' someone asked her.

'They moved to Florida. He hardly sees them.'

'Oh. No doting grandparents on the doorstep, then.'

Evelyn put a hand on her flat stomach. 'It won't be like at home, that's for sure. When my sister got married, she lived with us for a year and a half, and there were so many relatives poking their noses in when David was born, I'm surprised the little chap had any idea which one his mother was.'

We all laughed, then Maureen said, more seriously, 'Sometimes I think it must be nice to make a brand new start. Nobody saying, "Oh, you're Albert and Mona's eldest", and, "Aren't you like your mother?" and expecting you to behave in a certain way. You can be whoever you want to be.'

One night eight of us piled into two cars and set off for the airport to give Maureen a noisy send-off. She wore a new suit and hat, and looked very elegant. I couldn't help wondering where the boyish figure, in shorts and T-shirts, of a few weeks earlier had gone. When she caught sight of me looking at her, she struck a funny pose and I saw the old Maureen again.

'I haven't changed, you know, just because I'm wearing all this clobber, you silly thing,' she said, reading my mind.

'They're all going to be so proud when they see you back home.' I stood back to admire her properly, and she posed again.

'You will write to me, won't you, and let me know what happens here. I know what great correspondents you both are. And do give my love to Celia and Molly. I wish I'd seen them again.'

'Of course,' we promised, and Pat piped up, 'Oh, I'm so jealous! I wish it was me going back.'

'I know something that will make you both even more jealous. Someone reminded me that it's Proms season. I wonder if I can get a ticket for something at the Royal Albert Hall. A Beethoven symphony, perhaps?'

'Oh, stop!' said Pat. 'I want to be in London right now.'

It was Thursday, and Pat remembered that was tea-party day. We were both on earlies, so, for probably the first time ever, we got there on time.

'English tea or iced tea?' asked the plump, efficient girl who was serving.

'Iced, please.'

'Make that three,' said a familiar voice behind us.

It was Molly, grinning from ear to ear.

'When did you get back? Where are you staying? You look just the same!'

'What did you expect?' She shook her head. 'Let's go and find a seat.'

But before we had sat down, Agnes – one of the first nurses we had met in Cleveland – appeared, ushering two girls we hadn't seen before.

'Here they are! Pat and Gwenda, the two who turned up in time for tea!' Agnes beamed at us both. 'I've brought some new arrivals to meet you.'

'Nobody can understand my accent,' moaned one of them. 'One person thinks I'm German, someone else thinks I'm Dutch! I want to tell them that I'm actually speaking proper English.'

'Oh, we had that at first. Just smile sweetly,' said Pat.

'One of my patients asked me if we have ham in Scotland. What sort of a question is that?' said her friend, who came from Aberdeen.

Molly said that she was probably to blame for that, as she'd been overwhelmed by all the chicken when she arrived. The two girls looked at her, baffled.

'Everywhere I looked there was chicken. Half a chicken. A basket of chicken. A whole cooked chicken.'

'Molly thought a restaurant meant fish and chips,' I joked.

'No, gammon and pineapple,' she replied. 'We're very posh in Hamilton.'

We all laughed, except for one of the girls, who suddenly wailed, 'Oh, I'm so homesick! And whoever heard of putting ice in tea!'

Agnes introduced them to some other nurses, and we finally had the chance to catch up with Molly. She was staying with friends outside Cleveland, and was planning to work at Mount Sinai for a few more weeks.

'Will you be at the club tomorrow night?'

She said she would try to get there, but it wasn't so easy coming back into the city in the evening.

'How was Celia when you last saw her?' asked Pat.

'Ah, Celia!' I cried, remembering her last words to us. 'Let's have a toast to her now.'

We all raised our glasses in the air.

'To Celia! May you get better soon! And may we all meet again one day!'

As if it had worked its magic immediately, there was a letter from her back at the apartment, saying that she was out of hospital and staying with Ann and May, who had moved out of the nurses' home and rented a place of their own. Ann had bought a car, and the three of them had been on trips to San Francisco and out into the country.

'I'll be looking for a job soon,' she wrote. 'Perhaps you'll come and visit some time?'

A cable arrived from Montreal to say that the SS *Cairngowan* would be leaving for Leith around 18 September. We wrote straight back to book our passages. At the club, Herman said that if we travelled up at the weekend he would be happy to drive us. We were almost speechless with gratitude.

Aunt Anne and Uncle Bill came over from Detroit with our trunks, and we spent a day in Enrique's garage packing up. There was barely room to put a foot down. Barbara gasped when she saw everything and said she would leave us to it, but kept us supplied with drinks, and even left lunch on the kitchen table when she had to go to work.

A leaflet from the Hotel Colorado fluttered to the floor. I picked it up. 'Mansion of the West', it proclaimed. A pang of something that felt like homesickness twisted inside me. I swallowed. 'Did I tell you that I heard from Cleo yesterday? He hopes that I have a wonderful life.' I tried to sound breezy. 'I guess he's realized that we aren't going to meet again after all.'

Pat looked at me and nodded gravely.

'What are you going to do with the antlers?' she asked later, as we sat on a suitcase, drinking our umpteenth cup of coffee.

We had finally removed them from Flatus, and it had been decided that I would keep them.

'I'm not sure, but I've just got to play a trick on my parents with them. Perhaps I'll put them on my father's car and wait for the reaction. On second thoughts, perhaps not.'

'I think your parents are going to get a big enough shock just seeing all this stuff turn up,' said Pat, looking at the chaos around us.

Finally, it was done. I sent one trunk ahead to Montreal to travel home on the ship with me, and Enrique took charge of all the others. A true friend to the end, he labelled them all and arranged for them to be shipped directly to Newcastle.

One night, we showed our movie films at the club. Some of the old crowd were missing, now, but it still felt like home there, and it was always uplifting to see faces and hear voices from all over the world. We began with some film taken in Cleveland before we left, and the room resounded to cries of recognition, laughter and groans.

'Look at you, Tony, the barbecue expert. You almost set fire to our apartment,' said Pat.

'I seem to remember that it was your idea to light it inside,' he replied. 'Did you ever use that thing?'

'Did we use it? We ate so much steak I'm surprised we're not mooing.'

There was Celia, dancing at our leaving party with Herman, who had my oversized straw hat perched on his head.

'I even remember the music that was playing then,' said Herman nostalgically. '"Cherry Pink and Apple Blossom White". Whenever I hear it, I think of your parties.'

'Ah, Pat and Gwenda's parties!' someone called out.

There were Joan and Olov on their wedding day.

'Did you see Joan? How is she?'

'What's it like out west? Someone told me everyone there carries a gun.'

'Did you go to Hollywood?'

'I don't suppose you saw any film stars?'

Herman swore he would come and visit us all in England. 'And whoever marries first, I'll be at their wedding. You'll see.'

We spoke to Margaret on the phone a few times, but she had to go away and we didn't get to see her. She sounded happier than she had done in her recent letters. She was working for a very nice lady, she said, but still in touch with her old family.

'I've just posted a little parcel to you both to take home, and some gifts for your parents, too,' she said.

'You've been such a good friend, Margaret.'

'Och, one day you can do the same for me.'

I came home one evening to find a letter from one of our old sisters, offering both me and Pat a job at the leprosy hospital in Redhill, starting in September. It was like a dream come true, and we were all set to write back with our acceptances straight away when we stopped and thought about it.

'We can hardly skip off down south as soon as we get home,' said Pat. 'What will our families think if we say, "Hello! We're off to London next week"?'

It was with the deepest regret that we wrote to refuse them.

The man in the garage had offered fifteen dollars for Flatus, but it didn't feel right to let her go for that.

'He'd just break her up and use her for spare parts,' I said to Pat.

'What spare parts?' she laughed. 'There's not much on her worth having.'

Then Agnes and her friend Jean offered to buy her for fifty dollars, and we liked the idea of Flatus staying with British nurses and carting them off on adventures, though probably not so far-flung.

'I don't think she could manage the Alaska Highway again,' I said, apologetically.

'It might surprise you, but we don't actually intend to go that far,' said Agnes. 'However, there *is* one condition. Please can you take me out for some driving lessons before you leave?'

Herman almost had a fit when he saw the amount of luggage we had to take with us, despite having sent the larger items on ahead. We filled the boot and most of the back seat, then started on the roof-rack.

It was a sad parting, with what was left of the old gang – and some of the new – sitting on the steps as we prepared to leave. Enrique and Barbara. Andy and Tony, who joked that he would never have started that collection for us when we were in Hawaii if he had known we had spent all our money going shopping. Agnes and Jean. Sheila and Isabel, and Sheila's boyfriend, Eugene. And a few others who wandered down from their apartments to see what all the commotion was. But there was no Molly. She hadn't been at the club either, and we were bitterly disappointed.

'Keep in touch!'

'Tell us where you go in Flatus! Hope she lasts a bit longer.'

'She'd better!'

'Write! You must write.'

'We'll want to know what *you're* doing, too.'

'Don't forget us.'

'As if we could!'

Everyone was laughing and crying and promising to write, and saying they would see us again in Cleveland or London, or Newcastle or Edinburgh.

Then we were in the car, and we were actually leaving. I only realized, as I settled back in my seat, just how tiring the last few days had been, with so many people to say goodbye to. One day I had worked three shifts back-to-back, two at Mount Sinai and one at the Women's Hospital. Some of our friends ran alongside the car as we began to pick up speed.

'I think you've forgotten something.' Herman frowned, and glanced quickly behind him.

'They're just being silly,' I said, waving madly from the back seat.

He pulled up, and then I saw a small figure racing along the pavement behind the others, who were all now shouting, 'Stop!'

'It's Molly!' I cried, and Pat and I both leapt out of the car and ran to meet her.

'Oh, we thought we'd never see you again!'

We waited for her to get her breath back. She raised her eyebrows. 'I thought you two were the intrepid travellers. Hamilton isn't the end of the earth, you know, and I don't believe Newcastle was either when I last looked.'

Pat went back to the car, and when she returned she was hiding something behind her.

'Here you are.' She thrust Sammy at Molly.

Molly took the dog and fondly stroked a brown ear before handing him back. 'Keep him a bit longer. You can return him to me one day in England . . . or Ireland . . . or, I don't know . . . Fort Nelson.'

'Fort Nelson?'

'The place where the people from the Summit Café went shopping.'

'I remember it well, but what on earth would we be doing there?'

'Who knows. We might end up anywhere. A nurse's life, eh?'

Somewhere on the shores of the St Lawrence I woke up, confused with sleep. I could hear the low murmur of voices coming from another part of the car, and just for a second I thought that we were all together again, the five of us, driving on those long, straight roads in a car named Flatus, with a pair of stag antlers pointing the way.

The Trunk in the Attic

A Note From the Author

We all grow up hearing stories from our parents, and I was no exception. How many times, I wonder, did Gwenda begin a sentence with, 'When I was in America . . .'? Things were bigger there, and they were often better, too. Toys we had never seen the like of crossed the Atlantic from generous friends – a talking Bugs Bunny, crying dolls, giant balloons shaped like animals.

I was the oldest of three sisters and a brother, and I think all four of us shared the same favourite tales: the one about the patient who bore the imprint of a bear 'hug' after an all-too-close encounter down at the creek; or the one about the man who shot a bullet hole in the cowboy hat that we unearthed every so often from a trunk in the attic (that trunk turned up more recently in the garage of my parents' bungalow, and was found to contain many more treasures: airline tickets, matchbooks, old maps and letters being just a few of them). But others simply blew over us and settled like dust in the room. Perhaps, when aunts Pat and Molly were visiting, our ears pricked up as the sound of laughter and memories relived drowned out our childish games, but most of the time we affected boredom when my mother chose to regale us with yet another of her reminiscences.

More intriguing were the people from this vast and exotic country who dropped into our lives every now and then. I don't think we children bothered to enquire exactly how they fitted into the story, but they were 'from America' and that was interesting enough. Margaret Falconer was a regular visitor most summers for a large part of my childhood. She would arrive, a frail, bird-like figure, from the heat and humidity of Manhattan, her luggage spilling with expensive gifts. There were also second-hand clothes for me and my sisters, many of them bearing the label 'Saks Fifth Avenue', which meant nothing to us but made my mother and Margaret exchange meaningful looks over our heads. Margaret had gone to work as a live-in housekeeper to one of the sons of her former employer, and had moved to New York City with him and his wife, where she helped to bring up the couple's two daughters. She spent a lot of time in our house shivering and pulling cardigans around her thin shoulders, yet she seemed to enjoy the change of scene and returned year after year.

Bob and Mary Ann Jones came one year, and were named Lord and Lady of the Manor at the medieval banquet my parents took them to one night. They sat on grand chairs at the head of the table, while everyone else had to make do with benches. Bob had grown a beard by then, and looked quite the part.

Presents used to arrive from Florence and Lloyd Langer – the couple from Phoenix, Arizona, who are mentioned all too briefly – as well as a monthly magazine called *Arizona Highways*, full of pictures of red earth and a sky so blue it made your eyes water to look at it. Lloyd himself came over once, a widower then, travelling with his niece and her daughter.

And then there were the letters and Christmas cards, bearing photos of families gathered round swimming pools, looking tanned and happy.

So I suppose you could say that America has always been a backdrop to my life.

I visited for the first time when I was eighteen, on a family holiday in 1980. We flew to San Francisco, to the home of Bob and Mary Ann in the Bay Area, and stayed with them and their two younger children, Brad and Brenda (Laura had married and left home by then). We also visited Joan and Olov Modig and their sons, Mark and Alan, in Los Angeles, and Lloyd in Phoenix. He was in his eighties by then, but still took us camping in the Grand Canyon.

Eight years later, after a languages degree and a couple of jobs in publishing, I spent six months travelling in South America with a friend, then flew to New York, to Margaret and the Waldman household, to begin a Greyhound trip across the States, my route planned around the people I hoped to visit. I had traced some 'lost' friends by then. My mother had told me about the wonderful Enrique Kierulf, who had so generously and diligently forwarded their mail to them for eighteen months, and I managed to locate him – and Herman Leggon – before I left England. It wasn't quite as easy a task in 1988 as it would be now. I remember spending hours in Marylebone Library during my lunch-hour, going through the microfiche of US telephone directories, grateful, at least, that both men had unusual surnames.

Of course they were just as kind and hospitable as I had been told, as was Barbara, Enrique's wife. I felt with all three that I had made new friends of my own, rather than just got to know friends of my mother.

Later in the trip, now on the west coast, Bob and Mary Ann were their usual generous selves, and allowed me to treat their house like my home, as did Maureen, the only one of the five girls to settle in the US, in her home in Pacific Grove.

Tom and Margaret Byrne in Cleveland, good friends of Molly, and Joan Mensor in Truckee, California, another nurse from Cleveland days, all showed me hospitality on that trip, though they are not mentioned in the story.

We now jump forward about twenty years. I was in the northeast one summer with my family when my mother handed me a few pages of A4 paper. She had decided to type up the letters she had sent to her parents two or three times a week for the duration of her stay in the States. Perhaps one day, when they were older, she suggested modestly, her grandchildren would be interested to know what she had got up to. I started reading, and demanded to see more.

Why, I wondered, had I not been told about this? It was like watching a reel of film run before my eyes. I could see the keen, expectant faces of the two new arrivals as they were welcomed at the hospital tea-party that cold February afternoon, the wonder in the eyes of the girls who drove into New York City late one night and saw the lights of Manhattan for the first time. Perhaps remembering the sounds from the living room all those years ago, I could hear the laughter of the five who spent so many days – weeks, months even – squashed together in Flatus.

The story seemed too good to keep to myself, but it took another couple of years before I found a publisher who fell in love with it as much as I had. The support and enthusiasm of Antonia Hodgson and Hannah Boursnell at Little, Brown have been crucial in the book's development.

After I began writing, other characters came back into our lives. I could hardly believe it when I discovered – in a quick internet search – a Robert Loewe playing the piano in a Colorado café. Could it be the girls' old friend? It was, and he has since been in touch with them, even playing Pat a burst of *Salad Days* down the telephone line when they spoke.

And while searching for more information on the remarkable community in Carville, Louisiana, I discovered that a reporter for the BBC had been there only a few days earlier, and, even more incredibly, had been shown round by Pete, the nurses' guide half a century before. The hospital is now the National Hansen's Disease Museum, but a few former patients still live in its grounds.

Voices from the past

My primary resource for writing this book has been the correspondence of my mother Gwenda – primarily the letters she wrote home to her parents – as well as many long conversations about her wonderful adventures. When Pat offered to let me read her own letters home, I found that they shed new light on this more innocent age that I was now inhabiting. A lifelong friend of Gwenda's, Barbie Cawthorne, also shared with me the letters she received during that time.

Most of the characters in the book are real people, and I use their real names, with only a handful changed to protect confidentiality. A tiny minority are invented, but even they are usually drawn from actual details. In a few other instances, I have used the names of real people but turned them into characters of my own. I hope that these people will forgive me for any liberties I have taken.

As for the conversations in this book, some of them are as they were recounted in the letters, or later relayed to me, but I have often used my prerogative as author to imagine how they might have unfolded.

If I have a regret, it is that I was not able to include all of the encounters the five nurses had. Some good friends and interesting people have been omitted in order to keep this book a manageable size, and particular mention must be given to Liese Karabetian and Heidi Irvin, with whom happy times were spent;

Gloria and John Aitchison in Sarnia, Ontario, who extended hospitality at regular intervals; the Perkins family in San Francisco, who offered the girls the use of an apartment in the city, and looked after Flatus during their trip to Hawaii; Dr Mervyn Sopher, who arrived in Cleveland from Newcastle with the following instructions from Matron at the General: 'Look out for Beadle and Brady. They'll probably be halfway round America in an old banger, but you might just catch them.' How true those words turned out to be!

New beginnings

After recovering from her illness, Celia stayed in Los Angeles and worked in Mount Sinai Hospital on Sunset Boulevard for three years, before going back to Ireland to care for her mother. After her mother's death she married Michael Griffin. They live and farm in County Kilkenny.

Gwenda met Alder Gofton from Whitley Bay, who was training to be a priest in the Church of England, not long after her return to the UK. She found being married to a vicar a full-time job, and didn't work as a nurse after her marriage. She has lived in various locations in Newcastle and Northumberland with her husband and family. On their retirement she and Alder moved to Ponteland, a few miles out of Newcastle. She is still in touch with several of the friends she made in America.

Maureen went back to the US in January 1960, and settled first in the San Francisco Bay Area, where she brought up her daughter, Belinda, moving later to Pacific Grove on the Monterey Peninsula. She died on 4 July 1999. Belinda lives in Oregon with her husband, daughter and son.

Molly and Pat returned to Mount Sinai Hospital, Cleveland, in 1961, before buying another old car and travelling west with two German boys, visiting some of the friends they had made on the previous trip. They worked in Los Angeles before going by Greyhound to Miami to take a cruise home.

Molly married Scotsman David Murdoch, from Gourock, in 1965, and lives in Uddingston, near Glasgow. They have three sons and four grandchildren.

Pat married Scotsman Ian Small, from Coatbridge, in 1965, and settled in South Queensferry, near Edinburgh. She was widowed in 1998, and has two sons and two grandchildren.

Barbara Fox, 2011

Acknowledgements

This book owes a lot to many people. Thanks primarily to Celia, Gwenda, Molly and Pat for allowing me to write about their lives, to Belinda Marzi, Maureen's daughter, for her enthusiastic response to my writing about her mother, and to everyone else who finds themselves in these pages.

I am indebted to Gwenda and Pat, whose letters provide the backbone for this book, and to my late grandparents, Arthur and Gwen Brady, and Pat's late parents, Sidney and Kitty Beadle, for keeping the letters for all those years. Pat and Gwenda, along with Molly and Celia, answered all sorts of questions by letter, email and phone, while Belinda and her aunt, Betty Sherwood, provided helpful biographical details about a much-missed mother and sister. Some of the above also read drafts of the book and made helpful suggestions, while my friend Pat Methven read the early chapters and did likewise.

Barbie Cawthorne allowed me to read her own letters from Gwenda, where I learned some of the things she didn't tell her parents. Mary Ann Jones and Herman Leggon, who both feature in the story, have taken numerous trips down memory lane on my behalf, and relayed them to me so well.

A huge thank you to all at the Little, Brown Book Group, and especially Editor-in-Chief Antonia Hodgson, and my editor Hannah Boursnell, who both made their passion about the story clear from the start, while Hannah has supported and assisted me along the way. Helen Surman has created a truly memorable cover. Thanks are also due to production manager Marie Hrynczak and my publicist Kirsteen Astor, to cartographer John Gilkes and freelance editor Deborah Adams, who made invaluable improvements to the text.

The following people have racked their brains on my behalf: Ruth Morris, David Morris, Mollie Gallo, Les Gallo, Amy Gofton, Mark Gofton, Jennifer Gallo-Fox, Joe Fox, Sarah Jordan, Mike Fox, Carol Jarvis and Alder Gofton. My husband Mike has tried to help me sound as if I know what I'm talking about when it comes to cars. My sons, Joseph and Thomas, have laughed over my shoulder at the computer screen – though not always in the right places.

Last but not least, I am hugely grateful to the staff at Saga Magazine, especially David Allsop for commissioning 'The Incredible Journey' for the July 2009 edition, Sue Strange for making it look so good and Kirsty Lyon for helpfulness well beyond the call of duty. Photographer Murdo MacLeod took some pictures of Pat, Gwenda and Molly for the feature that are raising eyebrows to this day.